# THE CHESTER & HOLYHEAD RAILWAY

Volume One

## UNIFORM WITH THIS BOOK

|  |  |
|---|---|
| Graham S. Hudson | *The Aberford Railway and the History of the Garforth Colleries* |
| John Thomas | *The Callander & Oban Railway* |
| Rex Christiansen and R. W. Miller | *The Cambrian Railways Volume 1: 1852-1888, Volume 2: 1889-1968* |
| N. S. C. Macmillan | *The Campbeltown & Machrihanish Light Railway* |
| Patrick J. Flanagan | *The Cavan & Leitrim Railway* |
| Edward M. Patterson | *The Clogher Valley Railway* |
| H. A. Vallance | *The Great North of Scotland Railway* |
| H. A. Vallance | *The Highland Railway* |
| Edward M. Patterson | *A History of the Narrow-gauge Railways of North East Ireland Part One: The Ballycastle Railway Part Two: The Ballymena Lines* |
| Edward M. Patterson | *A History of the Narrow-gauge Railways of North West Ireland Part One: The County Donegal Railways* (second edition) *Part Two: The Londonderry & Lough Swilly Railway* |
| H. W. Paar | *A History of the Railways of the Forest of Dean Part One: The Severn & Wye Railway Part Two: The Great Western Railway in Dean* |
| John Marshall | *The Lancashire & Yorkshire Railway Volumes 1, 2 & 3* |
| David L. Smith | *The Little Railways of South West Scotland* |
| R. A. Williams | *The London & South Western Railway Volume 1* |
| G. A. Brown J. D. C. A. Prideaux and H. G. Radcliffe | *The Lynton & Barnstaple Railway* |
| Colin G. Maggs | *The Midland & South Western Junction Railway* |
| John Thomas | *The North British Railway Volume 1* |
| Rex Christiansen and R. W. Miller | *The North Staffordshire Railway* |
| G. Whittle | *The Railways of Consett and North West Durham* |
| Peter E. Baughan | *The Railways of Wharfedale* |
| W. J. K. Davies | *The Ravenglass & Eskdale Railway* |
| A. D. Farr | *The Royal Deeside Line* |
| Robin Atthill and O. S. Nock | *The Somerset & Dorset Railway* |
| Ralph Cartwright and R. T. Russell | *The Welshpool & Llanfair Light Railway* |
| John Thomas | *The West Highland Railway* |

Down Holyhead express headed by 2-2-2 No 531 *Lady of the Lake* leaving the Anglesey end of the Britannia Bridge in the late 1860s (*Victor Welch*)

# THE CHESTER & HOLYHEAD RAILWAY
## Volume One

*The Main Line up to 1880*

*by*
PETER E. BAUGHAN

DAVID & CHARLES : NEWTON ABBOT

0 7153 5617 8

© Peter E. Baughan 1972
All rights reserved. No part of this publication may be reproduced, stored in a retrieval system, or transmitted, in any form or by any means, electronic, mechanical, photocopying, recording or otherwise, without the prior permission of David and Charles (Publishers) Limited

In
Memory
of
Victor Edward Baughan

Set in eleven point Pilgrim
and printed in Great Britain
by Bristol Typesetting Company Limited
for David and Charles (Publishers) Limited
South Devon House   Newton Abbot   Devon

## Contents

LIST OF ILLUSTRATIONS                                       8

1 THE PRE-RAILWAY YEARS                                    11
  Early postal services – the sailing packets – the Act of Union – the Holyhead Road – Conway and Menai Bridges – Rennie's harbour works – first steam mail packets – last years of the Holyhead mail coach

2 FIRST RAILWAY SCHEMES                                    23
  Proposed London—Porth Dynllaen Railway 1836 – the Vignoles surveys – Brunel plans a route to Ireland – Irish Railway Commission – Holyhead v Porth Dynllean – Ormes Bay schemes 1836–8 – Chester & Crewe Railway – Great Holyhead Railway Project 1838–42 – the 'Hungry Forties'

3 SUCCESS IN PARLIAMENT                                    35
  Committee on London—Dublin Communication 1840 – Committee on Post Office Communication with Ireland 1842 – James Walker's report 1843 – Chester & Holyhead Bill in Parliament – the Chester & Holyhead Railway Act 1844 – dispute with the Grand Junction – the land mail contract

4 OPEN TO BANGOR                                           53
  The team – proposed atmospheric railway – Bill for crossing the Menai Straits – letting the contracts – the work force – work started – threat from the Great Western – the Mania year – sea

defences – Shrewsbury & Chester Railway – the first stations – preparations for opening – Board of Trade inspections—Saltney to Bangor – Chester joint station

5 BRIDGING THE CONWAY AND PREPARATIONS FOR MENAI    89
The first designs – genesis of the tubular principle – Chester & Holyhead Railway Completion Act 1845 – the experiments—letting the contracts – tragedy at the River Dee – General Pasley's letter – the Conway Tubular Bridge – floating the first Conway tube – raising the first Conway tube – Board of Trade inspection—first Conway tube – completion of the Conway Bridge

6 OPEN THROUGHOUT—THE BRITANNIA TUBULAR BRIDGE    120
Board of Trade inspection and opening Llanfair to Holyhead – financial difficulties – the Britannia Tubular Bridge – tube construction started – floating the first tube – raising the up line tubes – opening the up line – Fairbairn v Stephenson – completion of the bridge – final Board of Trade inspection

7 FROM OPENING TO AMALGAMATION    143
Steamer service authorised – 1847 working agreement – first Irish Mail train – mail contract lost – Peto in the chair – agreements and disagreements 1850–52 – government intervention – the LNWR takes over – 1860 mail service

8 LOCOMOTIVES AND ROLLING STOCK 1848–1880s    181
First CHR locomotive orders – motive power shortage on the LNWR – CHR engines go to Wolverton – preparations for working the line – early locomotives – Ramsbottom, the 'Ladies', and water troughs – the 'Trent' run – CHR rolling

stock – gas lighting, brakes, and rolling stock failures – sleeping carriages – early engine and carriage sheds

9 HOLYHEAD UP TO THE 1880s 208
Proposed refuge and packet harbour – proposed extension line 1847 – construction starts on harbour of refuge – proposed railway extensions 1855 – further schemes in refuge harbour – the great breakwater – broad gauge locomotives – steamship *Great Eastern* at Holyhead – abandonment of government packet harbour – first railway station – extension railway and second station – Holyhead tank engines – inner harbour works 1860s to 1880 – new harbour, station and hotel opened

10 OPERATING AND WAY & WORKS 1848–1880 244
Early trains and traffic – additional stations – Britannia Hotel, park, and station – freight traffic and facilities – Irish interlude 1860s to 1880 – permanent way and works 1850s to 1880 – Menai Bridge Junction 1865–1870 – the Abergele accident – signalling and telegraph works to 1880

APPENDICES 296
1a Dates of openings of main line – 1b Dates of station openings, &c and other works up to 1880 – 2 Officers of the CHR and LNWR Holyhead district 1844–1880 – 3 Opening passenger train service Chester—Bangor May 1848 – 4 CHR rail passengers 1848–1858

REFERENCES 303
ACKNOWLEDGEMENTS 312
INDEX 315

# List of Illustrations

### PLATES

| | page |
|---|---|
| Robert Stephenson (*Photo Science Museum, London*) | 65 |
| James Meadows Rendel (*courtesy the Trustees of the British Museum*) | 66 |
| Captain Constantine Richard Moorsom RN (*National Maritime Museum, London*) | 66 |
| Coach road, and railway tunnel, viaduct and sea wall at Penmaenmawr, 1849 (*Photo Science Museum, London*) | 83 |
| Britannia Bridge under construction, 1849 (*Photo Science Museum, London*) | 84 |
| Britannia Bridge conference of engineers (*By permission of the National Trust to whom the picture is loaned by Lady Janet Douglas Pennant*) | 133 |
| Britannia Bridge from the Anglesey shore (*London Midland Region*, BR) | 133 |
| Suspension and tubular bridges at Conway (*Author*) | 134 |
| Aerial view of Conway (*Aerofilms Ltd*) | 134 |
| Trevithick 2–2–2 'Crewe type' (*Photo Science Museum, London*) | 151 |
| Trevithick 2–4–0 'Crewe type' (*Locomotive & General Railway Photographs*) | 151 |
| Chester joint station, c 1860 (*Chester Public Library*) | 152 |
| Down train entering Bangor station in the early 1850s (*courtesy Roger Wilson, Hutton House Transport Collection*) | 152 |
| Flint station from the west, 1970 (*Author*) | 201 |
| The first Prestatyn station from the west, 1970 (*Author*) | 201 |
| Penmaenmawr station from the east, 1970 (*Author*) | 202 |
| Llanfairfechan station from the west, 1970 (*Author*) | 202 |
| The closed station at Aber from the west, 1970 (*Author*) | 202 |
| Experimental locomotive *Velocipede*, 1847 (*Photo Science Museum, London*) | 219 |

Ramsbottom 2-2-2 locomotive No 531 *Lady of the Lake*
at Crewe, 1862 (*London Midland Region*, BR)  219
Gaerwen station from the west, 1965 (*Author*)  220
Valley station from the south, 1970 (*Author*)  220
Admiralty Pier station, Holyhead (*Locomotive & General Railway Photographs*)  220
Aerial view of the railway harbour at Holyhead (*Aerofilms Ltd*)  269
CHR paddle steamer *Cambria*, 1848 (*London Midland Region*, BR)  270
LNWR paddle steamer *Eleanor*, 1873 (*London Midland Region*, BR)  270
Two views of Holyhead new harbour, June 1880 (*British Transport Historical Records*)  287
Holyhead new station and hotel, c 1880 (*London Midland Region*, BR)  288

IN THE TEXT

Map of main line, branches & connections  10
Penmaenmawr viaduct and tunnel  68
Abergele station 1848 (*Illustrated London News*)  75
Ogwen viaduct 1848 (*Illustrated London News*)  81
Chester joint station (*Chester Public Library*)  87
Broken span at the Dee Bridge (*Illustrated London News*)  105
Construction of tube for Britannia Bridge  125
Britannia Tubular Bridge—entrance from the Bangor side March 1850 (*Illustrated London News*)  136
Samuel Morton Peto 1851 (*Illustrated London News*)  160
Peto's signature (*Author's collection*)  161
Map of development at Holyhead 1846–1880  210
Map of Admiralty Pier, Holyhead 1848–1868  217
Map of first stations at Holyhead 1850–1854  229
The Queen at the Admiralty Pier, Holyhead 1853 (*Illustrated London News*)  234
Bangor station 1848 (*Illustrated London News*)  251
Map of Irish connections  265
The Abergele accident 1868 (*Illustrated London News*)  281

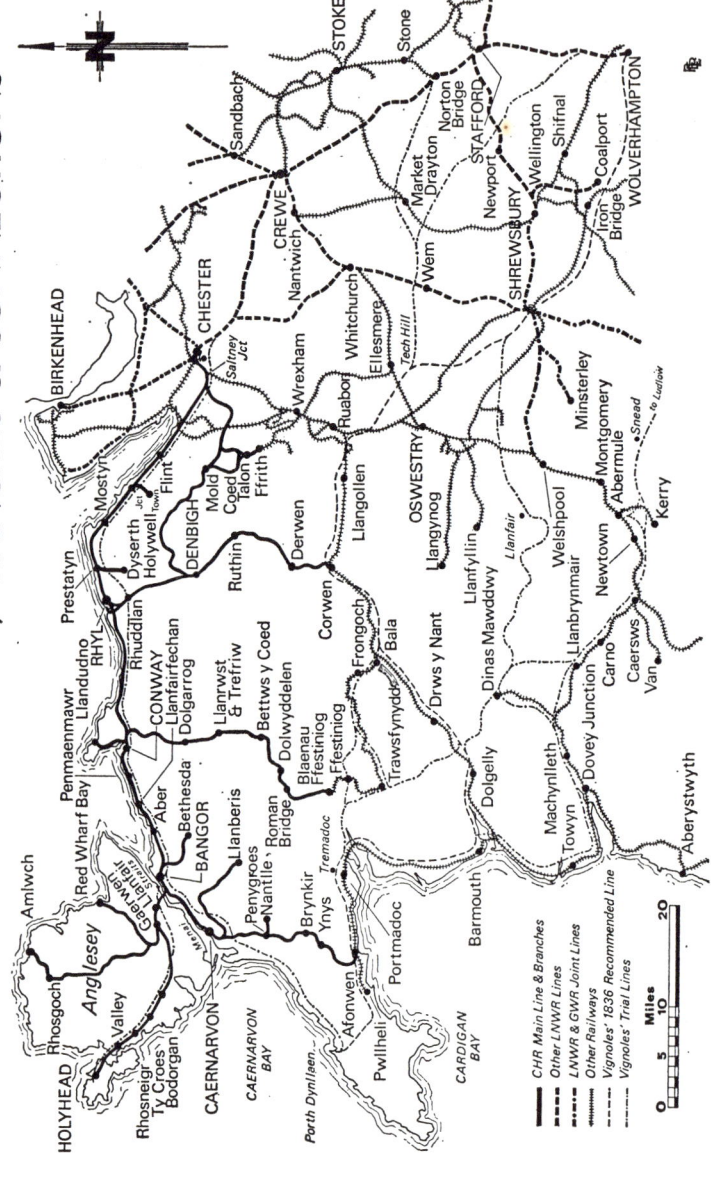

CHAPTER ONE

## *The pre-Railway Years*

Holyhead in the early 1800s, packet station for the Irish Mail service, was a quiet place of some two thousand inhabitants. Situated on Holy Island, off the north-west tip of the Isle of Anglesey, and with the Holyhead Mountain (so called though it be but 720ft high) to the west, the salt-sprayed harbour and huddle of stone and slate buildings faced out across Holyhead Bay. Through the mists and squalls of the Irish Sea, to and from the harbour, ventured small sailing packets under the overall charge of one-armed Captain John Macgregor Skinner, a veteran of many years in the marine service of the Postmaster General. As yet only a light on the Skerries Rocks, seven miles north of Holyhead and first lit in 1717, guided the packets into the harbour, though the South Stack lighthouse was under construction. (It started operating in February 1809.) Of great antiquity, Holyhead had altered little through the years. Irish politics, however, were shortly to bring to it a bustle and development which has lasted to the present day.

### EARLY POSTAL SERVICES

The postal service commenced in the time of Queen Elizabeth I when Irish affairs required regular communication between the Court and the Lord Lieutenant of Ireland. In October 1572 post stages were set up for a weekly mail service via Chester and Liverpool, with embarkation at the latter port. There was also another route via Reading, Bristol,

Swansea and Milford, to Waterford. Four years later the Midlands route was switched to Holyhead, with posts at Barnet, St Albans, Stony Stratford, Daventry, Coventry, Lichfield, Stone, Nantwich, Westchester, Denbigh, Conway, and Beaumaris. This latter route provided the shortest sea crossing and led direct to Dublin Castle. Court personages, military and civil, and messengers in the Queen's service, rode post on horseback in all weathers on appalling roads at an average speed in winter of five miles an hour. Though at first these were official posts, nevertheless, by permission, private persons could also send letters. Between 1582 and 1598 the London—Holyhead posts were withdrawn. On their reintroduction in the latter year the route was much the same as before, except that Brickhill and Towcester superseded Stony Stratford and Daventry, Coleshill was introduced as an additional post before the Lichfield stop, and Rhuddlan superseded Denbigh.

During the time of Cromwell the posts were tri-weekly, let under contract, but in 1660, Restoration year, an Act incorporated the Post Office, under control of the newly-appointed Postmaster General. In 1784 a separate, independent Irish Postmaster General was created, and October of the following year saw in England the inauguration of the Irish mail coach, operating free from tolls on the new turnpikes, its journey starting from the Swan with Two Necks in Lad Lane near Gresham Street in London, and ending at the Eagle and Child (later the Royal Hotel) at Holyhead.[1]

THE SAILING PACKETS

At first there appears to have been only one packet boat in regular use on the mail service but in March 1646 the House of Commons decided there should be two. The Restoration in 1660 saw three packets and in 1768 a further three were added, giving six sailings a week. In 1772 the Postmaster General ended the system whereby there was only one contractor, and provision was made for there to be five packets.

The commanders were appointed by warrant from the Postmaster General, had entire responsibility for providing and crewing their own boats, and relied on passenger receipts to realise a profit. Their crews were officially rendered free from the attentions of the Press Gang.

During the American War of Independence the packets generally were subject to considerable hostile action and the resultant shortage decided the government that henceforth it would build its own boats. Even the Irish Mail was not immune: in March 1780 the postmaster at Holyhead informed London that two American privateers had captured the packets *Hillsborough* and *Bessborough*, returning them after ransom had been paid. A third packet, *Le de Spencer*, narrowly avoided capture. The privateers were crewed by Irishmen and commissioned by Benjamin Franklin, then in Europe representing the infant United States.[2] (The other two packets making up the five then at Holyhead were *Dartmouth* and *Clermont*.)

The Irish mail packets (made up to six again in 1809) went unmolested through the Napoleonic Wars, and it was during that period that Captain Skinner was appointed commodore captain at Holyhead. In 1798, in command of the packet *Princess Royal* out of Falmouth, he fought a successful single ship action with a French brig, *L'Aventure*, thereby justifying Admiralty policy of arming the packets. Captain Skinner, a loyalist American who had seen service in the Royal Navy, was feted for his victory and given the plum job of the Holyhead station three years later.[3] There he was to rule until, on 30 October 1832, in his seventieth year, he was washed overboard from his ship *Escape* while approaching Holyhead in heavy seas. Earlier that year Skinner had told a Parliamentary committee that the Holyhead Post Office steam packets were meanly furnished and that their construction had been accompanied by penny-pinching. His death, occasioned by the failure of a bulwark, brought this fact home. He was a great character in the history of Holyhead and much loved by all accounts. He was accompanied by a tame raven which, left at

Holyhead when the captain was outward bound, would recognise the ship from afar on the inward approach and fly to meet it. Skinner's memory is perpetuated by an obelisk overlooking the harbour.

For a spell in the eighteenth century, Parkgate, on the Dee estuary a few miles north of Chester, was an alternative to Holyhead for the Irish service. Though the Post Office kept to the existing route, the public preferred the longer sea crossing from Parkgate as it obviated passage over the notoriously bad North Wales coast road and the sometimes downright dangerous crossing of the Menai Straits. There were two routes between Chester and Anglesey via Conway: the regular post road passed along the foreshore, under Penmaenbach and Penmaenmawr, and thence over the Lavan Sands and by ferry to Beaumaris; the other route, which was used when the tide was in or the weather bad, reached Penmaenmawr by way of a hilly inland road via the Sychnant Pass, whence a difficult 'cliff-hanging' route was followed to the sands below and thence across to Beaumaris or on to Bangor. For the dangerous passage over the sands, travellers were accompanied by local guides.

Other reasons for preferring Parkgate could be found in Holyhead itself for at that time the port had a somewhat raffish character and the few amenities tended to border on the disreputable. They catered for the sailing men and the local populace and discouraged the ordinary traveller from closer acquaintance. Dean Swift, in 1727, was delayed at Holyhead for nearly a month in what he considered were foreign surroundings: three packets were holed up in the harbour, nobody of consequence spoke English, the weather was foul, the lodgings smoky, and worst of all, the vicar could or would not play backgammon because they had not been introduced![4] Travellers were frequently so detained; contrary winds could keep outward bound vessels locked in the harbour, while others wishing to enter frequently found themselves beating about outside waiting for a westerly. To make matters worse the harbour went dry at low tide. Nevertheless,

Parkgate was doomed, for the Dee was slowly silting up, and by the early nineteenth century it was out of use.

## THE ACT OF UNION

As long as Ireland had her own Parliament, the authorities on the English and Welsh side made only perfunctory attempts to improve the land mail route. The Act of Union in May 1800, however, forced a change in this attitude. Ordinary travellers, lamenting their ordeal through the years, had received little sympathy, but now Irish MPs made to brave the journey to sit at Westminster became vociferous in loud complaint. In 1801 John Rennie, the celebrated civil engineer, and Joseph Huddart, merchant navy captain and hydrographer, were asked by Parliament to report on the best routes and port for the Irish mail service. They recommended Holyhead and suggested improvements to the road and the rerouting of the coaches via Shrewsbury, thus avoiding much of the North Wales coast road and the Conway ferry crossing. Not until 1810, however, was an Act passed for improvements at Holyhead, and at the harbour of Howth on the Irish side, at a cost of £10,000.

## THE HOLYHEAD ROAD

The condition of the road traversed by the Holyhead mail coaches and the uncertaintly of the ferry crossings at Conway and the Menai Straits caused late running and unreliable connections with the packets, themselves at the whim of the weather and subject to the tides. Occasional attempts were made to compel the turnpike trusts and parish councils, responsible for the road, to keep it in repair. But it was a losing battle and the road became more dangerous with the passing years: Sir Henry Parnell, MP for Queen's County, complained of his coach being overturned, the occupants being thrown into a pool of water. London coachmen frequently refused to work the Anglesey side, where there was indeed no made road in parts, and even riding post was fraught with suspense.

Samuel Smiles records that three horses broke their legs in one week.[5]

There was one man who could help at this time: Thomas Telford, Scottish genius of roads, canals, bridges and aqueducts. John Foster, Chancellor of the Irish Exchequer and moving spirit behind a better London—Dublin communication, asked Telford to survey a route for a new road between Shrewsbury and Holyhead. He first tried two routes across the Berwyns, following the Tanat and Ceiriog valleys, but found the gradients too severe and recommended instead a road through the Nant Ffrancon Pass.[6] His report, however, was pigeon-holed following the retirement of Foster. It was not until 1815 that someone else with fixed opinions and bruised feelings about the road came forward: Sir Henry Parnell's efforts in that year of Waterloo sparked off a series of Parliamentary reports from which came legislation effecting the improvement of the Holyhead Road. The 1815 report led to an Act in May of that year whereby a commission was appointed to supervise the spending of a Treasury grant of £20,000.[7] Telford, appointed engineer, made a survey of the whole route between London and Holyhead, together with the mail road from Lancashire to Holyhead along the North Wales coast.

The works, started in 1815 and substantially completed by 1819, included the Archway cutting on the Great North Road at Highgate and a number of regradings, widenings, diversions, and new lengths. These included the Nant Ffrancon cut-off route, avoiding the Conway crossing, by way of Bettws-y-Coed, where the old road was left and the Waterloo Bridge built, and thence by way of Capel Curig and Bethesda to Bangor. The gradients, some as bad as 1 in $6\frac{1}{2}$, were brought to a minimum of 1 in 20. On Anglesey an embankment of some 1,300 yards in length, 16ft high and 34ft wide at the top, was constructed for the road across the Stanley Sands to Holy Island.[8] On Telford's advice the seven turnpike trusts between Shrewsbury and Holyhead were bought out by the commissioners under an Act of 1819.

THE PRE-RAILWAY YEARS 17

Further committee reports in 1816, 1817, 1819, 1820, and 1822 culminated in 1823 in 'An Act for vesting in Commissioners the Bridges now building over the Menai Straits and the River Conway, and the Harbours of Howth and Holyhead, and the Road from Dublin to Howth; and for the further Improvement of the Road from London to Holyhead. Further Acts of 1825, 1826, and 1833 completed legislation concerning the Holyhead Road during this period, the last Act transferring to the Commissioners of His Majesty's Woods and Forests the powers vested in the Holyhead Road Commissioners.

CONWAY AND MENAI BRIDGES

If the Holyhead Road was tortuous, the ferries over the Conway and the Menai Straits were worse. Samuel Johnson in his diary of a journey into North Wales, noted in August 1774 that there were two ferry boats at Conway, a small one for passengers and a larger one for the coach, the latter being subject to the tides. If the coach was thus delayed, its occupants would wait at an inn at Conway, westbound passengers going across the river ahead of their coach. Of interest is the foreboding felt by Johnson for the precipitous Penmaenmawr route ahead of him. In fact he found to his relief that two years earlier the road had been improved and a protecting wall built.[9]

From the 1770s there were proposals for a bridge across the Menai Straits but on every occasion either the Admiralty objected on navigation grounds, or the plans proved to be technically unsound. John Rennie, in 1801, planned a great single cast iron arch of 450ft span, 150ft above high water. Considered to be too ahead of its time, its very magnitude condemned it in the eyes of the timid. In his fruitless 1810 proposals, Telford brought out two designs which were rejected by the Admiralty, one for three cast iron arches each of 260ft span at the Swilly Rock, and the other, outdoing Rennie, for a single cast iron arch of 500ft span at Ynys-y-

B

Moch, 100ft above high water.[10] In 1814 Telford designed a suspension bridge of 1,000ft central span over the Mersey at Runcorn, and though this too became so much waste paper, the valuable experience was translated to his successful 1818 plans for bridging the Menai Straits, submitted at a time when the commissioners were becoming increasingly concerned with this one remaining weak link in the Holyhead Road. Again Ynys-y-Moch was the site. The bridge, 100ft above high water, had a central span of 550ft approached by four great stone arches on the Anglesey side and three on the Caernarvonshire. In the following year a construction Act was passed, though preliminary work was started on the piers during 1818. The first stone of the main pier at Ynys-y-Moch was laid on 10 August 1819 by W. A. Provis, the resident engineer. By April 1825 work had reached a point where a start could be made on raising the sixteen massive suspension chains and this was completed by 9 July. Concurrent with the Menai operations, Telford constructed the Conway Suspension Bridge, the first stone of which was laid on 3 April 1822.[11] Both bridges were opened in 1826, that at Menai on Monday 30 January, and the Conway on 1 July.[12] Very aptly the first vehicle to pass over the great bridges was the Holyhead mail.

### RENNIE'S HARBOUR WORKS

For years the sailing packets were small vessels of less than 100 tons, crewed by some ten men, and taking between 18 and 40 hours to fight their way across the Irish Sea. At Holyhead from early times they anchored off Parry's Island (otherwise Ynys Rug). In 1810, however, the Act for improvements at Holyhead and Howth having been passed, construction commenced at Holyhead of a pier—known as the 'Admiralty Pier'—1,150ft long and 50ft wide, with a lighthouse at its head, running due east from the inner side of Salt Island, with a 60ft jetty at right angles to the pier and 8oft from its head. At the same time a small pier, 550ft long, was constructed on the opposite shore from the Pilbeo Rock, leaving an opening between it and the Admiralty Pier of 420ft. This small pier was also provided with a jetty and had a graving dock for merchant vessels on its west side. The works, planned and executed by John Rennie, were completed in 1824, and provided a harbour area of six acres at low water at a total cost of about £142,000.[13] Rennie had originally proposed additional works in the inner harbour and on the outer side of Salt Island which, had they been carried out, would have saved much time and labour in later years. (Further history of Holyhead harbour is discussed in chapter 9.)

On the Irish side the packets moored at first off Ringsend but from 1796 they used the new Pigeon House Dock in the mouth of the River Liffey. On 1 August 1818 they were transferred to Rennie's new harbour at Howth, some nine miles north-east of Dublin. In 1817, however, Rennie commenced harbour works at Dun Laoghaire which, with the introduction of deeper draught steam vessels on the mail and passenger services, and renamed Kingstown in honour of a visit from King George IV, was gradually to take traffic away from Howth. Also in 1817 it was decided to make a small landing place in the little cove at Porth Dafarch, on the westerley coast of Holy Island, to land mails during easterly winds. It went out of use with the demise of the sailing packets.[14]

### FIRST STEAM MAIL PACKETS

Steamers first started operating from Holyhead in 1819, put on by the New Steam Packet Company. There were then seven sailing packets on the Holyhead mail service, and the coming of the steamers, with their superior accommodation and improved timekeeping, threatened the passenger business of the sailing vessels. By the spring of 1820 the Post Office was giving consideration to the use of steam and the New Steam Packet Company offered to take the mails in their Napier-built paddle steamers *Talbot* (150 tons) and *Ivanhoe* (170 tons). The Post Office preferred to compete, however, and two paddlers were constructed on the Thames, the *Lightning* (205 tons) and *Meteor* (189 tons). Crews from Holyhead went south to fetch them in May 1821 and on going into service it was noted with satisfaction that their performance was superior to that of their rivals.[15] Captain Skinner got the *Lightning*. The new steam service received royal blessing when soon after its commencement George IV crossed over to Ireland with Skinner. The two men had long been acquainted and the King gave permission that the *Lightning* should be renamed *Royal Sovereign* in memory of the event. The large arch at the entrance to the Admiralty Pier at Holyhead also commemorated the royal visit. So successful were the Post Office packets that the New Steam Packet Company withdrew its vessels, though the *Ivanhoe* was later purchased by the Post Office and returned to Holyhead.[16]

The Holyhead steamers caused concern in Liverpool. The Dublin mails still went via Chester and Holyhead, with consequent delays in transit, and Liverpool demanded its own service. The Post Office thereupon decided once more to construct new steam packets, and the Liverpool—Kingstown mail steamers, calling at Holyhead, commenced operating on 29 August 1826.[17] The Holyhead steamers, however, continued in the main to use Howth until 22 January 1834 when all the services went to Kingstown.[18] On 17 December 1834 the Dublin & Kingstown Railway was opened, the mail being carried from that day. Authorised by Act of 6 September 1831 to make a line from Westland Row, near the Post Office in Sackville Street, Dublin, and thence along the south shore of Dublin Bay to terminate near the southwest angle of Kingstown harbour, the railway as constructed was of double track throughout with two additional lines at Westland Row.[19]

The Liverpool packets cut into the Holyhead passenger traffic; during the first eight years of steam at Holyhead the expenses there totalled £231,000 and the receipts £140,000.[20] The expense of running two packet stations for the Dublin mails, and the increased costs of steam over sail provoked criticism in the 1830s, some of which alleged Post Office mismanagement. In 1832 the English and Irish Post Offices were amalgamated, and the opportunity thus given to reconsider the operation of the Irish mail traffic resulted in 1837 in all Post Office packet services being transferred to the Admiralty. The Post Office continued to stipulate the timetable requirements, the Admiralty ran the ships, and the Treasury paid.[21] Repairs to the packets on the Irish service were done at Holyhead.

### LAST YEARS OF THE HOLYHEAD MAIL COACH

The mail coach timetable in 1797 provided for a total journey time of just under 45 hours. The down coach left Charing Cross at 8pm, breakfasted at Northampton, took dinner at Lichfield and tea at Stafford. Arrival at Chester was at midnight with a stop of one hour for supper. By about 5.30am the coach had reached St Asaph where breakfast was taken. Ferryside, on the Conway estuary, was reached at 9am and at 9.30 the coach passed through Conway. It reached Bangor Ferry House at 12.20pm where an hour was allowed for dinner and the crossing. Arrival time at Holyhead was at about 4.50pm. Return departure from Holyhead was at 7am, with dinner at Conway, supper at Chester, breakfast at Stafford, dinner at Hinckley, and arrival in London at 4am.[22] Post Office business was transacted at the meal stops and at other places along the route.

Improvements to the Holyhead Road resulted in a new schedule introduced from 5 April 1819 whereby a time of 36 hours was attained,[23] the mail leaving London at 8pm as before and, with favourable winds for the packets, arriving in Dublin in about 48 hours. At about the same time as the Act of Union a telegraph was erected at Holyhead so that the mail coach could be held on the approach of a late arriving packet, thereby saving a whole day. Of all the mail and stage coaches, that to Holyhead was perhaps the most famous, and strenuous efforts were always made to improve the timings. By 1832 the time was down to 28 hours 6 minutes, including stops at Birmingham, Shrewsbury, Corwen and Bangor. Arrival at Holyhead was at midday, twenty-five minutes before the Howth packet sailed. The return mail coach left Holyhead at 12.15am and was due in London shortly after six on the second morning. By 1836 the London—Holyhead timing was down to 26 hours 55 minutes.

For a few years, however, Holyhead was to lose the mail service. With the opening of the London & Birmingham Railway in 1838, and its connections by way of the Grand Junction and the Liverpool & Manchester Railways to Liverpool, the Post Office transferred the Irish and other mails to rail. By an Act of 14 August 1838 the Postmaster General was empowered to call on railway companies to take the mails, and the first travelling post office came into use that year. A contract was entered into with the City of Dublin Steam Packet Company—a concern which was later to be a rival of the Chester & Holyhead Railway and its successor in tendering for the Holyhead mail service—whereby from 24 January 1839 a new schedule was operated between Liverpool and Kingstown giving an overall London—Dublin timing of about $22\frac{1}{2}$ hours, and Holyhead was left merely with the local mails and those for the Chester area. Two of the Admiralty packets were taken off the Holyhead service, leaving four Admiralty vessels to continue there for just over a decade: *Zephyr, Doterel, Otter,* and *Sprightly.* Holyhead was to resume a portion of the London—Dublin mail service on the opening of the Chester & Crewe Railway (chapter 2) but did not regain the whole traffic until the opening throughout of the Chester & Holyhead Railway.

CHAPTER 2

*First Railway Schemes*

PROPOSED LONDON—PORTH DYNLLAEN RAILWAY 1836

The question of further improvement to the Irish mail route was to occupy the attention of the government for a decade commencing in the mid 1830s. There was, however, some early private initiative. Had the Menai Straits not been such an obstacle to a rail link, the established port of Holyhead might have been considered from the outset. At a meeting in Dublin on 9 August 1835, however, Henry Archer, manager of the Festiniog Railway, proposed a rail and steamer link with London via Porth Dynllaen, about 20 miles south-west of Caernarvon. Not unexpectedly, he thought that the rail route should pass through Portmadoc. In January 1836 a meeting in Caernarvon confirmed the opinion that Porth Dynllaen was a suitable location for a harbour on the Welsh side, as it was capable of sheltering the largest steam packets. A railway to London was planned through Merionethshire, Montgomeryshire, the Teme Valley, and thence through Ludlow, Worcester, Stratford, and Oxford. Such a route, of 220 miles, promised to beat all others as to speed and would, the meeting proclaimed, be 'the means of introducing into Ireland what she most wants, not only in capital and enterprise, but the mind of England'.[1] Following this, a committee was appointed to seek the help of the Lord Lieutenant of Ireland in publicising the project in high places, and the eminent engineers, Charles Vignoles and John Urpeth Rastrick, were asked to survey possible routes from Porth Dynllaen through the

Welsh mountains to join existing railways to the south.[2] These surveys were carried out in the spring and early summer of 1836 (map page 10).

### THE VIGNOLES SURVEYS

Vignoles' most direct route was a trial line via Tremadoc, Ffestiniog, Bala, Llangollen, Shrewsbury, Iron Bridge, and Wolverhampton; the distance from Porth Dynllaen to London was 244 miles. There were, however, gradients of 1 in 16 and 17 for two miles immediately after Tan-y-Bwlch, leading to a ten mile stretch of 1 in 153 through Trawsfynydd to a two mile tunnel under the Pass of Treweryd. A second trial line went by Barmouth, Towyn, Machynlleth, Dinas Mawddwy, and Llanfair to join the first at Shrewsbury, the total distance to London being 267 miles. Again gradients were heavy: two miles at 1 in 38 east of Dinas Mawddwy led to a tunnel of three miles under the Pass of Bwlch-y-Fedwen. A third trial line left the second east of Machynlleth and proceeded via Newtown, Snead, Bishops Castle, and Ludlow, towards Worcester and Oxford; from Porth Dynllaen to London was 260 miles. The ruling gradient on this line was 1 in 52 over two miles leading to a tunnel of $1\frac{1}{2}$ miles under Carno Pass. To avoid the worst gradients Vignoles recommended a fourth route which, with a ruling gradient of 1 in 150, ran via Barmouth, Bala, and Llangollen where it joined the first trial line to Wolverhampton, giving a mileage to London of 260. While the foregoing routes were being examined, the committee also asked Vignoles to survey from Chester to Holyhead and from Bangor to Porth Dynllaen.[3] These instructions were sparked off by reports of the promotion of a railway from Ruabon to Chester, and by the Chester & Crewe and Chester & Birkenhead projects, all of which pointed to Chester shortly becoming a railway of some importance.

# FIRST RAILWAY SCHEMES

## BRUNEL PLANS A ROUTE TO IRELAND

While Vignoles was thus engaged, July 1836 saw the appearance, albeit from a distance, of the Great Western Railway's engineer, Isambard Kingdom Brunel, who was reported to be surveying a railway route from Gloucester to New Quay on Cardigan Bay. This was envisaged as being a direct link in a route to Ireland. For the time being this proposal faded out of the picture but it was to re-appear later in different guise. With Brunel working up from Gloucester and Vignoles covering the North Wales area there was considerable difference of opinion as to which route might be best. At this point the government took a direct hand in the question.

## IRISH RAILWAY COMMISSION

It was becoming increasingly apparent that there should be some government policy regarding railway construction in Ireland, both to secure the best strategic routes and to provide employment. In December 1836 commissioners were appointed to consider and report upon a general system of railways in Ireland. The commissioners were Thomas Drummond, Under Secretary of State in Ireland; Col John Fox Burgoyne, an engineer officer and chairman of the Irish Public Board of Works; Peter Barlow, professor of mathematics at Woolwich Military Academy; and Richard Griffith, civil engineer, who had recently completed his famous geological survey of Ireland. They appointed Vignoles as engineer and on 31 March instructed him to report on the investigations already made as to the connecting railway and port on the English and Welsh side.

Vignoles then made additional surveys to complete permutations of the mid Wales lines and also laid down two new routes for exploration, from Tech Hill near Ellesmere to Norton Bridge via Market Drayton, and from Tech Hill to Wolverhampton via Newport, both to join the Grand Junction

Railway. The results showed, as far as Vignoles was concerned, that he still considered his original recommended line to be the most suitable, and that he believed that if the Ruabon—Chester line was constructed, the Liverpool traffic for Ireland would go via Bala. He ruled out the direct route from Chester to Holyhead or Porth Dynllaen: two lengthy tunnels would be required at Penmaenbach and Penmaenmawr, and he foresaw great difficulties at Bangor on account of awkward levels and disruption to property. 'The construction of a second bridge across the Straits of Menai', said Vignoles, 'is too great an undertaking to be seriously contemplated', and, 'the present bridge across the Menai Straits must be made use of, the locomotive engines starting from, and stopping at each end', if the Holyhead line were to be made. The alternative Bangor—Porth Dynllaen line would be very expensive, requiring four tunnels and as many viaducts. The northern route was nearly 20 miles further from London than that via Bala; whereas the first would be between sea and mountains, inaccessible for 90 miles of its length, the latter, though passing through a mountainous area, would be an artery serving both sides. Vignoles thought that the northern route should be viewed only as a means of attaining by railway either Holyhead or Ormes Bay (the latter, now Llandudno, being seen as a possible site for a harbour), and that this at once raised the question of the comparative merits of Ormes Bay, Porth Dynllaen, and Holyhead as packet stations for the Irish mail steamers.

### HOLYHEAD V PORTH DYNLLAEN

The commissioners' first essential task was to choose the best port which combined shortness of sea journey with good harbour facilities; the railway route was of secondary importance. They envisaged the coming removal of the mails to Liverpool on the opening of the London & Birmingham Railway and forecast a journey time to Dublin by that route of $22\frac{1}{4}$ hours, four hours quicker than by the coach service to Holyhead. Ormes Bay, between Great and Little Ormes Heads, was noted as giving a probable improvement on the Liverpool timing if a railway could be constructed thereto, the sea journey to Kingstown being 96 miles, the rail distance to London calculated at 230 miles, and the overall time $19\frac{1}{2}$ hours. However, $1\frac{1}{2}$ hours could be gained over Ormes Bay by using Porth Dynllaen, the sea distance thence to Kingstown being 70 miles, and the prevailing wind more favourable.

Lieutenant W. L. Sheringham RN reported favourably to the commissioners on the potential harbour facilities at Porth Dynllaen in June 1838. The commissioners also had a report from Captain Beaufort RN, an Admiralty hydrographer (later Rear Admiral Sir Francis Beaufort whose name is perpetuated in the 'Beaufort Scale' of wind forces) who, in October 1836, had been instructed by the Treasury to carry out surveys for harbours best suited for the packet stations. His report, dated 4 December 1836, came down, indirectly, in favour of Holyhead: 'As long as Dublin mails are carried by coaches, on common roads, the best place of embarkation, in every respect, will be Holyhead, which is only 62 statute miles from Kingstown harbour, and which only requires a little elongation of the pier in order to admit a larger class of steam vessels at low water'. However, as a naval man (and thus somewhat unsuited to judge the matter), he proclaimed flatly that a railway to Holyhead would be impossible, and suggested Porth Dynllaen as the only alternative. Vignoles, in his report to the commissioners, backed him up: '. . . the advantages are decidedly in favour of Porth Dynllaen as a packet station, and if Holyhead had not already existed as such, no hesitation could have arisen as to the determination of the question'.

The commissioners decided otherwise. Their main business was concerned with Ireland, however, and it was to be left to a committee on Post Office communication with Ireland, which heard evidence in 1842, finally to decide the matter. The 1838 commissioners' feelings are revealed in their comment on a letter to them from William (later Sir William) Cubitt, civil engineer, dated 2 July 1838. Cubitt had been investigating the problem of communications with Ireland for some five years. In 1836 private parties had asked him to make a survey for a new harbour at Ormes Bay and for a connecting railway thereto. He could think of no less expensive way than to go via Ormes Bay but believed that an extension of the line to Holyhead would serve best the object of speed and shortness in the London—Dublin communication. Cubitt's views, which arrived just in time to be included in the commissioners' report, were in fact close to their own: 'Our opinions, in every essential, are in a great degree confirmed by so good an authority'.[4] It was 'Round One' to Holyhead.

### ORMES BAY SCHEMES 1836–8

The Ormes Bay proposal of 1836 was for a railway via the North Wales coast to Chester, and thence to Crewe and the Grand Junction Railway by way of Waverton and Tattenhall. Plans were prepared in November 1836 for Parliamentary approval.[5] In the session of 1837, however, the St George's Harbour & Railway Bill was unsuccessful as against the rival Chester & Birkenhead and Chester & Crewe Bills, both of which obtained Royal Assent. In September 1838 there was a revivalist meeting in Chester to promote the St George's Harbour & Chester Railway. The estimated cost of the harbour and breakwater was £200,000, and that of the railway, which was planned to join the authorised Chester & Crewe at Rowton, about three miles south-east of Chester, £600,000. This, it was said, compared very favourably with the current Vignoles project of a mountainous mid-Wales line costing an estimated £3½ million.[6] A private enterprise view of the matter appeared in Herepath's *Railway Magazine* in October 1838 when a correspondent opined that Porth Dynllaen was an extremely difficult place to which to make a railway. 'Our men of business also hesitate on other grounds; they say "If people from Ireland will pass by Holyhead, why should they stop at the Ormesheads, and not proceed to Liverpool?" Again, the Government may project some other line, and then their outlay would be totally lost. For myself, I am perfectly satisfied that the only rational plan is to lay down a railway from Chester to Holyhead, by way of the Ormesheads. No half measures will stand long in these days'. The directors of the Chester & Crewe had, he said, been urged to take up the Ormes Head line, but were holding back for the reasons he had given. Despite this, it was not to be too long before the Chester company was aspiring to make a line to Holyhead.

### CHESTER & CREWE RAILWAY

The Chester & Crewe was incorporated by Act of 30 June 1837, with a capital of £250,000, to make a railway commencing from the north-west side of Brook Street, Chester, to join the Grand Junction Railway near Crewe Hall. At Chester the C & C joined the Chester & Birkenhead Railway, authorised by Act of 12 July 1837. The chairman of the C & C was John Uniacke, mayor of Chester and chairman of the River Dee Navigation improvement committee. At a C & C meeting in October 1839 Uniacke said that the directors had been seeking access to the Potteries by a new line to Harecastle. The proprietors had rejected the proposal, however, and it was now thought best to amalgamate with the Grand Junction Railway. In return, the GJR was to pledge itself to a Potteries line, and to completion of the C & C if the latter's capital ran out. To this the GJR was only too amenable; it had for some time feared that the C & C might fall into the hands of the Manchester & Birmingham Railway which also joined it at Crewe. The Bill for incorporating the C & C in the GJR received Royal Assent on 19 May 1840.

The works on the Chester & Crewe and the Chester & Birkenhead were completed fairly quickly despite flooding in the winter of 1839–40 and the usual navvy fights, one of which, on the C & B, necessitated having the military called out. The Birkenhead was opened to the public on 23 September, and the C & C on 1 October 1840. That month Herepath's *Railway Magazine* noted that the C & C was considered by the

GJR to be an important auxiliary; that company was giving thought to the removal of its locomotive establishment at Edge Hill to Crewe. From 6 April 1841 the Dublin mails commenced taking the C & C and C & B route to Birkenhead where they were taken aboard the packets, Liverpool passengers and mails coming over the Mersey to make connection.[7]

Though the C & C was purchased as a protective measure by the Grand Junction, that company was none too pleased with early C & C traffic receipts. The GJR board was not without hope, however, that its acquisition would ultimately prove a source of profit and in fact 1842 was to see the culmination, in a government report, of inquiries into the viability of extending the C & C to Holyhead.

### GREAT HOLYHEAD RAILWAY PROJECT 1838-42

Between 1838 and 1842 attempts were made to secure official blessing for a line to Holyhead. On 29 October 1838 a large meeting at Bangor heard Francis Giles, engineer, speak on a survey he had made from Chester to Holyhead. His proposed line was 87 miles in length, 60 of which were level. He suggested a new bridge over the Conway estuary but proposed that the existing Menai Suspension Bridge be used for the railway, the locomotives being detached and the carriages worked over by rope and stationary engines. The estimated cost was £2½ million. Giles did not approve of a line to Porth Dynllaen and said that as regards Shrewsbury or Chester being the point of departure for a new railway for the Irish traffic, the latter was preferable as it would permit access from Liverpool and Manchester.

George Stephenson was of similar mind. A letter from him to that effect to Uniacke was published in the *Chester Gazette* in October, and at a meeting of the C & C on 14 November support was pledged for the scheme. Thus committed, the C & C sought a second opinion to that of Giles, and Stephenson was asked to carry out surveys, also taking Porth Dynllaen into consideration. On 19 December 1838 Stephenson reported in favour of Holyhead and against Vignoles' line from Shrewsbury via Bala, which he considered impracticable.[8] Like Giles, however, he proposed rope haulage of railway carriages over the Menai Bridge. With the pace warming up, January 1839 saw further meetings, in Shrewsbury and Chester, supporting Vignoles and Stephenson respectively. The *Railway Magazine* for February 1839 commented:

> It is . . . curious to see the manifestos of impracticability published against each other's projects by the rival engineers, Mr. G. Stephenson and Mr. Vignoles. The latter gentleman makes several charges of unfairness against Mr. Stephenson's statements in the engineering difficulties and measures of distances respecting the Porth-Dynllaen line, which we suppose will be answered by Mr. Stephenson. We are ourselves sorry to see the charges and recriminations, which must tend much to shake the faith and confidence of the public in professional statements.

According to Samuel Smiles, Vignoles published a defence of his line, confessing at the same time that to go against Stephenson was 'almost bearding the lion in his den'. If anyone, Vignoles had the ability to do some bearding. Among the great number of brilliant, self-reliant, men of his time he must stand with the foremost. His career, indeed his whole life, had been exceptional. After hectic early years of soldiering and exploration, the latter including surveys of South Carolina and the neighbouring states in 1816, he had emerged more than ready for the Railway Age. The Rennies introduced Vignoles to railways in 1825, employing him on their projected Brighton Railway and Liverpool & Manchester Railway surveys. The Oxford Canal, Wigan Branch Railway, North Union, and Sheffield Ashton-under-Lyne & Manchester followed. He was, by common consent, by the early 1840s accepted as one of the leading civil engineers in the country.[9] Vignoles' Irish interests had particular bearing on his arguments with Stephenson; he was engineer-in-chief to the Dublin & Kingstown Railway.

While the opposing merits of Holyhead and Porth Dynllaen

were being argued out, John Jenkins, engineer to the proposed St George's Harbour & Chester Railway, decided the public required reminding that his scheme was still in being. In a letter to Herepath published in January 1839 he emphasised the excellent harbour potential of Ormes Bay, and the cheapness of the railway thence to Chester, with its light gradients and cost of but £10,000 per mile. He claimed that 'this route has met with the unqualified preference of a great majority of the most influential citizens of Dublin, and that with their . . . support, the company are now proceeding with vigour in the prosecution of their project'.

The *Railway Magazine* also reported in January 1839 that a deputation from the St George's Harbour & Chester concern had met the Chancellor of the Exchequer. They were told there would be no grant of public money towards either the Stephenson or Vignoles projects. Two recent events also boosted the hopes of the promoters: heavy gales had slightly damaged the Menai Bridge, making it all the more unlikely that Stephenson's trains would be allowed near it; and those same gales had caused two vessels to founder with the loss of sixty lives which could have been saved had a harbour existed in Ormes Bay.[10]

To all this the main protagonists paid scant heed, and in March 1839 a prospectus for the 'Great Holyhead Railway', nominally independent but backed by the Chester & Crewe, was published by Herepath. In the following month Stephenson spoke before a general meeting of the C & C. He had, he said, levelled the two lines to their respective ports; the Vignoles' line to Porth Dynllaen he characterised as 'one that ought never to have been attempted', while his own, to Holyhead, he described as being 'as smooth as the waters which flowed beside it'.[11] At this point, when Stephenson's Holyhead line seemed fairly set on course, Herepath put his finger on the one weak link. In an editorial in the *Railway Magazine* in June 1839 he criticised the suggested crossing of the Menai:

> Mr. Stephenson's notion, however, of passing the Menai is perfectly absurd; in fact, it is monstrous. The bridge between

the centres of the pillars is 579 feet; each carriage, therefore, if drawn by a horse, could not have to be drawn less than 1,000 or 1,200 feet. Supposing there were 10 carriages besides engine and tender, from 12,000 to 14,000 feet, between 2 to 3 miles would have to be traversed in the middle of the line by horse-power, which, including unhooking, &c., could not be done in less than a-half or three-quarters of an hour. That is, from 15 to 20 miles would be lost by a passage of only 580 feet. The only rational way of passing the Menai is by another bridge, either wooden as Mr. Stephenson suggests, or iron as the late Mr. Rennie and Mr. Telford proposed.

Herepath's argument was to prove fruitful. Indeed it seems probable that the great engineer had already decided to alter the mode of crossing the Straits, for in the July issue of the magazine it was again rumoured that a separate wooden bridge was planned. That month saw another rumour, from the same source, that the 'Great Holyhead Railway has died a natural death', an impertinence quickly denied by the Chester & Crewe. Any blame for delay was put on the present position of the money market.

### THE 'HUNGRY FORTIES'

There was in fact a trade recession which delayed many railway projects, and in the Parliamentary session of 1840 not one new company was to be incorporated. The mid 1830s had seen the passing of a number of Acts for main line railways, and capital had largely been exhausted. Promoters were sitting back, awaiting openings of lines and first receipts, before committing themselves further. Of greater importance were the difficulties, in 1836, of some of the Irish banks, which in turn brought pressure on the City of London. Disastrous harvests of 1838 and 1839, coupled to a period of speculation which left millions of pounds in accepted bills outstanding, a cotton price war with American planters, and an outflow of capital to finance American expansion, had produced an effect where investors were few and circumspect.

By June 1839 the Bank of England was seeking aid from the bankers of Paris. This then was the situation in which it seemed that a railway from Chester to Holyhead was but a pipe dream.

CHAPTER 3

*Success in Parliament*

COMMITTEE ON LONDON—DUBLIN COMMUNICATION 1840

Development of national communications was not entirely stifled by the depression of the early 1840s. Though for the time being the grand strategy could not be pursued in terms of pick and shovel work, important routes were planned which could be commenced when times were better. Two such routes were still largely undetermined: London to Glasgow and Edinburgh, and London to Dublin. In November 1839 the Treasury appointed Lieut-Col Sir Frederick Smith and Professor Peter Barlow as commissioners to inquire into and report upon the alternative lines. Their findings on the London—Dublin question were reported in April 1840.[1] There were of course the multiple Vignoles lines already discussed, two by Stephenson and Giles from Chester to Holyhead, and the Ormes Bay line by Jenkins. The commissioners' report commenced by casting gloom over the Vignoles camp:

> It also appears that a line was surveyed between Wolverhampton and Shrewsbury, on which Mr. Locke has made a report . . . but we do not learn that any survey has hitherto been made for determining the best line between Shrewsbury and Chirk, so that the project for a railway to Porthdynllaen by Mr. Vignoles' route is apparently still incomplete.

The commissioners left London on 30 December to inspect the various routes on the ground. From Chester, Stephenson and Jenkins accompanied them over their respective projects.

They also met Henry Archer (chapter 2), who claimed he was the promoter of the Bangor—Porth Dynllaen line, somewhat to the commissioners' surprise as they had not received any plans and believed the scheme to be unsupported. Giles and Vignoles were not in attendance. Giles had consistently opposed Stephenson since the latter had proved him wrong over crossing Chat Moss on the Liverpool & Manchester Railway (Giles had said it could not be done); and Vignoles had written to the commissioners saying he had nothing to add to his 1837 report on the Porth Dynllaen lines, but pleading for a fuller investigation which would prove his case. The commissioners were not impressed:

> We here think it right to remark, that had there seemed to us, after an inspection of the country, any ground for supposing that a line more easy of execution than that from Chester to Holyhead was to be found between Porthdynllaen and Shrewsbury, by the Bala Pass, which Mr. Vignoles has stated to be the lowest in this part of North Wales, or had there appeared statistical reasons for preferring the Inland line, we might have felt the propriety of pressing upon the consideration of their Lordships the foregoing suggestion of Mr. Vignoles, but we have seen no cause for so departing from the strict letter of our instructions.

Nevertheless, as will be seen, they did examine the country through which the Vignoles routes were projected.

The commissioners noted that all three coastal lines took nearly the same route. Jenkins' line had hardly any difficulties—only a tunnel near the Ormes Bay termination. As to the Holyhead lines, in the main Stephenson's was cheaper than that of Giles. At the Penmaenbach headland, for instance, Stephenson's tunnel was 500 yards in length; Giles had provided for one of 1,408 yards. Stephenson went around Penmaenmawr, protecting his railway with a sea wall; Giles bored through the clay and slate for 1,628 yards. Both engineers planned an embankment over the Malltraeth Marsh on Anglesey but Giles, to avoid as much of the marsh as possible, deviated the line and landed himself instead with a tunnel of 1,065 yards at Trefdraeth. The commissioners also met Brunel who, in April, submitted details of a line he was surveying as part of a railway from Didcot on the GWR, to Worcester, and thence by Vignoles' route via Newtown, Carno, Dolgelly, and Barmouth to Porth Dynllaen.

From the evidence they had gathered, the commissioners favoured the North Wales coast route and once again the final decision hung on the question of the most suitable harbour. For this the Admiralty was called in. Rear-Admiral Sir James Gordon and Captain Beechey RN, reporting to the commissioners in January 1840, had rejected Porth Dynllaen and Ormes Bay. Referring to them as mere roadsteads, they were considered to be 'totally out of the question'. Holyhead, they thought, offered the best opportunity for development into a good packet station and harbour of refuge. There was no river to discharge silt, the harbour was in a bay, and the government already had an establishment there. The Treasury was left in no doubt by the summing up in the commissioners' report:

> Holyhead being selected as the port for the Dublin packets we are of opinion that the best line of railway for the communication between London and Dublin is that proposed by Mr. George Stephenson, namely, by Chester and Bangor to Holyhead.

So that there should be no misunderstanding, a statement was appended to the effect that had Porth Dynllaen been found the most suitable, the recommendation would still have been for a railway along the coast from Chester. There was an immediate response from the Chester & Crewe. On 18 May 1840 Uniacke told a meeting of MPs and others friendly to the Great Holyhead Railway that the reason there had been no application to Parliament for a Bill in the previous March was because the commissioners' report had been delayed by a petition which compelled them to examine the Vignoles routes. This Uniacke thought to be fair grounds for seeking suspension of the standing orders of Parliament relating to the giving of notice for their Bill in March. The meeting voted to construct the Great Holyhead line and to apply to Parliament for assistance.[2] On 23 May a deputation from the promoters of the Chester & Holyhead Railway (they had dropped the earlier title) met the Chancellor of the Exchequer. They pointed out that the government could save £77,953 per annum by concentrating the packets at Holyhead, and requests were made to drop the standing orders relating to the giving of notice for the Bill as well as the customary 10 per cent deposit required on capital.

Meanwhile, Herepath's *Railway Magazine* of 16 May, still rumbling angrily on about the Menai Bridge proposal, criticised the commissioners' report. The bridge, said Herepath, vibrated 'most fearfully' in high winds. It was not thought by many to be as safe as the commissioners would have it, and the accuracy of their calculations as to its safe loading was questioned. Even if the commissioners were right, why then did both Stephenson and Giles avoid taking locomotives over the bridge and propose instead the inconvenience of either horse traction or a fixed engine with stations on each side?

> To our comprehension, these propositions do not show much confidence in the strength of the bridge. If what we have heard be true, we should not well relish being a passenger in a train going over it in a high wind. Is it quite certain, in such a case the carriages could keep on the rails?

Herepath thought that as the local traffic would be negligible no company would finance the line; the commissioners would have done better to recommend Ormes Bay. Perhaps this attitude was not surprising. Herepath's leaders were much against Sir Frederick Smith and the Railway Department generally. Sir Frederick had been appointed Inspector-General of Railways on 2 December 1840 and had since then been subjected to criticism from the railway press against what was considered to be meddling in private business by a government department headed by a person who was deemed incompetent. Sir Signal Smith (one of the less obnoxious epithets by which he was tagged) put up with the job until December 1841, when he resigned to become director of the Royal Engineers' establishment at Chatham. He was, in fact, very highly qualified by his Royal Engineer training to assess the nature of heavy engineering works.[3] He was to reappear on other government commissions concerning railways and was to pronounce on the harbour of refuge at Holyhead (chapter 9).

On 23 June 1840, Lord Grosvenor, on the provisional committee of the Chester & Holyhead Railway, moved in Parliament that the promoters be permitted to bring in a Bill in the next session, and that the standing orders be dispensed with. Sir Robert Peel, and Henry Labouchere, President of the Board of Trade, accepted that the railway would be of national importance but refused, reluctantly, to a departure from the strict Parliamentary rules laid down for private business. By 120 to 110 votes Lord Grosvenor's motion was defeated. In August Herepath was able gleefully to say that 'at present this project is at a stand still'. During 1841, the height of the depression, nothing further was done until December when a meeting of the promoters, held at Bangor, decided to give Parliamentary notices on the railways of Stephenson and Giles.[4]

### COMMITTEE ON POST OFFICE COMMUNICATION WITH IRELAND 1842

The next move was made by the government. In June 1842 a select committee of the House of Commons was set up to examine the question of Post Office communication with Ireland. Once more the merits of Holyhead and Porth Dynllaen were reviewed. By inference, the committee preferred Holyhead, the main reason being that as the speed by rail was about three times faster than by steamer, the shortest sea route should be adopted. Liverpool returned fleetingly to the discussion, only to be dismissed as inconvenient and unsafe as a packet station. Ormes Bay rated no interest.

The evidence heard by the committee is of interest. William Cubitt made the point that Vignoles' line would inevitably get blocked by snow. George Bidder, civil engineer, saw no engineering difficulties in the Chester—Holyhead route and thought no other line would be as cheap. As local traffic would be small, he suggested a single line, with passing places, protected by the electric telegraph (Bidder was a founder of the Electric Telegraph Company). The Bangor—Porth Dynllaen line he considered impracticable. Bidder's opinion carried weight; he was noted for his immense powers of mental calculation, and was a terror in giving Parliamentary evidence by his ability to spot a flaw in an opponent's case. His friendship with the Stephensons dated from 1822 when he was with Robert at Edinburgh University.[5]

George Stephenson explained that as to crossing the Menai Bridge, each carriage weighed about five tons, equal to a coach and four horses; if taken across by rope there would be no oscillation. He had laid out the line so that it could be carried either across the bridge or under one of the arches to a place at which another bridge might be made. It was perfectly safe to take trains on the bridge and the delay would only amount to ten minutes. Like Bidder, he believed the coastal line to be the cheapest possible. Of the Bala route he stated: 'I am not bold enough to project such a line; indeed, I consider it is quite out of the question to attempt it'. Asked if he was referring to the inland line or the Bangor—Porth Dynllaen route, he replied: 'I have examined both lines; in fact, there is not a creek, or ravine, or valley, which I have not examined, with a view to getting the cheapest line possible'. The Bangor—Porth Dynllaen line would terminate 80 feet above sea level, requiring a stationary engine to transfer goods.

The 1842 report appears to have decided the issue as to the best railway route. From here on the promoters went ahead, with the guarded approval of Sir Robert Peel who had become Prime Minister in 1841. Faced with war in China, an invasion of Afghanistan, open enmity from France, Canada, and the

United States, virtual anarchy at home from the Anti-Corn Law League and the Chartists, and with the effects of the depression, he was engaged in shaking a discredited British government into a programme aimed at overcoming the crisis. Peel's Irish background was of importance in fostering his interest in the nascent Chester & Holyhead Railway for, should home troubles spread across the St George's Channel, a fast railway and steamer communication with the Irish capital would be invaluable. During the previous Whig administration there had been much talk and no action; Sir Robert felt it was time to move.

In March 1843 the Earl of Wicklow was host to a meeting of members of both Houses of Parliament and it was agreed to ask Peel if government aid would be forthcoming to carry out the 1842 recommendations.[6] In April the Grand Jury of Cork addressed a memorial to the government in favour of the CHR.[7] Next month the government appointed Captains Back and Fair RN, to make further surveys of the harbours at Holyhead and Porth Dynllaen, and James Walker, civil engineer, was also asked for his observations. By October 1843 both reports were available. The naval officers favoured Holyhead.[8]

### JAMES WALKER'S REPORT 1843

James Walker's report, dated 6 October 1843, was made to the Admiralty, who had turned all the previous evidence over to him.[9] Inspections of Holyhead and Porth Dynllaen harbours took Walker until late August, when he commenced examination of the CHR and Bangor—Porth Dynllaen lines. As to the CHR, he objected to using the Menai Bridge and to making the line single with passing places, 'an expedient which may have a saving in the first cost to recommend it, but which the danger, the difficulty of repairing, the uncertainty, and the delay, ought much to outweigh'. He preferred a separate arched bridge over the Menai:

> The unfitness for a railway of the present suspension bridge

which is approached by a slope of 1 in 25; the interference by engines and trains with the present use of it, which interference will, I am sure, be more frequent and annoying than appears to have been contemplated; the delay at all times, and particularly in stormy weather; the having to cross Bangor with an embankment 70 feet in the deepest part; the numerous curves to reach the bridge, and the repetition of similar curves on the Anglesea side, are all objectionable. I think neither the Holyhead Road, nor the Menai Bridge, should be injuriously interfered with. . . . The railway bridge may cross at the Swilly or Gorred Goch rocks. The position and width of the latter are taken from a survey by Mr. Vignoles; they are nearest the direct line. The late Mr. Rennie and Mr. Telford both proposed fixed bridges over the Straits; the cost was, I believe, the only objection. The ironwork of bridges may be done now at half the cost, and the traffic will be very much greater than was then calculated upon.

I think Mr. Stephenson's plan* of terminating on the west, better than that of Mr. Giles, which takes the east side of Holyhead Harbour.

(*If there is any inaccuracy in my statement of Mr. Stephenson's line it must be ascribed in part to my not receiving from him any explanation of his line, beyond what the documents he had previously sent in afforded me.)

Walker had not examined the southerly mountainous approach, which he stated was backed by the GWR. He had received much help from George Carr Glyn and Messrs Creed and Bury regarding the alternative London & Birmingham and Grand Junction approach through Crewe and Chester. As to train speeds over the proposed CHR, he thought London —Dublin could be done in 14 hours: 'Dublin time is 25min 22sec later. Much confusion and disappointment would be prevented by the clocks in the United Kingdom being all kept to Greenwich time. The true time for astronomical purposes might also be shown upon the dial'. Finally, the Bangor— Porth Dynllaen line was four miles longer than to Holyhead, 'but of the two I consider that to Porth-dyn-llaen the easier, and if an inland line to Holyhead, whether through Worcester, or Shrewsbury can be shown, which shall be as good as by far the greater portion of the Bangor to Porth-dyn-llaen line, it will be superior to the coast line, which has some heavy rock in parts, and which in some places upon the coast, will be much exposed to storms'.

### CHESTER & HOLYHEAD BILL IN PARLIAMENT

Despite Walker's implied resurrection of the Vignoles line, on 10 November 1843 the CHR promoters published the first notice in the *London Gazette* of their intention to apply for an Act of incorporation. At this point came a final attempt for a Chester to Ormes Bay line. Entitling themselves as the North Wales & Dublin Railway & Harbour Company, and with John Braithwaite and Thomas Page as railway and harbour engineers respectively, the promoters suggested that their line, to terminate either at Conway or Ormes Bay, would save £2 million over the CHR scheme. Additional railway mileage to Holyhead was, they said, a waste of public money and out of proportion to the time saved. Events had gone too far, however, and one can only marvel at the persistence of these people in view of official preference for the CHR.

The deposited plans and sections for the CHR Bill showed the main line commencing at or near the stations of the Chester & Crewe and Chester & Birkenhead Railways at Chester, and terminating on or near the old Customs House Quay at Holyhead. There was to be a branch from the main line, two miles south-west of Chester, running due east through Handbridge to the Chester & Crewe at Rowton Moor, about 1½ miles north of Waverton station, which would permit through running from Crewe to Holyhead, by-passing Chester. Powers were sought to lay down rails on the Menai Bridge, and for the LBR and GJR companies to contribute towards the CHR, with options to purchase or lease.

In February 1844 the LBR voted in favour of supporting the CHR.[10] There was some dissent. George Hudson was rampant at this time and put fear into 'Junius', writing in the *Railway*

*Times* of 24 February. 'Abandon your Holyhead folly!', he pleaded, imploring the LBR to retreat to its natural boundaries and strengthen itself against Hudson. The Grand Junction's meeting in February was cautious; the company was not now in negotiation with the CHR promoters, as it currently appeared that there was some doubt of there being any government help. There was something behind this; Peel had been playing 'hard to get'. A discussion had recently taken place in the House of Commons on the general subject of existing harbours of refuge where shipping could take shelter from storms. Holyhead was one such and Peel, referring to it, had also mentioned the CHR:

> With regard to the railway, there had been some negotiation respecting the conveyance of the mails, in the course of which the company had come down from £80,000 a year to £40,000, and he did not know what the effect of holding out a little longer might be (a laugh). Only yesterday a new company had made a proposition for constructing a line by way of Great Ormsby [sic], but at present he could make no further statements upon this subject.

This appeared in the *Railway Times* on 2 March. An editorial followed up with:

> The progress of this undertaking seems to be a novelty in the railway world. It has been formed, exists, and is in Parliament, with £165,000 deposit paid into Court, and no prospectus. It has crept up silently enough, without scheming, without advertisement...

The CHR Bill, presented by Owen Stanley MP, was read for the first time in the Commons on 14 March 1844 and for the second time eleven days later, when it was referred to committee. Much of the evidence repeated what had gone before to the various inquiries. George Stephenson said he now intended to tunnel through Penmaenbach as well as Penmaenmawr; he thought the seas too rough to risk going round the former. (During March the CHR directors noted that James Meadows Rendel (p 208) had been instructed by the

Admiralty to inspect the route of the railway along the sea beaches.) The Commissioners of Woods and Forests objected to the railway crossing by the Menai Bridge except under certain restrictions, and Stephenson recommended construction of a new bridge using the Britannia Rock. During the hearing a government representative was added to the committee on the request of Mr Gladstone, Vice-President of the Board of Trade, who required that if government money was involved the executive should be represented. This was a rare occurrence for a private Bill and, despite some remonstrance that the presence of the new member, Sir George Clerk of the Treasury, would involve additional time, both Peel and Labouchere insisted that the Bill was too important. When the Bill reached the Lords only the land portion had been approved. It would be necessary to introduce a further Bill for the Menai crossing in the next session. This was partly Stephenson's doing: he said that he would prefer to start work in 1844 rather than wait a year, reasoning that he could be proceeding with the tunnels which would take some three years to complete. The portion of the line left over until 1845 was that from the west bank of the River Ogwen, two miles south-east of Bangor, to Llanfairpwllgwyngyll (Llanfair PG) on Anglesey.

While the Bill was in the Lords the Duke of Wellington suggested that it should once again be deferred while the government further pondered upon the merits of Holyhead and Porth Dynllaen. To this Glyn of the LBR replied that if the Bill was lost in 1844 his company would abandon it.[11] Fortunately, Peel felt that the harbour question should not be permitted to interfere with what was a purely railway Bill, and the Lords agreed that if an acceptable line could be got to Holyhead the government would recommend a public grant to make Holyhead a complete packet station and harbour. By 24 June the Bill, less the Ogwen—Llanfair portion, was only awaiting Royal Assent to become law. The CHR directors resolved that, as soon as assent was obtained, they would inform the Treasury that a new route had already been surveyed across the Straits, and would formally seek assurance as to the works at Holyhead.

## THE CHESTER & HOLYHEAD RAILWAY ACT 1844

The Bill received Royal Assent on 4 July 1844 (7–8 Vic cap lxv). The company was incorporated, and empowered to raise £2,100,000 in £50 shares, of which the LBR might contribute £1 million. Powers were given to construct the main line, except between the Ogwen and Llanfair. The Chester cut-off to Rowton Moor was not authorised.

In face of common threats from new railways, which would be in competition, the LBR and GJR were in alliance at this time. One result was the GJR's acquiescence to the LBR's backing of the CHR which had nine LBR directors among its first directorate: James B. Boothby, Edward Cropper, George Carr Glyn, Pascoe St Leger Grenfell, Christopher Hird Jones, Joseph Frederick Ledsam, Ross Donnelly Mangles, Captain Constantine Richard Moorsom RN, and Thomas Smith. Three directors were appointed by the Chester & Birkenhead: William Jackson, John Laird, and William Potter. Six more directors, making a total of eighteen, were elected by the original CHR undertaking—that started by the Chester & Crewe —and these were: William Rickford Collett, Adam Duff, William Edmund Ferrers, Sir John Josiah Guest, William Henri Thomas, and William Thompson.

Provisions in the Act included the following: the company was to construct a station at Flint; the cuts through the walls at Chester and Conway should be in an approved manner; the slopes of the existing road embankments at Conway and over the Stanley Sands south of Holyhead could be used on payment of annual rent; the Conway was to be bridged so as to give an equivalent clearance to that of Telford's suspension bridge, with which any new structure should be in harmony; a sea wall was to be made near Abergele; and Penmaenbach was specifically to be tunnelled through. Powers were given to cross existing railways on the level, namely at Eyton's

## SUCCESS IN PARLIAMENT

collieries and works at Mostyn and Lletty, and at his foundry and ship-building yards at Flint. Admiral Dundas's private railway from Buckley to the River Dee was to be crossed by an arch bridge.

It is of interest to delve back into the minutes of the CHR directors' meetings during the critical months before the passing of the Act. Two themes emerge: the argument with the Grand Junction as to financial aid; and the laborious negotiations with the government concerning the mail contract.

### DISPUTE WITH THE GRAND JUNCTION

In mid November 1843 Timothy Tyrrell, solicitor to the CHR, wrote to Richard Creed and Captain Mark Huish, the respective secretaries of the LBR and GJR, seeking to agree terms for their companies' financial participation.[12] From the Grand Junction there came a cautious reply:

> GRAND JUNCTION RAILWAY
> Secretary's Office, Liverpool
> Nov$^r$. 24th 1843
>
> Sir,
> Your letter of the 18th was laid before the Directors of this Railway at the special meeting this day.
> The Scheme of a Chester & Holyhead Railway involves in many ways the interests of the Grand Junction Coy and the working of their line. Yet until now no communication of any kind has been made to this Board on the subject. You do not now tell us who are the promoters of the project, what is the line decided upon, what is the probable cost of it, what the terms asked from Government, what the services to be performed for them, or to what extent the negotiations have succeeded.
> Until informed on these points you must see that the Grand Junction Directors are not in a condition to enter upon the consideration of the offer contained in your letter.
> You state that until our reply is received you shall not again

approach the Government, and I am desired to assure you that we shall not, as we had intended, make any tender to Government while this correspondence is pending.

Your obed<sup>t</sup>. Servant<br>Mark Huish

Tyrrell replied that the LBR and GJR had only been approached so that they could have some influence on the CHR board. 'Your various enquiries cannot be duly answered until the intentions of the government are known, and the terms agreed with them.' He suggested that if the GJR would accept a quarter of the CHR capital and direction, then the LBR should also be asked to join in.

The GJR, however, declined the offer; it wished to join with the LBR in an extension from Chester but until the latter's intentions were known it preferred not to negotiate with third parties. Early in December the LBR replied favourably, Tyrell again pressed Huish for a decision, and a meeting of the three companies was arranged. The CHR thereupon decided to offer the other two a third each of the capital. The meeting, on 13 December, was not a success; the LBR and GJR asked that Joseph Locke, the GJR's engineer, should act jointly with George Stephenson in the construction of the CHR. This provoked an unqualified negative from the latter's deputation, for such an arrangement would have been a spanner in the works of no mean order. There had for some time been an antagonism towards Locke on Stephenson's part. Locke, originally a pupil of Stephenson in the Liverpool & Manchester days, had since proved himself superior to George in survey and specification work and had brought to light serious and costly errors on both counts by Stephenson, both before and during the latter's time as engineer to the Grand Junction. This had eventually led to Locke superseding Stephenson on that line. Though, therefore, understandable from the GJR's point of view, the idea of reuniting the two engineers on the CHR was not a sound one. As a compromise it was agreed that Locke and Robert Stephenson should make joint observations on Walker's report, but apparently Locke was embarrassed by the whole business and refused the job when approached in February 1844.

Meanwhile, the Grand Junction had further cause for concern, for the CHR was at this time making overtures to acquire the Chester & Birkenhead Railway. Talks had been in progress since January 1844, with the approval of the LBR, but the operation was considered by the GJR to be premature. In a letter to the CHR on 8 February, Huish pointed out that the traffic potential of the CHR had not been ascertained, nor the practicability and cost of bridging the Menai Straits. The government, he said, appeared unwilling to enter into a stipulated-price mail contract, and it was not even yet certain that the Irish traffic would be concentrated at Holyhead. Believing for these reasons, apart from the extra £500,000 which would be required for the purchase of the C & B, that 'there is no probability of any adequate return for Money to be invested in the new Project, this Board feel that they cannot, in justice to their proprietors, take any part therein'.

In view of this it was ironic that, though negotiations between the CHR and the C & B went on for some time, nothing was to be settled. Though unwilling to participate, however, the Grand Junction was certainly not hostile. It undertook that it would not, either by a disproportionate reduction of rates to and from Liverpool, or by arrangement with the Irish steamboat proprietors thence, compete with the CHR for the Irish traffic, but would let it take its natural course.[13] Such a policy was necessary: the GWR-backed South Wales Railway, with its goal of Southern Ireland via Fishguard, was at this time bringing out its prospectus. The threat was real and the CHR provided a counter to it. The CHR offer was accepted by the London & Birmingham. That company intimated its wish to have one half of the direction and to take £1 million capital. To this the CHR agreed.[14]

THE LAND MAIL CONTRACT

In April 1843 the CHR directors informed the government

that they would construct the railway as far as the Menai Straits within two years, and the remainder within three years of its commencement, and would then be prepared to contract for the conveyance of the mails from Chester to the packet port, in return for £80,000 per annum for the service. It was suggested that payment should commence as soon as the line was open to Bangor, the contract to be for twenty years. Despite subsequent meetings between the directors, Sir Robert Peel, and the Chancellor of the Exchequer, the government withheld an answer pending receipt of the Treasury and Admiralty reports. In November 1843 the company asked whether the government wished Walker's suggested alterations to be adopted, as they would seriously affect estimates both of making and working the line, and also the official view about required train speeds for the mails. The Chancellor, Henry Goulbourn, replied that Walker's report was intended to supply information to all parties interested; it did not refer specifically to one company. As to train speeds, this was a matter for the Post Office.

On 10 January 1844 the chairmen of the LBR, GJR and CHR went to the Treasury where they were received by Peel, Goulborn, Sir James Graham (the Home Secretary), and Sir George Clerk. Anxious to reach agreement, the chairmen offered £60,000 per annum to work the mails, but Peel said he thought this to be too much; he had already received an offer for £50,000, from a party backed by 'a powerful capitalist'. As the government intended spending £½ million on the port of Holyhead as part of the deal, he said, they were in fact providing the chief terminus of the company and saving it considerable expense. Peel also said that the government had considered the principle of the atmospheric railway as being applicable to the CHR and recommended its adoption. This was a wily move; it raised the old bogey of a broad gauge advance to the North Wales coast without actually saying so. Lastly, the Prime Minister inferred that all were agreed that a new bridge would be necessary over the Menai.

Considerably worried, and with rather more now to think

about than just the mail contract, the chairmen returned to Collett's London home and there decided to reduce the offer to £40,000. Peel was so informed on 11 January, but when the CHR Bill received the Royal Assent—nearly six months later— no response had been made. On 9 July, five days after the Act, and with the CHR directors in a state of suspense, they warned the Treasury that if the shareholders were to learn of the government refusal to agree terms, they might be so discouraged as to abandon the undertaking. The company did not expect the government to pay for the new bridge; it merely pointed out that the increased cost would require additional remuneration to that of £40,000.

On 20 July 1844 Collett headed a deputation to see Peel at Downing Street. After being told that the shareholders would not proceed unless arrangements had been made as to the mails, the Prime Minister promised to consult with the Earl of Lonsdale (the Postmaster General). Ten days later Peel informed a CHR deputation that the Postmaster General would require two mail trains daily each way over the CHR, the payment for which, if reckoned at the rate paid to the North Midland Railway of a shilling per mile, would amount to about £6,500 per annum. Collett told Peel that this was very much below the average payment for lines on the western side of the country and that nothing less that £40,000 would satisfy the proprietors. Thus entrenched, the two sides parted. On the following day, at Peel's request, the CHR board sent him a letter setting out the reasons for demanding £40,000: the rate for the western side of the country was 1s $11\frac{7}{8}$d per mile, and as the CHR trains would be required to travel faster than on other lines, the cost would be at least 25 per cent more. Concentration of the packet services at Holyhead on the opening of the railway would save the public about £48,000 a year which, allowing for the claimed £40,000, left £8,000 of direct savings. The mileage paid to the Grand Junction for the mails was 699 miles per day, an annual cost of £17,940. The opening of the CHR would cut this by nearly £8,000. Increased passenger duty consequent on Holyhead superseding

Liverpool would bring in an additional estimated £2,000.

At the end of August the Treasury replied that in view of these savings and the unlikelihood of the line being built without government help, their Lordships felt justified 'in making an exception in this case to the general practice by which they have hitherto been governed in making agreements for conveyance of the mails'. The terms, however, would be £30,000 per annum for five years, and then for a further five years, subject to review. The CHR board resolved, on 26 August 1844, that it was not expedient to reject the offer but that the second period should be for ten years. Further correspondence followed, ending with a Treasury minute of 17 September giving the final terms, to which the CHR agreed on the same day. Two up and two down mail trains were to be run daily. For the first five years the annual payment was agreed at £30,000. The second period, to be for seven years, was also at £30,000 maximum but was subject to a reduction by a sum computed on a minimum mileage basis (equal to about £7,270 per annum) which, fluctuating between those two amounts, would give a return to the CHR of 5 per cent on the capital subscribed.

Now, at last, the way was clear. With the Act obtained, the backing of the LBR, plans ready for crossing the Menai, and hard-won agreement with the government as to Holyhead harbour and the land mail contract, the Chester & Holyhead Railway Company could get on with the business of constructing its line.

CHAPTER 4

## Open to Bangor

### THE TEAM

During construction of the railway the Chester & Holyhead Railway Company had its headquarters in Moorgate, London. In February 1844 George King was appointed secretary, and in March was given an assistant, Alexander Gifford. After the passing of the incorporation Act in July 1844, Collett and Thomas were elected chairman and deputy chairman respectively and the board decided to appoint a resident director to head a works committee, based at Chester, at a salary of £1,000 per annum. Captain Moorsom was asked to take on the job. Charles Mills was made treasurer, and Robert Stephenson appointed engineer-in-chief. This was at a time when his father was anything but pleased with the CHR:

> 24 Great George Street,
> Westminster   22 Nov 1844

Dear Sir,

I received with much pain and disappointment a Communication that the Holyhead Railway Board had reduced the amount of my account furnished you to £500— This is the first time in my professional career that my charges have been so treated. In this case not nearly the time employed by me nor any thing like the expenses I have been put to have been charged. When I gave up the Line after having projected & matured it & when in fact it was in my own hands I did so on the implied understanding that I should be remunerated for my services & I am much hurt that my services should be looked upon as they are by your present

Company. I beg you will lay this communication & my account again before the Board.

      Yours truly
        Geo. Stephenson

G. King Esq. re

The board minutes are discreetly silent as to any answer to this letter.

Captain Moorsom took until September 1844 to make up his mind to accept the onerous duties of resident director. His colleagues could hardly have picked a better man. Born in 1792, son of Admiral Sir Robert Moorsom, the young Constantine had made an excellent career in the Royal Navy where he distinguished himself by his ability and inventiveness. He received post rank in 1818 after which, on a number of stations, he experimented with and improved upon the sailing qualities of naval vessels. He remained on the Navy list and reached the rank of Vice-Admiral in 1857. His ability with the land works of the CHR may be said to have been as a 'trouble-shooter' in handling men and representing the board on the spot, but most of all it was his considerable knowledge of sea-going vessels which was to be of value later when the CHR commenced the steamer service to Ireland.[1] Added to these virtues were soundness of judgement, level-headedness, foresight, and a good humour which were to be a source of strength in the years ahead.[2]

PROPOSED ATMOSPHERIC RAILWAY

At this point it is of interest to note one of those fascinating historical possibilities which occur from time to time. Sir Robert Peel's statement in January 1844 concerning atmospheric traction was not ignored: on 26 January the CHR board noted that the proposals of Messrs Samuda to grant a licence to operate the line as an atmospheric railway were approved in principle, and Robert Stephenson was asked to comment. In evidence to the Select Committee on Atmospheric Railways in April 1845 Stephenson said that the directors 'desired me to proceed to Dalkey, and there make such experiments as I thought proper, for the purpose of satisfying myself whether it would or would not be a proper mode of propulsion'. (This was the Kingstown & Dalkey Railway which had commenced operating in August 1843.) Stephenson reported to the CHR board in June 1844 that the atmospheric system 'is not an economical mode of transmitting power, and inferior, in this respect both to locomotive engines & stationary engines, with ropes . . . it is not practically calculated to acquire and maintain higher velocities than are comprised in the present working of locomotive engines'. He thought it could be used advantageously on short stretches, or where the gradients were bad for locomotives, where short high velocity journeys were made, but the system was too inflexible on a long line of railway. The idea was not taken further so far as the CHR was concerned.

### BILL FOR CROSSING THE MENAI STRAITS

In September 1844 the board decided to seek Parliamentary powers for the line between the west bank of the River Ogwen and Llanfair PG, including the crossing of the Straits. In November 1843 Stephenson had planned a circuitous route north of Bangor, largely avoiding heavy engineering works. James Walker, however, had then proposed an alternative straight line which saved about ¾ mile but entailed formidable works including 2,500 yards of tunnelling through extremely hard rock and at extra cost of £100,000. By August 1844 a third route had emerged, taking a mean course. Stephenson's line was opposed by Christopher Bethell, Bishop of Bangor, who complained that it came too near to his palace. Glyn suggested that the Bishop (who incidentally spoke only English in a diocese where 195,000 out of 200,000 people understood little more than their native tongue[3]) might be persuaded to set aside his private feelings if he were offered £15,000 for the purpose of founding and endowing a school. There was hope that this sweetener might pay off, but on 23 November the

Treasury said that in any case it would oppose Stephenson's line on public grounds. The board must have anticipated this for on the same day it noted that plans for the Bangor line had been deposited in Parliament and standing orders complied with. The plans showed Stephenson's line and an 'alternative line', the latter being that of August 1844 and which was passed in the forthcoming Act. Powers were received for the Ogwen —Llanfair line in the company's Act of 1845 (chapter 5).

### LETTING THE CONTRACTS

In anticipation that because of government involvement the Bill would succeed, land purchases went ahead. In early 1844 the landowners appeared generally well disposed towards the railway but in April there was a hint of trouble. Francis Sandars and Francis Fuller, the company's land agents, reported that at about £157 an acre the cost of land alone would be £143,928; with buildings and compensation it would be £170,318. Their report ended:

> We have had interviews with several Freeholders as well as Agents upon the Line, all of whom appear anxious for the Railway, but we are sorry to say from what we hear, unless a very large price be given or agreed upon for such Land and Buildings, in those instances before the passing of the Bill, there will be many petitions against it, and we learn that no great faith ought to be placed on the Welch Jurors doing their duty.

In September 1844 Stephenson was asked to prepare the construction contracts. The drawings for the Chester—Rhyl contracts were to be ready to go to tender by the end of January 1845, from Rhyl to the Ogwen by early March, and thence through Anglesey shortly after. Stephenson went over the route on 18 and 19 December 1844 and suggested that the tramways at Flint, in constant use, be not crossed on the level but that the line should be raised west of the town (altered levels in the Counties of Flint, Denbigh, Caernarvon, and Anglesey were sanctioned by the Chester & Holyhead Railway.

Chester Extension and Amendment Act of 9 July 1847). There were delays. On 15 November 1844, for instance, Moorsom wrote to King . . . 'I have written to Mr. Stephenson to urge on the Contracts, but you cannot get Engineers to attend to these matters till after the 30th,' (the last date for depositing plans in Parliament) . . . '& every man is now at double pay'.

Nevertheless, by May 1845 contracts had been let as follows: No 1, Chester to Shotton, 8 miles, to Edward Ladd Betts (*Herepath's Journal* of 22 February 1845 had him as plain 'Mr Bates') for £118,996; No 2, Shotton to Rhyl, 22 miles, to William Mackenzie for £202,000; No 3, Rhyl to Old Colwyn, 9 miles, to William Mackenzie, Thomas Brassey, and John Stephenson for £159,753; No 4, Old Colwyn to about ¼ mile west of the site of Llandudno Junction, 5¾ miles, to Messrs Gregson for £45,937; No 6, across the Conway, but excluding the bridge and its approaches, 2 miles, to John Evans for £36,721; No 7, Penmaenbach tunnel and approaches, about one mile, to John Harding and John Cropper for £59,611. As to contract No 9, from about 1½ miles west of Aber to just short of the Menai, 6¼ miles, and known as the 'Bangor contract', this went to Thomas Jackson. The board had wanted competitive tenders but Stephenson was strongly of the opinion that no lower offer would be made than that from Jackson, who thereby got the contract in May 1845. The price was £255,800, completion to be by 1 August 1847.

Tenders for contracts 8 and 12, 7¾ miles from Penmaenbach to the Bangor contract, and 5½ miles across the Malltraeth Marsh in Anglesey respectively, were considered in June. Evans and Harding & Cropper had tendered for No 8 but Stephenson considered that they had sufficient on hand, 'according to their means', and it was let to Messrs Warton & Warden for £89,664. (Though the firm was thus spelt in the CHR minutes, other sources have them as Wharton & Warden.) No 12 contract, for which only Evans had tendered, was readvertised with the remainder of the Angelsey line. Thus contracts 11 to 14 came before the board in August 1845. Out of several tenders, only one contractor, Betts, put in for the whole lot.

His advent was welcomed. Stephenson told the board that as the district was very poor for accommodating railway navvies he thought that all the contracts should be let to one efficient party, unless considerable saving could be effected by dividing them. Betts therefore got the Anglesey line at £395,000. Stephenson's estimate was for £374,000. Contract No 10 was the biggest plum of all—the Britannia Tubular Bridge. Construction of this and the Conway Bridge (contract No 5) is discussed in chapters 5 and 6.

Many of the contractors for the main works were personally known to Stephenson. To take just one line, the North Midland, in 1837 Harding & Cropper, John Stephenson, and Thomas Jackson had been among contractors employed under him. Thomas Brassey had constructed part of the Chester & Crewe and was well into his career as one of the most eminent of railway builders. Betts, contractor on the South Eastern Railway between Reigate and Folkestone, was already well known and was to join later with Brassey and Samuel Morton Peto in a partnerhip which constructed many famous works. Peto was in time to become the chairman of the CHR (chapter 7).

### THE WORK FORCE

For the most part these contractors took care of their men, pioneering some of the improvements in industrial relations in early Victorian England. In 1846, following reports in previous years of the harsh, brutish conditions under which railway navvies lived and worked, a Select Committee on Railway Labourers heard evidence on the matter, during which some interesting facts came to light regarding conditions on the CHR. The company had put £300 towards the employment of scripture readers from the Town Missionary Reader and Scripture Society. Six worked between Chester and Bangor and another two on Angelsey. Their business was to go whereever large groups of men worked. They were to talk to them during their meal breaks, persuading them to attend Divine worship and send their children to school. William Breakey, one of the readers, said that the Welsh, many of whom had been miners and who formed the majority of the work force on the CHR, had a great desire to learn the English language. Most of the young men had bought pocket Bibles and Testaments. 'The Welsh labourers', said Breakey, 'were very steady, sober men; I had never seen anything like it.' Perhaps one reason for the sobriety was that they were paid in money, fortnightly and on Saturdays. This, said Moorsom, effectively stopped the usual Friday night carousal and kept them at work for a further day. They had, one imagines, to fear hellfire and damnation if not sober for Sunday. Then, except for essential shift work in the tunnels, all operations ceased and the scripture readers came into their own.

Proper shops were provided along the line for the supply of the navvy families. Wooden huts, with slated roofs, were put up on Anglesey, the local habitations, in Moorsom's opinion, being for the most part more impoverished even than those in the north of England. Nevertheless, the company's cottages were thought to be too fine by the Welsh labourers who sought local accommodation. Thomas Jackson thought that it was more profitable and efficient if his workers were housed properly. He built timber cottages, with three rooms, double-boarded and with two windows, for his married men on the Bangor contract. The maximum number of occupants allowed was five. Rents were 1s 6d (7½p) to 2s (10p) a week. This apparently pleased the men as the current rent for two rooms in Bangor was as much as 10s (50p) a week. Sometimes arrangements made by the contractors got across local interests. In December 1845 the innkeepers of Bangor petitioned the CHR against Jackson erecting huts for the sale of beer. Religious education was one thing; cheap beer was quite another.

On the mixing of Welsh and English labourers, Moorsom noted 'the effect that is being produced upon the Welsh population by being brought into intercourse with the English labourers; how very much they are improved in their method of managing their work; how much better they feed; and how they are emulating the English in the extent of work they can do. The proportion at the beginning was five Welshmen to three Englishmen in filling waggons, and now they are coming to par'. Moorsom summed up his running of the works in the language of the sea: 'The best disciplined ship has always the fewest accidents, and does the thing the quickest'. Asked if there was the same chain of command on railway works as on a man-of-war—'Not the same, certainly, but a supervision conducted on a similar principle'.

From the evidence it would seem that the CHR was one of the few companies blessed with a minimum of trouble from its navvies unlike, say, the Lancaster & Carlisle, then under construction, where national rivalries between English, Irish, and Scots erupted into bloody battles. But in case someone should break bounds, and they did on rare occasions, the CHR employed policemen, paid for by the contractors, the uniforms being similar to those of the police on the London & Birmingham Railway.

### WORK STARTED

Appropriately, the first sod was cut and the first shot fired at the Conway tunnel on St David's Day, 1 March 1845. Betts also started in early March and, at the end of May, Jackson commenced the Bangor contract, land purchases having been made. On 12 May work started on felling trees at the Rope Walk, Chester.[4] That month also saw the first call on shares, there being a second call in June.

In June, Edward Parry wrote to the board. He was preparing a descriptive account of the railway and requested that when published it might appear under the sanction of the directors. *Parry's Railway Companion from Chester to Holyhead*, of some 150 pages and mixing hard detail and poetic whimsy so beloved by the Victorian paterfamilias, came out in 1848. It was dedicated to the CHR directors and it seems a pity to have to relate that, having prepared what was an excellent publicity job, when Parry applied for a permanent post on the company's staff in January 1848 he was turned down.

By November 1845 there were some 5,000 men and 500 horses and drivers on the works. The *Carnarvon Herald* of 6 December described a visit to the Bangor contract. Four shafts of Llandegai tunnel were down to formation level, five were being sunk for Bangor tunnel, one being down to formation level, and two out of the four shafts in Belmont tunnel were completed and headings being driven. Jackson had 1,095 men employed and was praised for 'erecting convenient and comfortable temporary cottages for the men, in which to reside, and to have their meals as human beings ought to have them'. It was hoped that the local quarrymen would benefit when the slate owners saw what could be provided by a railway contractor.

### THREAT FROM THE GREAT WESTERN

Since August 1845 the CHR board had become increasingly worried over a renewal of the Porth Dynllaen railway scheme. At the August half-yearly meeting of their company, the Great Western directors had recommended promotion of a broad gauge line from Worcester to Porth Dynllaen. Collett was quick to reassure the CHR shareholders: the GWR proposal could not give a shorter route than via the CHR and he thought that the government would not sanction such a line in view of its involvement with the CHR. It was necessary, said Collett, to obtain another narrow gauge outlet to London to counter the broad gauge thrust to the north, and the shareholders voted to support to the extent of £300,000 a proposal from the Chester & Ellesmere and the Liverpool & Birmingham Canal Companies that they should convert their canals to railways, thus giving a new and shorter route from Chester to Stafford and Wolverhampton (volume 2).

Others sought to thwart the Great Western. Also in August the prospectus from an intended Great Welsh Junction Railway, planned by Sir John Rennie, proposed taking a double departure from Bangor and Porth Dynllaen, to run thence by Harlech, Dolgelly, Shrewsbury, Ludlow, Hereford, Monmouth, Merthyr, Swansea, and Carmarthen, to terminate at Pembroke. There were branches to Gloucester, Chepstow, Newport, and Cardiff.[5] A rival affair was the Great North & South Wales & Worcester Railway which in August proposed a line from Worcester to Porth Dynllaen. The promoters soon backed down in favour of the Great Western scheme, however, contenting themselves with a link between the latter and the South Wales Railway.[6] Lack of financial support caused the Bill to be withdrawn. If Paddington was smugly appreciative of all these scurryings around, others were not. There was some rude comment on the Worcester—Porth Dynllaen line in *Herepath's Journal* in December 1845:

> It is to be lamented that Brunel has no more consideration for the credit of the profession to which he belongs, and of which, with reasonable care, he might have made a distinguished ornament. Should any of his professional rivals lay hold of this section, get it lithographed, and print in large letters over it, 'BRUNEL'S RAILWAY', it would be a standing joke against him in Committee and out, to the end of his life.

A correspondent wrote, . . . 'Of all the droll things in the shape of railway sections that have been perpetrated during the last few months, this one of Mr Brunel's must, I think, certainly be the drollest'. There were to be some $6\frac{1}{2}$ miles of 1 in 60 gradient and no less than $10\frac{1}{2}$ miles of tunnelling. 'The total length of this precious line is $128\frac{3}{4}$ miles, having just 15 miles of level scattered over it, in patches averaging something less than half a mile each'. The writer, who signed himself 'SUUM CUIQUE', from Caernarvon, ended with the following:

> Do you know whether Mr. Brunel proposes to the shareholders to employ atmospheric or steam locomotive power for working the line? Imagine, in either case, a Manchester and Leeds goods train, or a North Midland excursion train, on a pass of 1 in 60; it would be mesmerized to a certainty. Atmospheric power will no doubt be recommended, some engineers having found that a force of 8 lbs per square inch

is far more powerful in propulsion than a force of 70 lbs. In case of atmospheric, I would beg to suggest that the tube should be of sufficient size to admit of the carriages being worked either withinside or without. Medhurst's plan of inside propulsion would answer best, having the double advantage of allowing the shareholders to run through their property, and keeping them at the same time in the dark; which is what engineers so much like, and which is done with such effect on one or two lines, with which you and I are acquainted.

In January 1846 Glyn told the CHR board that the Oxford Worcester & Wolverhampton and the Oxford & Birmingham were likely to join the GWR in promoting the Porth Dynllaen line in Parliament. Frank Forster, assistant engineer at Bangor under Stephenson, was told to copy plans of the proposed line. The sections undoubtedly presented an engineering nightmare, with some embankments shown as being 80ft high, and the CHR board obviously hoped that some fault in the calculations would be sufficient to damage the GWR Bill in Parliament.

Meanwhile, Collett kept his nerve; at the half-yearly meeting in February 1846 he stated that there was but one rival project to the CHR, 'and that could scarcely be estimated at more than a mere burlesque upon engineering'. The coming amalgamation of the Grand Junction and London & Birmingham companies, he said, would protect the CHR from competitors. (The two companies were to join with the Manchester & Birmingham to form the London & North Western Railway by Act of 16 July 1846 (9–10 Vic cap cciv). Nevertheless, the Worcester & Porth Dynllaen Bill went to Parliament and passed the first and second readings. In desperation, the CHR supported any opposing petition which seemed likely to be effective in July came anti-climax. All along the Bill had been dependent for GWR support on the understanding that it would authorise a broad gauge line. The Gauge Commissioners' report of 1846, advocating that the spread of the broad gauge should henceforth be restricted, effectively killed Great Western interest and the Porth Dynllaen Bill was withdrawn.

## THE MANIA YEAR

The year 1846 started with a slight misunderstanding between Stephenson and the CHR board. The latter had noticed with some surprise that, unbeknown to the directors, Betts' completion dates for the Anglesey contracts had been extended to October 1848, some ten months later than agreed. Stephenson explained that as the Britannia Bridge could not be completed before October 1848, and he considered it inadvisable to work the Anglesey line before its connection with the remainder of the railway, he had at Betts' request extended the completion dates. He knew of the directors' wishes to hold back on calls on shares, and he had thought the delay would help them. In 'the multiplicity of business at the time just preceding his departure for the continent', the matter of seeking board approval had been lost sight of. He greatly regretted the omission, and assured the directors that he would attempt to get the bridge open by June 1848 and would tell Betts that his completion date must now be 1 May of that year. A contributory factor to Betts' request was that much of his equipment came by sea and had been delayed by bad weather.

In May 1846 the Post Office told the company that the mails would be sent over the line when there was sufficient of it open to effect a saving of an hour in the London—Dublin time, and the Treasury advised the erection of the electric telegraph along the route, indicating that the government would pay to use it.[7] By August there were no less than 12,388 men and 861 horses and drivers at work, hacking away at the cuttings, forming embankments, building sea walls, viaducts and bridges, and blasting through tunnels with gunpowder.[8] When not working, the navvies occasionally rioted. Contracts 8 and 9 were in trouble on 22 May 1846 and the military had to be called out from Chester to put a stop to the fighting. Warton & Warden were told to maintain four regular police and 50 special constables, recruited from the men, and Jackson six police and and 50 specials.

Page 65

*Robert Stephenson. Photograph taken shortly before death*

*James Meadows Rendel. Mezzotint by Bellin from a painting by Opie*

*Captain Constantine Richard Moorsom R.N. Engraving by Holl*

In June there was some heartsearching among members of the CHR's finance committee. They reported that, taking into account expenditure estimated on works, stock, and equipment, together with the CHR's involvement in branch line schemes (volume 2), the future outlay of money must be very great:

> On the 21st of July a further call of £5 per share will be payable by the Shareholders when the Company's borrowing powers will come into operation, and some prospect of relief was held out to the Shareholders by deferring any further calls for some considerable time—unless however something should arise to prevent the great mass of Railway Bills now before Parliament passing in the present session, your committee feel that some difficulty will arise in obtaining the necessary Loans.

Despite this, the directors put on a brave face at the opening of Penmaenbach tunnel on 16 November 1846, the event being celebrated in Conway with 'flags, banners, mirth, and music, being rife in every quarter, and the shipping in the river being handsomely decorated for the occasion'.[9]

### SEA DEFENCES

In October 1846 heavy seas damaged the sea wall on the west side of Penmaenmawr tunnel on contract 8. On either side of the tunnel the rock was either blasted to form a terrace for the railway or built up to make an embankment. Though most of the tunnel had been completed, parts of the embankment and parapet wall were still not much above beach level. Stephenson reported to the board:

> On the morning of the 22nd (October) I visited Penmaen Mawr during a heavy spring tide and a very heavy gale of wind from the north, and to my surprise although I did not reach the spot until three-quarters of an hour after high water, the sea was breaking over the wall full 40 feet high, —such masses of water being thrown over the wall soon dislodged the backing which being of rubble was washed

away leaving the wall ... incapable of resisting the heavy impulses from the waves ...

About twelve chains of the wall required rebuilding.

Before however deciding upon the mode of reconstructing the damaged part of the wall, I wish to make another examination upon the spot; for having witnessed the force and height with which the sea breaks over the proposed levels of the Railway—I am satisfied that the intended parapet upon the Wall must be carried much higher than designed, and probably continued by an arch over the Railway, resting against the cliff which forms the land boundary of the line of Railway.

I am not prepared at once to submit this as the final plan to the Board, it is simply what has occurred to me; but I propose to suspend all procedings on this part of the work until the Spring.

Penmaenmawr viaduct and tunnel

In the following March, Frank Forster wrote to Stephenson saying that Warton & Warden were not to blame for the damage in October. He admitted that he had not been prepared for a storm of such force, 'and it has always since that time been a satisfaction to me that you were there, and witnessed its power and effects, which I doubt not convinced you as they did me, that a perpendicular wall is not the proper form for the most exposed part of Penmaen Mawr'. Forster suggested an ashlar foreshore, commencing about 3ft above high level of ordinary spring tides, extending seawards, level at the top, for about 15ft, and then descending to the beach at an inclination of about 1 in 3. Clay and stone for the filling could be got from the cutting east of the tunnel. This additional work was priced so that it gave the contractor only a small margin.[10] The plan was agreed but in July 1847 it was decided to substitute a 550ft viaduct of 13 piers and cast iron girders in lieu of a portion of the sea wall at Penmaenmawr, so as to allow the surf to beat on the shore underneath the railway. At the same time the tunnel was found to be so full of fissures in the rock that it was decided to line it for half its length. According to Smiles, Stephenson afterwards 'confessed that if a long tunnel had been made in the first instance through the solid rock of Penmaen Mawr, a saving of from £25,000 to £30,000 would have been effected . . . in railway works engineers should endeavour as far as possible to avoid the necessity of contending with the sea . . .'

## SHREWSBURY & CHESTER RAILWAY

Originally projected in 1839, the North Wales Mineral Railway Company was incorporated by Act of 1844 for a line from the coal district of Ruabon to join the proposed CHR at Saltney, about 1¾ miles west of the latter's commencement at Chester. In November 1844 the NWM asked whether the CHR would immediately construct the Saltney to Chester portion of its line, and support the NWM in ensuring that the intending Shrewsbury Oswestry & Chester Junction Railway, then before

Parliament to make a line from Shrewsbury to Chester, would carry its route between Rossett and Chester over the NWM. Negotiations between the CHR and NMW as to tolls and construction dragged on until May 1846 when Collett told the NWM chairman that the Saltney—Chester portion might be ready by the following October. In June the NWM agreed to pay £2,000 per month minimum as tolls, the balance to be determined by traffic. On 14 October 1846 Moorsom reported:

> I have been over the Line between the Birkenhead Station (Chester and the Shrewsbury Junction (Saltney) which was to have been inspected by Gen$^l$. Pasley on the 10th inst; but in consequence of the Line between the junction and Ruabon not being ready he postponed his visit. The down line of rails is ready and the other will be ready next week with the exception of the Dee Bridge which will require from 6 weeks to 2 months to complete; by which time the sidings at the junction will also be complete.
>
> I have requested Mr. Lee to apply to Mr. Dockray (resident engineer on the LNWR) for such signal Discs as are required, and I have instructed him that till Mr. Betts has completed both Lines of Rails he must maintain the switch and signalmen after which it will devolve on the Shrewsbury Company to do so.

By this time the NWM had amalgamated with the SO & CJ to become the Shrewsbury & Chester Railway. On 21 October, General Pasley of the Board of Trade inspected the line and sanctioned the opening. Ten days later the S & C completed an agreement with the CHR as to use of the line; it took possession on 2 November and opened it for public traffic two days later.[11]

The Chester—Saltney Junction section of the CHR commences 17 chains to the west of Chester station (discussed later), though future CHR mileages will be given from the centre of the station. After leaving the triangular junction to the Birkenhead line the railway as constructed passed through a long tunnel under Northgate Street and adjacent gardens. The length of the tunnel was noted by Parry in 1848 as being 300 yd, and by Edwin Clark in 1850 at 405yd through red sandstone, but a deposited plan of 1852 for a proposed Birkenhead Railway branch to Saltney, planned by Brunel and which passed nearby, clearly shows the CHR tunnel as having been about 475yd. In 1865 the Chester & West Cheshire Junction Railway (later part of the Cheshire Lines Committee's undertaking) was authorised to make its terminus to the east of Northgate Street and to carry its line over the CHR. During the construction the CHR tunnel was opened out in several places, and further by the LNWR in 1874–5. In later years the CHR was widened (volume 2) and the railway now passes through two tunnels, the four-tracked Windmill Lane tunnel (under the CLC) of 111yd, and the Northgate Street tunnels, two bores, of 216 and 218yd. After leaving the latter a further 200yd takes the line over the Chester & Ellesmere Canal and then by viaduct, with the Roodee racecourse to the south, on the approach to the Dee Bridge. From there it was under half a mile to Saltney Junction and the S & C, 1 mile and 67 chains from Chester General station. In July 1848 the CHR traffic committee considered making a connecting line with the S & C at Saltney giving through running to traffic coming from Wales but nothing came of the idea.

The S & C was opened throughout on 12 October 1848,[12] and within a year became involved, together with the Shrewsbury & Birmingham, in a battle with the newly-formed London & North Western Railway. While the Grand Junction and the London & Birmingham had been rivals, the latter had backed the Shrewsbury lines as a future investment and protection for its northern traffic. On the formation of the LNWR, however, that company saw the Shrewsburys as competitors for the Birkenhead traffic, an opinion which was confirmed when the two small companies announced that they intended reducing fares between the Black Country and Chester. Euston then decided to use every means to ruin them. It was particularly anxious to keep the Shrewsburys' trains from using the Chester & Birkenhead (by then the Birkenhead Lancashire & Cheshire Junction), and Chester station became the scene of some undignified examples of personal assault by North Western employees on the servants and passengers of the S & C.

By 1851 the Shrewsburys had made traffic agreements with the expanding Great Western, and all three, known as the 'Associated Companies', were busy appealing to the BL & CJ to join with them against the LNWR. In place of the existing agreement with the CHR, the S & C obtained statutory running powers to Chester and thence to Birkenhead in 1851, and in November of that year the BL & CJ agreed to lease its line to the associated companies. The LNWR, however, by dint of promoting two rival lines between Chester and Birkenhead, one a LNWR offspring and the other sired by the CHR, succeeded in frightening the BL & CJ into switching sides and the leasing Bill was withdrawn. From October 1851 the S & C commenced running into Birkenhead and in the following year the BL & CJ asked for increased mileage receipts. The S & C thus ceased entering Birkenhead from 1 December 1852, thereby forcing on the BL & CJ the onus of itself taking the S & C traffic on to the town. Now came a proposal for an independent 'Birkenhead Railway', with a branch to Saltney and a main line on to Birkenhead, noted above, which entirely avoided the CHR and BL & CJ lines. It was not proceeded with. The BL & CJ was renamed the Birkenhead Railway in 1859. Its further history does not concern the CHR; the disputes between Paddington and Euston ended with the Birkenhead vesting jointly in the GWR and LNWR by Act of 1861.

Apart from the question of lease or amalgamation with the Shrewsbury companies, the GWR applied separately in November 1852 for running powers through to Birkenhead. This would have entailed laying down the broad gauge over the CHR from Saltney Junction to Chester. Opposition was left to the LNWR but in any event the Bill failed. Amalgamation of the associated companies took place by Act of 1854, the Great Western thus arriving in Chester on the standard gauge via a small portion of the CHR. In Parliamentary evidence and by a clause in the amalgamation Act, the GWR undertook not to promote any extension of the broad gauge north of Wolverhampton unless sanctioned by the Board of Trade. As will be seen later, the broad gauge was to be found at Holyhead, though not as might be imagined from the foregoing.

### THE FIRST STATIONS

In May 1844 the CHR board decided there were to be fourteen intermediate stations: at Queens Ferry, Flint, Holywell, Mostyn Quay, Rhyl, Abergele, Colwyn, Conway, Aber, Bangor, Menai Bridge, Penmynydd, Trefdraeth, and Llanfaelog. The last three were to be known as Llanfair PG, Bodorgan, and Ty Croes. Bodorgan was specifically provided for in the company's Act of 1849. In May 1846 there was a successful petition from local inhabitants for a station at 'the Valley' on the eastern side of the Stanley Embankment on Anglesey. By the following November, Stephenson had prepared the station ground plans and it was decided to start work on the Queens Ferry to Conway stations as soon as the land was obtained. Moorsom told the board that there would probably be need for small stations at Connah's Quay, Bagilt (sic), and Prestatyn, but that he and Stephenson thought that they, and Colwyn and Aber, had better wait, presumably because of the prevailing financial stringency. In March 1847 a station committee was formed to agree upon the elevations of the buildings and the staff necessary for opening the line. Also that month, with the Conway Bridge under construction, a temporary Memel timber platform and booking office were ordered for the east side of the Conway.

The station elevations were in the hands of Francis Thompson, the architect, who had been responsible under Stephenson for all the stations on the North Midland Railway.[13] For the CHR, Thompson designed two-storey rectangular buildings, producing variety in the treatment of the roofs and introducing flanking pavilions to enclose the platform canopy. The buildings, many of which are still standing, albeit some in a rather woebegone state, are late Georgian in character, a feature being their stone-framed windows and quoins in white Penmon stone brought from the quarries near Beaumaris. For some of the stations serving the less important stopping places, Thompson produced smaller house-like designs with a low-pitched roof to the main building and an all-round roof to the ground floor giving cover to the platform and offices. Living accommodation of some six rooms for the station master was provided on the first floor. All the early stations, save Bodorgan and Valley, are of brick in Flemish bond; the two exceptions are of stone. The low-pitched slate roof appears on all except Conway and Mostyn which have parapets.

Apart from Chester, the Thompson stations still in existence at the time of writing are Flint, Holywell (closed), Mostyn (closed), Prestatyn, Conway and Aber (both closed), Bangor, Bodorgan, and Valley (closed). They differ little from their original appearance. Flint has two single storey outhouses which are later additions, Holywell at one time had four flanking pavilions, and Mostyn, which is like Flint in design, is probably least altered of all, though the building is derelict and the platforms cut back. Conway, in Gothic style, to harmonise with the castle, has mullioned windows and stepped gables surmounted by finials. Prestatyn, Aber, Bodorgan, and Valley, built for small communities where the accommodation required was minimal, formed a group distinct from the others. Abergele station, since rebuilt, was similar to Flint and Mostyn, with characteristic pavilions and an arcade on the ground floor elevation.

As constructed, Bangor station, which was on a grander scale than the other intermediates, had two main platforms. One was on the up side, and this had a bay at the west end for the local trains. The other, as now, was on the down side. The front elevation of the station building on the up side was identical to the platform elevation and formed the station front to the yard. Passengers reached the booking office either by staircase from street level or by a sloping cab approach. The entrance side fell steeply away by embankment strengthened by a retaining wall. Between the station and Bangor

Abergele station 1848

tunnel at the east end, the railway passes over the Caernarvon Road, depicted by an early print (p 152). Further minor alterations at Bangor up to 1880 are noted in chapter 10, and those after that year in volume 2.

Relative sizes of the first stations may be gauged from the following tenders accepted by the CHR board on 9 June 1847: Queens Ferry to Peto & Betts at £1,449, and all the following to Thomas Hughes: Flint £4,101, Greenfield (Holywell) £5,375, Mostyn £3,938, Prestatyn £1,113, Rhyl £5,806, Abergele £4,541, and Aber £1,233. Construction of Bagilt and Colwyn was not authorised until November 1848 and July 1849 respectively. Conway and Bangor were let respectively to Hughes for £4,600 and John Morris of Birkenhead for £6,960 in August 1847. The Anglesey stations went to Betts. December 1847 saw half the stations between Chester and Bangor completed and the remainder well in hand, supposedly to be ready for the opening, then optimistically fixed for 1 January next. The subsequent rebuilding of some of the first stations, later stations brought into use during the early years, and the freight facilities, are discussed in chapter 10. A complete list of stations with distances, dates of openings, alterations, and closures, etc up to 1880, is given in appendices 1a and 1b.

PREPARATIONS FOR OPENING

In February 1847 Stephenson reported to the company's half-yearly meeting. There were about 12,560 men at work. Contract No 1 would be ready in under three months (as will be recalled Saltney to Chester was already open). Half the permanent way was in on contract No 2. On No 3 only 60,000 of the 158,000 cubic yards of the Llandulas embankment and 70 out of 530 yards of Penmaenrhos tunnel (this was to be shortened later) remained to be done. Contracts 4 and 6, either side of the Conway, would be finished in two months. Nos 7 and 8 included the sea defences and Penmaenbach tunnel, already noted. No 9 was also progressing satisfactorily and

Stephenson thought that the line to Bangor, contingent on completion of the Conway Tubular Bridge, could be ready, together with the line through Anglesey, by the end of 1847. *Herepath's Journal* remarked in April 1847 that five tons of gunpowder were expended weekly on blasting in the three tunnels on the Bangor contract. Jackson had at that time some 1,700 men at work.

By August, however, it was apparent that Jackson would have difficulty finishing the Bangor contract on time. His was not the only contract in trouble. Moorsom reported that at all points where masonry was required the works were behind. The closing of the Foryd estuary at Rhyl, by the approach embankments to the bridge, had caused such surges to the tide as to threaten the foundations of the piers. Stephenson therefore decided to open out a portion of the embankment on each side. In October he noted, of Penmaenmawr, 'I have given to Mr. Forster instructions to extend the Tunnel a short distance at both ends by walling and a sloping timber roof to protect the Line as far as practicable from any loose stones which hang on the steep sides of the cliff between the Line of Railway and the Turnpike Road. This extension appeared tc me absolutely necessary when on the spot'.

In October, Moorsom called the board's attention to 'the peculiar circumstances which will attend the management of the goods, agricultural produce and minerals with a view to the selection now of a suitable manager and it should be borne in mind that he will have to carry on business with persons who can speak no English'. Moorsom also suggested the appointment of a resident engineer. The matter was referred to the station and establishment committee and interviews were held in November. Out of the four applicants for the position of goods manager the committee chose W. M. Comber. Aged twenty-seven, he was employed under Braithwaite Poole, the LNWR goods manager, and had, of his own accord, prepared a table of goods and cattle rates for the CHR. His uncle was goods manager on the Liverpool & Manchester. Comber was appointed at £300 per annum, and Hedworth

Lee, assistant engineer under Alexander Ross at the Chester end of the line, was made resident engineer at £350 per annum. At the same time it was agreed that the station staff should be bi-lingual, and a traffic committee was formed to make arrangements for opening the line and superintendence of the traffic. It superseded the station committee and was to sit at Chester.

Meanwhile, on 23 October 1847, Herepath was able to report that 'on Thursday week, about 30 miles of this line, from Chester to Rhyl, were run over by an experimental train'. By 10 November the directors had informed the Railway Commissioners that Chester to Bangor was to be opened on 1 December, but on learning from Moorsom that the masonry works were still retarded it was decided to postpone the event until 1 January. All this time the directors were concerned as to when the Post Office would consider the line sufficiently open to send the mails by it. They were told in December that one mail would be conveyed by rail as soon as Bangor was reached. Hard on this came a report from Moorsom, 'that on the 16th of last month (November) I accompanied Mr. Stephenson in a Train from Chester to Conway and found the line with the exception of the parts not yet completed in good order'. Jackson's Bangor contract, however, was still proving difficult and he was informed in December that the company would take all measures to see that it was duly carried out. Towards the end of the board meeting at which this was decided upon, Collett fell ill. His health had been poor for some time and he left shortly after for a few months' relaxation on the continent.

Thomas chaired the next meeting, on 12 January 1848, at which it was agreed that the opening from Saltney to Bangor should be put back to 1 March. As this was also St David's Day it was hoped the decision would be final, but in the event the board was again to be frustrated. The Post Office let it be known at this point that the only mail which would at first be transferred to Holyhead was the night mail, then going by Birkenhead. This led to some discussion on the board as to the Anglesey line and the passenger facilities to be provided there. Clearly the unfinished state of the Britannia Bridge must not interfere with potential revenue from the mails.

Despite previous proposed opening dates it was only at this late stage in January 1848 that the traffic committee recommended various operating requirements and staff appointments. The maintenance of the permanent way was to be the responsibility of Lee, the resident engineer, unlike the position on some railways, where this was given to an outside contractor. Nevertheless, this did happen subsequently, when Cropper & Bell were given the job at £120 per mile in May 1849. It was proposed that the total of twenty-three semaphore signals required between Chester and Bangor should be of LNWR pattern, supplied by Stevens & Sons of Southwark Bridge Road. This was to be expected; the CHR had already come to an agreement with Euston for the LNWR to work the line from the opening (chapter 7). Signals were to be erected at the following places: the junctions with the Shrewsbury & Chester and Mold Railways, at all the stations, on either side of the Foryd Bridge and the Conway Bridge, and at the tunnels. Level crossing keepers were appointed for the first 48½ miles; all posts, except at Flint, went to men maimed during construction of the line. Signal boxes, crossing keepers' huts, station furniture, and Edmundson ticket machines were ordered, and a list prepared of staff and rates of pay. Staff uniforms were to be similar to those of the LNWR, with 'CHR' on the buttons, but it was later agreed that porters at Bangor and on Anglesey should have capes. To control the railway James Owen Binger was appointed as general superintendent at £350 per annum. Binger had started his career on the London & Birmingham and had then gone to the North Midland, where he was superintendent of part of the line. After that he had assisted in winding up the affairs of the St George (Irish) Steam Packet Company. He had glowing references.[14]

By March 1848, with the Bangor contract still in arrears, Jackson had been served with notice to put an extra 850 men on the works. On 31 March the members of the traffic committee passed over the line between Chester and Conway, and the Menai and Holyhead, and it was noted with satisfaction that Betts had completed his contract. Journey times were Chester to Conway 1hr 17min, and Menai to Holyhead 55min.[15] The works were so near completion that it was decided to open to Bangor as soon as the Conway Bridge was passable, expected to be on 1 May; the portions of Jackson's contract behind schedule were beyond Bangor. The opening from Llanfair to Holyhead was fixed for Monday 5 June, provided the Post Office steamers were operated from that date. Passengers were to be taken by road between Bangor and Llanfair. In fact this latter opening was not to be until 1 August 1848 (chapter 7). The first Conway tube was in place by April (chapter 5), and on Easter Monday, 24 April 1848, excursion trains ran to Conway for the public to view the tube, an idea suggested by Captain Huish of the LNWR. The S & C asked if it could put on a train to inspect the tube and permission was willingly given.[16]

### BOARD OF TRADE INSPECTIONS
### Saltney to Bangor

On 19 and 20 April 1848 Captain Wynne of the Board of Trade inspected the line from Saltney Junction to just east of the Conway estuary. The works being so numerous and the company wishing to work the excursions on Easter Monday, his first report, dated 22 April, was a mere summary sufficient to approve the opening. He did, however, mention the Foryd Bridge. This was an iron girder structure carried on piers with approach embankments. In the centre was a 45ft wide opening section which was to remain closed except when required to allow vessels through. The captain commented that it took ten minutes to open the bridge, twenty minutes to warp a vessel through, and a further ten to close it.

Captain Wynne reported fully on 25 April. He considered the first 17 miles of earthworks unimportant, but thereafter

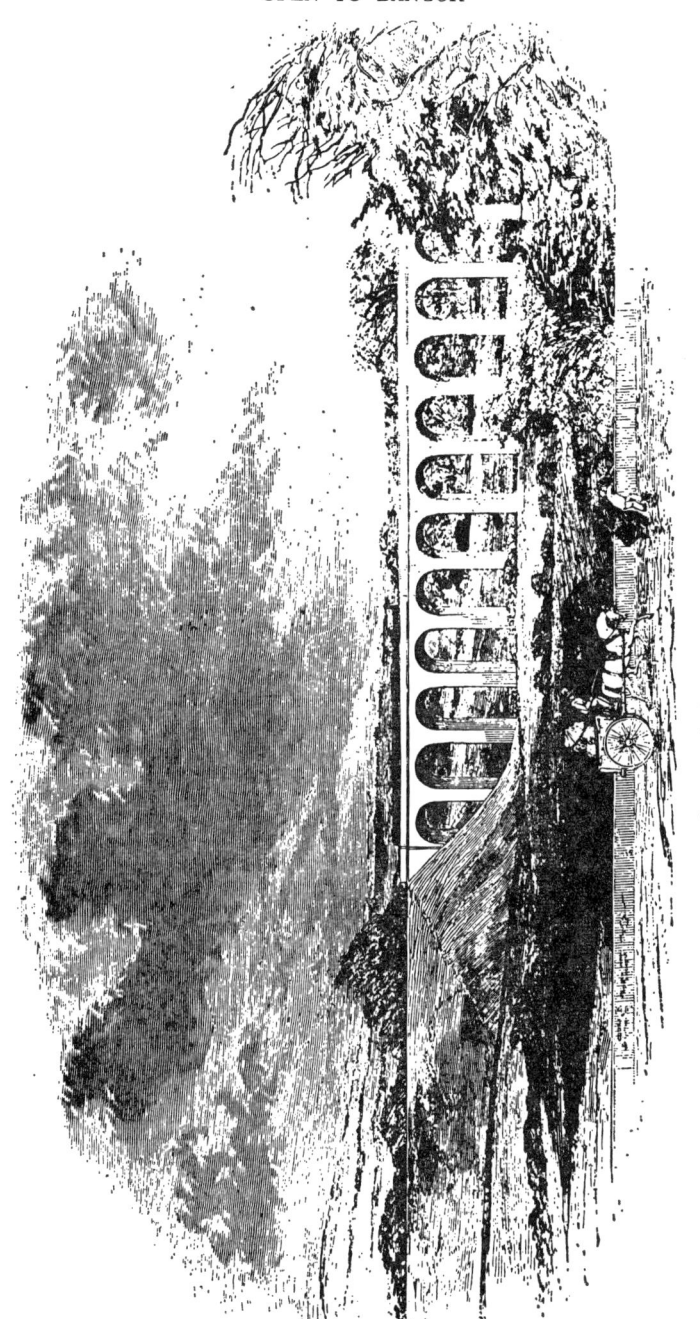

Ogwen viaduct 1848

they gradually increased in magnitude until within a short distance of Conway they were considerable, with 70ft deep cuttings and 35ft high embankments. Fifty-one bridges passed over roads or watercourses, thirty-four being of iron girders. Seven, with spans under 12ft, were of whole timbers, and the remainder of stone with interior brick arches. There were fifty-nine level crossings, eight of which were over public roads and had lodges, and thirteen road overbridges.

The section had two tunnels: Rockcliffe, between 10 and 11 miles from Chester, 98yd in length, executed as open cutting through sandstone and then arched over, with only 7ft of cover; and Penmaenrhos, between 38 and 39 miles, 488yd (BR records say 487), excavated through limestone, partly lined, and straight throughout. The plain east entrance contrasts with the fine castellated west portal. There was double permanent way throughout with 75lb/yd rails of double T form, secured to 20 and 24lb chairs by fir wedges, the chairs being spiked to triangular or rectangular section 9ft sleepers laid transversely. The ballast was 2ft deep and the width of formation level 33ft.

The line on to Bangor, including the Conway Bridge, was inspected by Captain J. L. A. Simmons of the Board of Trade in late April. As before, the company sought early approval in time for the public opening on Monday 1 May 1848. Captain Simmons obliged with a short favourable report. The works, he said, were 'stupendous', all well executed, and he was confident of their stability. 'The line is to be worked by the London and North Western Railway Company which is a guarantee of the sufficiency of the establishment'—a statement after Euston's heart.

The captain's detailed report was made on 14 June 1848 (for that part dealing with the Conway Bridge see chapter 5). He thought the earthworks light, excepting the last two miles into Bangor where the material appeared treacherous and there had been several slips. The Holyhead Road was carried over the railway on three bridges, one of stone $57\frac{1}{2}$ miles from Chester, and two others, of cast iron girders on masonry

Coach road, and railway tunnel, viaduct and sea wall at Penmaenmawr. Drawing by Russell, June 1849

Britannia Bridge from the Anglesey side, showing construction of a water tube on the Caernarvon shore, and the land tubes on the scaffolding. Drawing by Hawkins, May 1849

piers either side of Penmaenbach tunnel. The Ogwen viaduct, 58 miles, was of masonry piers with twenty-two semi-circular stone-faced brick arches of 26ft span and an extreme height of 42ft. (Moorsom, writing to King in November 1844, said the viaduct was to be erected to satisfy Colonel Pennant, the landowner; the line was originally to have been on embankment.) The Cegyn viaduct, 59 miles, was of similar construction, 57ft high, and with seven semi-circular arches of 35ft span. Four public highways were crossed on the level, and two tramways from stone quarries to the sea were carried over the railway.

The first tunnel on the section is that at Conway, $45\frac{1}{2}$ miles immediately west of the station and 74yd in length. Penmaenbach tunnel, at $47\frac{1}{4}$ miles, was reported as being 632yd in length (now 700yd according to BR records). Driven through basalt on a 40 chain curve, it was worked from adits to the beach. Penmaenmawr tunnel, at $50\frac{3}{4}$ miles, was given as 254yd in length, through greenstone and lined with greenstone rubble masonry. Differences in recorded lengths are explained in the case of Penmaenmawr, where a 130yd timber gallery covered the railway at the east end of the tunnel. It has been noted that Stephenson was also arranging for a similar extension at the other end. The 14 inch thick gallery roof was angled at 30 degrees, one side resting on the sea wall and the other on the hillside 40ft above the rails. There was an intermediate timber support and strut every 6ft. The avalanche tunnels were redecked through the years, the ends further extended, and the timber roofing replaced by wrought iron girders in 1864–5 and later by reinforced concrete. The total length today is 453yd. The fourth tunnel, Llandegai, at $58\frac{1}{2}$ miles, 506yd in length, was driven through shale and was brick-lined throughout. A mile further on, Bangor tunnel invested the line with an imaginative Thompson design, for its portal was in the Egyptian style, used with such dramatic effect on the Britannia Tubular Bridge. Bangor tunnel was given as being 924yd in length (BR records say 913). It too was through shale and was in process of being lined in brickwork.

F

The inspection stopped at Bangor, from there to Llanfair, including the bridge, not being ready for opening. At the west end of Bangor station is Belmont tunnel, originally 726yd in length.[17] Whereas the west portal is original, the east end of the tunnel was opened out in later years to enlarge Bangor station area (volume 2). The tunnel length is now 615yd; it was lined in 1870-1.

### CHESTER JOINT STATION

Chester station differed from the others for it was constructed as joint property. In August 1845, in the atmosphere of amalgamation then prevailing, the Chester & Birkenhead suggested such a venture and in the following October the Grand Junction proposed a station common to it, the C & B and the CHR.[18] The CHR board asked Stephenson to report but, though discussions took place between the companies, he told the board in July 1846 that nothing had been settled. J. M. Rendel, engineer to the C & B, had prepared station plans but these did not please the CHR directors who next instructed Stephenson to design a station wholly on the Crewe side of Brook Street bridge. By September it was understood that the LNWR, as successor to the GJR, and the BL & CJ and the Shropshire Union Railways & Canal companies would join the CHR in making the station. (The CHR had an option on SU company shares which had been acquired at the time of the proposed counter to the Worcester and Porth Dynllaen Bill mentioned earlier. The shares were transferred to the LNWR in December 1846.[19]) In November 1846, the S & C having been opened, Stephenson was asked to plan the station to include that company. It was agreed that construction and management expenses would be divided equally, a committee of directors of the four companies to run the station.

On 2 July 1847 the CHR directors for their part signed a contract with Thomas Brassey for construction of the station. On 9 July came Royal Assent to two Bills: the Shrewsbury & Chester Railway Act authorised construction of the station, and the Chester & Holyhead Railway, Chester Extension and Amendment Act (10-11 Vic cap cxlvii) the making of an extension line from the CHR into the joint property.

Francis Thompson was responsible for the station architecture which he conceived as being similar to that at Derby, built seven years before. The train shed and other features differed, however, for at Chester there was a central brick arcade between bays which took the place of cast iron columns.[20] As at Derby the façade was some 1,050ft in length. The central two-storey office block has a bracket-supported marquee placed between broad projecting blocks on either end themselves accented by corner loggia towers. The front elevation is virtually unaltered since the station was opened. The ground floor contained the usual waiting and refreshment rooms and booking office, with offices above for the CHR, the S & C, and the joint committee. Originally there was a single departure platform, 750ft long and 20ft wide, approached

Chester joint station

from the main block and, in between and in line with the office building, two three-tracked arrival bay sheds of 290ft by 24ft. Behind the departure platform and its three through tracks, and separated from it by a 24ft high arcade of pillars and brick arches, there was a carriage shed 450ft long and 52ft wide. An overall iron and glass roof covered the different sheds. Thirty-six turntables permitted carriage movements within the station. The goods shed, built at the same time, measured 270ft by 170ft.[21] By December 1852 all CHR business had been transferred to the Chester station offices, and the

London accommodation, latterly at Euston, had been vacated.

Construction of the station was under the direction of 27-year old George Grove, assistant to C. H. Wild on Stephenson's staff. Grove afterwards went to Bangor under Edwin Clark on the Britannia Bridge contract, but soon left engineering to devote himself to the Arts. He became secretary to the Royal Society of Arts in 1849, later compiled his *Dictionary of Music and Musicians*, and was knighted in 1883, the year he became first director of the Royal College of Music.[22] The foundation stone for the station was laid in August 1847 and, though not quite completed, the building was opened on 1 August 1848 (chapter 7). From then until 1890, when a large island platform was added on the far side, all the up and down through traffic used the one long platform, the northern portion serving the down trains and the southern the up, a scissors crossing enabling trains to pass each other.[23] Details of later works at Chester are give in volume 2.

CHAPTER 5

## Bridging the Conway and Preparations for Menai

Robert Stephenson's finest works, the Conway and Britannia Tubular Bridges, were constructed during financial difficulties, and under increasing pressure from worried directors to get the line open. Once the works had been started government encouragement waned, and it is clear that the CHR was most badly used by the politicians. The railway, built at enormous expense, and of national importance, virtually bankrupted the company. The Post Office and other authorities were enabled to improve vital communications to an extent undreamed of a decade or two before, and the Welsh and Irish tourist industries were given a flying start. But the whole effort depended upon the crossing of the Menai Straits. Stephenson, his first bridge design rejected by the Admiralty, produced in the Britannia Tubular Bridge what Glyn called 'one of the greatest triumphs in science ever achieved in this country'. He did so against numerous constructional problems, the agony of the Dee Bridge accident at a critical time, and despite doubters in the engineering world. Perhaps worst of all, he was involved in an unpleasant dispute over the originality of his design. At the end of it all he was offered a knighthood which he refused. Of all his works, the Britannia Tubular Bridge was his most enduring monument.

### THE FIRST DESIGNS

The first mention of the Menai crossing in the CHR board minutes concerns the possibility of using Telford's bridge: on

11 March 1844 Stephenson's assistant, Alexander Ross, was asked to report on the cost of its strengthening, with an alternative estimate for the construction of a new bridge.

Stephenson had examined various crossing points. In March he reported on three alternatives between Tal-y-bont, where James Walker's suggested line left the 1844 company route, and Llanfair PG where it rejoined it on Anglesey. The first, Walker's line, of 4½ miles, proposed crossing the Straits at the Gored Goch Rock by a bridge 600 yards in length. The second was the line then before Parliament, using Telford's bridge, the strengthening of which would cost £70,000. The third crossed at the Britannia Rock and was that which Stephenson recommended. The difficulties and expense of approaching the suspension bridge were uneconomic as its use could only be temporary; the Commissioners of Woods and Forests insisted that a railway over the bridge should be worked by horse power so as to permit its use by other traffic. Nevertheless, the directors decided for the time being to proceed with the line before Parliament, leaving it to future consideration as to whether to divert the railway to the Britannia route.[1]

Though the sites of Stephenson's Britannia and Conway Tubular Bridges were distant, certain circumstances were similar . . . 'in the first instance, every inquiry had reference to the construction of a bridge at the Straits, which would evidently, with slight alteration, be equally applicable to Conway; and thus special attention was never given to the detail of the latter bridge, until the general principles experimented on were fully confirmed as applicable to the larger structure. Thus the design of both bridges was simultaneous, and the early records of their progress are too closely interwoven to be separated'. So spoke Edwin Clark, resident engineer at the two bridges, in 1850.[2] But though the Conway Bridge thus appeared to be riding in on the coat-tails of Britannia, it was in fact the smaller bridge that got under way first, proving a most useful testing ground for the raising of the tubes.

By August 1844 the Britannia route had been decided upon.

Stephenson's proposal then was for a bridge of two cast iron arches, each of 350ft span, the railway to be 105ft above high water. The estimated cost, including abutments, was £250,000. A similar but single span bridge of 350ft was planned for the Conway, the railway there being a mere 20ft above high water. The anticipated mode of construction at Conway was to use centering to make the arch and then to float it into position on pontoons. At Britannia, however, where centering and scaffolding would be impracticable, it was intended that the arches be built up by placing equal and corresponding voussoirs on opposite sides of the piers at the same time, joining them by horizontal tie-bolts.

### GENESIS OF THE TUBULAR PRINCIPLE

So the proposals remained until plans were deposited for the Ogwen—Llanfair line for the Parliamentary session of 1845. There was an immediate outcry from navigation interests against the bridge scheme: there would not be a clear overall headroom similar to that afforded by the Menai Suspension Bridge and the area occupied by the spandrils and piers would restrict vessels to a narrowing channel and shelter them from much needed wind. In February 1845 Sir Robert Peel advised the company to seek the opinion of the Board of Trade on the proposed bridge. This was done but though the bridge drawings met with the approval of General Pasley of the BOT, the company was told that it was really a matter for the Admiralty. On 19 February there came a letter from the Admiralty enclosing a sketch of a scheme from a Mr Williams for crossing the Straits at the Gored Goch Rock by a suspension bridge. The sketch was forwarded to Stephenson.[3]

Meanwhile the CHR chairman, Collett, exuded confidence in the existing design. At the half-yearly meeting he crowed over the difficulties of the rival South Wales route . . . 'An idea has been entertained that a large portion of the Irish traffic will go by way of Wexford, and thence by the South Wales Railway.

This idea has been strengthened by the presumed difficulty of getting a bridge over the Menai Straits; but I can only say, that the difficulties of crossing the Severn are much greater. Besides, our difficulties have been surmounted, but those of the South Wales Company remain to be overcome'. This was premature; only a week later Stephenson told the directors that he was to meet Admiralty engineers at the Straits to confer on the site for the bridge and on its structure. 'In this position of affairs I felt the necessity of re-considering the question, whether it was not possible to stiffen the platform of a suspension-bridge so effectually as to make it available for the passage of railway trains at high velocity'.[4] It would be of interest to know whether Williams' proposed suspension bridge had any bearing on his reasoning. He had considered past projects, one of which was for a wrought iron cellular platform which he had designed for a road bridge over the River Lea at Ware. From there his thoughts progressed to a structure of separate wrought iron girders, made up of plates riveted together, but arranged in similar fashion to that of an ordinary cast iron girder bridge, and thence to a wrought iron rectangular tube, sufficiently large to take a train within it, and with suspension chains on either side. The tube should preferably, he considered, be circular or elliptical in form to mitigate against wind pressure. Thus far had his views come when the meeting with the Admiralty engineers was decided upon. In March 1845 he instructed two of his assistants to prepare drawings of a tubular bridge, based upon his ideas so far, the tubes to have a double thickness of plates at top and bottom.[5] Stephenson's own words describe his predicament:

> At this juncture I was placed in a most difficult position. Those interested in the navigation of the Menai Straits, as well as those who had, prior to this period, strenuously advocated Dynllaen in opposition to Holyhead as the proper terminus for a railway, had succeeded in inducing the Admiralty to give instructions to Sir John Rennie, Mr. J. M. Rendel, and Captain Vidal, to visit the Straits forthwith and report upon the probable injury which might accrue to the

navigation of its waters by the erection of the proposed arches at the Britannia Rock. I was too well acquainted with the overwhelming weight which is almost invariably given in such investigations to a long-established public interest, and the extreme jealousy with which any interference with it is watched, not to feel that the fate of my first designs was sealed. I stood, therefore, on the verge of a responsibility from which I confess I had nearly shrunk: the construction of a tubular beam of such gigantic dimensions, on a platform elevated and supported by chains at such a height, did at first present itself as a difficulty of a very formidable nature.[6]

He was nevertheless sure of his basic design and of his calculations. And so, when the Admiralty report went against the arched bridge and called for a clear headroom throughout of 100ft, Stephenson was ready:

It became my duty, then to announce to the Directors of the Chester and Holyhead Railway Company that I was prepared to carry out a bridge of this description. They did me the honour of giving me their confidence after I had generally explained my views; not, I believe, without some misgivings on their part.[7]

On 28 April the CHR board minutes noted . . . 'Mr. Stephenson stated that in the event of opposition to his proposed Bridge, he was prepared with another plan equally applicable for Railway purposes, and to which the Admiralty objections would not apply'. Added to this entry was a pencil note . . . 'That of an Iron Tunnel Models of which Mr. Stephenson was authorized to have prepared'.

CHESTER & HOLYHEAD RAILWAY COMPLETION ACT 1845

Thus committed, Stephenson prepared for the ordeal of the select committee stage of the Bill in Parliament. He consulted freely with his friends, especially Bidder, and showed his new drawings to General Pasley who, while agreeing to the principle of the design, objected to Stephenson's latest modification which was to remove the suspension chains, letting the tubes be self-supporting. John Laird, a CHR board member, and a prominent shipbuilder, offered useful advice on the strength of iron hulls. Messrs Miller & Ravenhill, shipbuilders, told Stephenson of the case of the *Prince of Wales* steamship which, when being launched, went astray so far as to form a natural bridge of 180ft span, between bow and stern, which was unsupported and yet had suffered little damage. Stephenson was grateful . . . 'The circumstances here brought to light were so confirmatory of the calculations I had made on the strength of tubular structures that it greatly relieved my anxiety, and converted my confidence into a certainty that I had not undertaken an impracticable task'.

Stephenson spent much time with his father discussing the problems of the design, during which he met William Fairbairn who in turn introduced him to Eaton Hodgkinson. Both 56 years of age, Fairbairn and Hodgkinson between them commanded a wealth of theoretical and practical knowledge which was to be invaluable in the design work for the tubular bridges. As an apprentice millwright at the Percy Main Colliery in 1804, inventive and largely self-taught, Fairbairn had there become friendly with George Stephenson, a kindred spirit. In 1830 Fairbairn and Robert Stephenson had together become members of the Institution of Civil Engineers. While Robert had followed his father in railway engineering, Fairbairn chose to go into shipbuilding. His son, Thomas, joined him at Millwall but later William went to Manchester where he experimented into the properties of iron, and invented a riveting machine. In the early 1840s he had advised the government on the causes of accidents from machinery. He was to be created a baronet in 1869. Eaton Hodgkinson was one of the foremost researchers and writers on scientific matters. In 1822, when Robert Stephenson was still at Edinburgh University, Hodgkinson had brought out a paper on the transverse strain and strength of materials, followed six years later by one on suspension bridges. In 1830 he had written on the strength and best forms of iron beams. He had been elected a Fellow of the

## BRIDGING THE CONWAY AND PREPARATIONS FOR MENAI

Royal Society in 1840 for a paper on the strength of pillars of cast iron and other materials.[8] Such then were the two men who, already collaborators, came fortuitously into Robert Stephenson's life at this time. One can imagine the satisfaction and relief of the younger man to find how impressed was Fairbairn with the concept of a tubular bridge, and how Fairbairn's appetite for research must have been whetted by the project. Forthwith he invited Stephenson to his yard at Millwall. It was a most useful visit, and the two men agreed upon a programme of experiments which Fairbairn was to carry out. On 5 May 1845 the Bill for the Ogwen—Llanfair line came before a select committee of the House of Commons. Stephenson tells what happened:

> The evidence which I gave before the Committee on the above day was received with much evident incredulity; so much so, that towards the end of that day's proceedings the Committee stated they would require further evidence, and especially that of the Inspector-general of Railways, before they could pass the Bill authorising the erection of such a bridge as that which I had proposed. The preamble of the Bill was passed, but a resolution come to which left the question of the bridge entirely open for further consideration. In this position of things it became evident, from my knowledge of the decided opinions held by the Inspector-general respecting the propriety of not dispensing with the chains, that I should not persist in the opinion that they were unnecessary; accordingly it will be observed, that whilst I expressed an unequivocal opinion as to the sufficiency of the tube alone, I was driven, from the circumstances that surrounded me, to leave the impression upon the minds of the Committee that at all events the chains might be left as auxiliaries to the tube if necessary.

A glimpse of the evidence given by Stephenson is illuminating as to the wish of counsel for the CHR to convey to the committee the engineer's ability to do the job:

> Q Have your calculations been submitted to many other engineers?

A I have made them in conjunction with Mr. Fairbairn of Manchester, whose experience is greater than any other man's in England.
Q There is no experience of a bridge being formed of a tube of this kind; is there?
A No, there is no experience of it; nor was there of the iron vessel some time ago. There is now one building by Mr. Fairbairn, 220 feet in length, and he says that he will engage that when it is finished that it shall be put down in the stocks at each end, and she shall have a thousand tons of machinery in the middle of her, and it will not affect her.
Q What is the length?
A 220 feet: but that is not so strong as a tube; and therefore any experience that this would carry out the tube would fully bear.
Q I wish to ask you whether this is your own suggestion?
A It is entirely.
Q From the experiments you have made, and from the inquiries you have also made, are you satisfied that that suggestion of yours is a practicable and safe one?
A I am not only satisfied that it is practicable, but I must confess that I cannot see my way at present to adopting anything else.[9]

James Meadows Rendel, examined by counsel for the CHR, said that he had advised the Admiralty to leave the principle of the design entirely to the railway company. He was sure that Stephenson's bridge would be safe. Stephenson, recalled on the second day of the hearing, told how he had originally thought of using a rigid timber platform. This, however, would eventually fail. He now believed he would still use a wooden platform, suspended from chains, on which he would construct two elliptical tubes, in situ, the chains being one on either side and one between the tubes. Two tubes were necessary so that there should be no tilting when the trains passed through. The select committee found the preamble of the Bill proved on 5 May, and the Chester & Holyhead Railway Completion Act received Royal Assent on 30 June 1845 (8–9 Vic cap xxxiii). It authorised the alternative line between the Ogwen and Llanfair, of 4 miles 46 chains, and construction of the bridge over the Straits.

### THE EXPERIMENTS—LETTING THE CONTRACTS

In August 1845 Hodgkinson was asked to assist in experiments to determine the form of the tubes. These commenced with simple cylindrical tubes of sheet iron which were tested to breaking point at Fairbairn's yard. At the half-yearly meeting of the CHR that month the directors reported that 'So satisfied is Mr. Stephenson with the comparative strength, durability and economy of this new method of Bridge Building that he purposes (sic) adopting it also for the crossing of the river at Conway'.

Stephenson was still concerned as to the method of raising the tubes. Briefly, a suspension bridge was to be made first, then embanked platforms at each end to and on the same level as the bridge platform. A railway was to be laid throughout the platforms and bridge. The tubes were to be erected on the outside platforms while an equal distributed load was laid on the bridge. When the tubes were ready they were to be rolled on to the bridge and the distributed load simultaneously rolled off. The suspension chains would take the weight of the tubes though these were to be constructed so as to be self-supporting.[10]

The experiments proved to be lengthy and in October 1845 the directors asked for a progress report. Hodgkinson suggested additional research, however, and Stephenson played for time. One point emerged: the circular tubes had proved unsatisfactory. The report was ready for the half-yearly meeting in February 1846, however, at which an artist's impression of the Britannia Tubular Bridge was hung above the chair, presumably to convince doubters and inspire the faint-hearted. The first series of experiments had been with plain circular tubes, the second with elliptical, and the third with rectangular. 'In the whole of these', said Stephenson, 'this remarkable and unexpected fact was brought to light, viz: that in such tubes the power of wrought iron to resist compression was much less than its power to resist tension, being exactly the reverse of that which holds with cast iron'. The rectangular tube had proved to be the strongest and it had been decided to abandon the others. Hodgkinson was now testing the strength of rectangular tubes of different dimensions.

The directors now decided there should be no further delays to construction. At a board meeting on 11 February 1846 Stephenson produced Thompson's drawings for the masonry and it was ordered that this work should commence forthwith. On 25 March tenders were received from Betts, Jackson, and Mackenzie singly, and from Benjamin J. Nowell, John Hemingway, and Charles Pearson jointly, for construction of the Britannia piers. The latter joint tender was accepted at £130,000, and on Good Friday, 10 April 1846, Frank Forster laid the first stone of the foundations at Britannia.[11]

The contract for the Conway Bridge masonry and bridge approaches was let on 6 May. There were six tenders. The lowest, and that accepted, was from John Evans for £26,500. Six days later Alexander Ross laid the first stone in the north-east corner of the Conway tower.[12] For the foundations of both towers, the rock was stepped and levelled at near the low water mark. At the south-east corner of the Conway tower, however, the rock shelved abruptly into deep water, and piles had to be driven into the silt for a platform to take the masonry.[13]

On 13 May, Stephenson and Fairbairn reported on their proposals for construction and erection of the tubes for both bridges. Stephenson then recommended that Fairbairn should superintend, 'in conjunction with him', the building of the two bridges. To this Fairbairn agreed, and he was formally appointed on those terms at a salary of £1,250 per annum—a handsome amount for those days. Both Fairbairn and Stephenson were empowered to appoint and hire extra assistants and workmen as necessary.[14]

Although the form of the Conway Bridge had been decided upon it was thought prudent to leave the Britannia until all the experiments were completed. Fairbairn made a model to one sixth of the size of the Britannia Bridge to test the rigidity, strength, and other properties of the design, after which work was to begin on the Conway tubes. As to these, Fairbairn suggested that the contract might be divided between 'the leading Iron Ship Builders, amongst whom may be reckoned my son Mr. Thos. Fairbairn at Millwall Poplar, Mr. John Laird at Birkenhead, Messrs Vernon & Co. Liverpool, and such other Builders as we could depend upon for the very first quality of work'.[15]

There were to be two workshops at the Menai and one at Conway and, on 8 July, George Pauling's tender was accepted for their construction; the foundations for that at Conway were already in progress. Stephenson recommended that the Conway chains should be made to the patent of Messrs Howard & Company for rolling the links without a weld. The firm fought shy of doing the job themselves but permitted use of their patent right on being paid 10s (50p) a ton, which would, upon the quantity of chains required, amount to about £1,500.[16] The early experiments with the one-sixth scale model were summarised by Stephenson in a report to the board on 29 July 1846:

> In such a model we should of course expect to have a very accurate exhibition of the merits or demerits of the tubular system.
>
> It will be in your recollection that the preliminary experiments led to the conclusion that great care would be required to prevent the upper side of the Tube from crushing,—that in short, the main object to be aimed at, was to give the top of the Tube the requisite stiffness.

The dimensions of the scale tube, which weighed a little over 5 tons, were: length 75ft between the supports, depth 4ft 6in, width 2ft 6in, with the upper side composed of cellular compartments running lengthwise along the tube.

When progressively loaded, the mean deflection was about one-tenth of an inch per ton, and with a load of thirty five tons suspended in the middle, it gave way on the underside, the upper part not having exhibited the least sign of failure up to the moment of fracture.

Hence therefore we have arrived at a most interesting result, viz:— that the liability of the plates on the upper side to crush, has been completely removed by the construction in compartments . . .

Stephenson said that contracts could now be let for the tube construction. The results of the experiments had been so satisfactory that suspension chains would only be required for their erection; he therefore proposed to dispense with chains, float the tubes to the piers, and raise them to the top of the towers by means of hydraulic presses. The tubes would be built, and the necessary platforms and shops provided on the shore instead of on the approach embankments as at first proposed.[17] The new mode of raising the tubes owed much to Edwin Clark. On 14 July he had been at Crewe station and while there had watched some workmen raising a water tank on brick piers by means of screw jacks. Clark saw that this method could be used for raising the Conway tubes if suitable recesses were made in the towers, hydraulic jacks being employed for the lifting. Stephenson had required some convincing as he was at first against floating the tubes on the tide, but Clark and Fairbairn had prevailed in favour of the scheme which shortly thereafter was adopted for the Britannia Bridge too.[18]

On 29 July 1846 the board accepted tenders for 8,000 tons of 'best' iron from the following: Walter Williams of the Albion Ironworks, West Bromwich; Bramah, Barrows & Hall, Bloomfield Ironworks, Tipton; John Bradley & Co of the Stourbridge Ironworks; the Butterley Iron Co; the Coalbrookdale Co; and G. B. Thorneycroft & Co, of the Shrubbery Ironworks, Wolverhampton. Each plate was to be marked 'C & H Co' and was to carry the name of the supplying contractor. In August 1846 Clark, Fairbairn, Forster, and Moorsom met at the sites of the two bridges to agree on the necessary construction platforms, workshops and huts. Those at Britannia were to be on the mainland, on the Caernarvon shore, while at Conway the river shore on the south-west side was chosen. Pauling was offered altered terms to his contract but he declined and the contract was cancelled. In March 1847 Nowell & Co contracted to erect cottages at the Straits. These, to take ten persons, each had five bedsteads and a table. There was further discussion on tube design in October 1846. It had apparently been suggested that the land spans of the Britannia Bridge should be in masonry but Stephenson saw little to be gained thereby and pointed out that such construction would affect the calculations as to the water spans. Even if a lattice girder bridge could be constructed—presumably suggested at even this late stage—it would not afford the same strength, weight for weight, as a tubular span with closed sides.[19]

By this time the construction tenders were in. There were twelve, including one from Fairbairn, and six refusals. John Evans was given the contract for the Conway Bridge at £37 per ton fixed complete, the price including materials at £15 per ton and the provision of platforms, workshops, machinery and huts for the men. As to Britannia, Garforth's tender for 1,000 tons, either delivered on board a vessel at Runcorn or constructed on site at the bridge, and Joshua Horton's tender for 1,500 tons, delivered on board vessel at Liverpool, were accepted on 14 October. The CHR finance committee was instructed to enter into contracts for the further portions of the tubes for which tenders had not so far been accepted, about 3,900 tons, and on 11 November 1846 tenders were accepted from William Fairbairn & Son and Ditchburn & Mare for the remaining portions in equal quantities at £32 per ton, to include delivery at the Straits. In January 1847, after a dispute concerning erection costs, Stephenson ruled that when sections had been delivered, the company would bear the expense of reconstructing the tubes to their state previous to being taken down in the contractors' yards. The contractors were to pay for riveting where necessary to complete each section to a length of 24ft. At the CHR half-yearly meeting in February 1847, Stephenson sounded a cautious note of optimism concerning the Britannia Bridge:

> In order to finish this contract by the end of March, 1848, it will be necessary to set about 3,000 cubic feet of masonry per day, which may, I believe, be accomplished by the extensive and efficient apparatus which the contractor has erected. Until some further advance is made in the construction of the tube, I am, of course, unable to speak with confidence of the rate of progress which may be calculated upon; but, as it is a description of work, upon which, when once fairly commenced, an almost unlimited force of men can be employed, I do not anticipate that it will materially delay the final completion of the line beyond the expected time.

The platform at Conway was of timber, 420ft by 40ft, piled into the beach, midway between high and low water. With a minimum of excavation, pontoons could later be got underneath for the purpose of floating the tube, which rested on longitudinal timbers on one side of the platform. On the other side were rails on which two travelling cranes hoisted the plates into position. At the north-west corner of the platform another crane unloaded the incoming plates. Alongside the platform, and also on piles, were workshops, a 20hp steam engine with shafting to three punching and shearing machines, a vertical drill and lathe, and a fan blower to the rivet furnaces. By February 1847 Evans had many of these items erected and in use and had commenced punching the plates and angle irons. The contractors at Britannia had not then started, owing to lack of iron, though two platforms were under way and the machinery was almost complete.[20] Later, two more platforms were constructed at Britannia to hasten work on the water tubes. The total length of the Britannia platforms was 2,199ft; they were similar to those at Conway but were on a larger scale. A tramway served nearly $3\frac{1}{2}$ acres of staging around the platforms which carried some forty-eight riveting machines, besides numerous travelling cranes, workshops, and furnaces.

To make the plates the contractors had to order additional steam power and special plate rolls and other machinery for their yards. The Coalbrookdale Iron Company got off to a bad start; their first attempt resulted in ten tons of defective plates and Fairbairn condemned the lot. The Butterley Company only began delivery in February 1847.[21] Nevertheless by the following June the lower part of the first Conway tube was completely riveted and the sides commenced. The plates were delivered slightly convex in shape. At Conway they were laboriously hammered flat but at Britannia iron rollers did the job.[22]

Only the hydraulic presses and lifting chains remained to be ordered. The latter require some explanation. It was decided, from experiments, not to have the presses under the tubes, where they required separate staging and support, but to place them inside so as to exert their power on chains hung from girders on top of the piers. The ram of the press was to be clamped to the chain; on its descent it would thereby lift the tube. Packing would then be placed underneath the tube and the ram would ascend and be re-clamped to the chain.[23] Chains and pumps were ordered on 12 May 1847 from Messrs Howard & Ravenhill, and Messrs Easton & Amos of the Grove Iron Works, Southwark, respectively.

On that day Clark reported that Evans and Garforth were progressing well but that all Horton's work had been condemned. Ditchburn & Mare had started work but Fairbairn, who had himself originally wanted to contract for the whole bridge, had arranged for Mare to take over his contract, and this without a word to the directors. They were understandably annoyed, and Fairbairn promised that if Mare appeared not to be making progress with the contract after a month he would surrender it to the company. In the outcome it stayed with Mare. That gentleman also took over Horton's contract in June 1847 so that, excepting one large tube put up by Garforth, Mare was responsible for the whole of the ironwork on the Britannia Bridge. All was now ready for the cacophony of hammering and clanging which was to reverberate over the Menai Straits for the next three years or so, while the masonry slowly rose and the tubes were riveted and joined by an ant-like army of workmen. On 13 June 1847 the first vessel, laden with iron, arrived at Britannia.[24]

### TRAGEDY AT THE RIVER DEE

As construction of the tubular bridges was starting, and when he was standing as a candidate for Parliament, a blow fell upon Stephenson which for lesser men might have had graver conequences. The Dee Bridge, for the design of which he was responsible, failed. The original intention had been for a brick bridge of five arches, completing the brick viaduct approach to the river, $1\frac{1}{2}$ miles from Chester. At an early date, however, Stephenson substituted a design of three cast iron spans of 98ft each, on a 51 degree skew to the river, resting on stone abutments and two stone piers. Each railway line was supported between the piers on two parallel 107ft 6in cast iron composite girders in three sections joined by semicircular castings secured to their upper flanges (illustration p 105). Connecting the composite girders were thirteen wrought iron tie bars, the distance of 12ft between the girders being spanned by oak joists, laid loose on the bottom flanges, serving as transverse sleepers to the railway. Above these, longitudinal planking formed the floor upon which iron chairs and rails were laid, including check rails. At the end of each composite girder was bolted a quadrant shaped casting from which eight wrought iron tension bars, clamped together, linked to a similar centre set of bars and a return link to the far quadrant. Each set of girders was independent from its neighbour alongside. One track of the bridge was opened in September 1846 for use by the contractors and on one occasion three engines and tenders, together weighing 90 tons, passed over without any apparent damage. Since November 1846 the bridge had been in regular use by the trains of the Shrewsbury & Chester Railway.

On 24 May 1847 the southern girder on the western span broke as the 6.15pm S & C train from Chester was passing over

*Broken span at the Dee Bridge*

it. The train was running five minutes late and at an estimated speed of 30mph. Although the engine got across, dragging its derailed tender with it, the carriages fell 36ft into the river. The fireman and five passengers were killed and eight injured. At the coroner's inquest early in June evidence was heard from workmen on the bridge of vibration and girder deflection when trains passed over, and the inference was that they were unsafe. General Pasley, however, remarked at the inquest that of a number of similar railway bridges erected both before and after he had been Inspector General of Railways, none, with the exception of the Dee Bridge, had failed. But, he went on . . .

It has been stated, that sometime after the Shrewsbury & Chester Railway was opened, and after I had inspected it, a girder was cracked and replaced by a new girder. This circumstance, which I did not know, coupled with the fracture of this one, induces me to think that they are not safe, and that it is the mere cast of a die between their safety and danger. By examining the bridge on Thursday, I consider that the tension-rods are of very little use indeed. I saw nothing to throw the carriages off the rails on the bridge, which had strong guard rails.

Stephenson, giving evidence, saw nothing to indicate weakness or imperfection in the bridge works. The wing parapet on the Saltney side was much shattered and displaced; the locomotive tender had clearly given a violent side blow to the masonry. The thirteen lateral ties had all been either torn from their sockets or wrenched off near to the sockets of the girder left standing. The main fracture of the girder suggested that the carriages had become derailed and had struck it a lateral blow. It had been argued, said Stephenson, that the check rails precluded a derailment. But in any violent collision these hardly ever prevailed; they only counteracted any moderate tendency to leave the rail. The hearing was adjourned to allow time for the Commissioners of Railways to report on the accident.

On 9 June Stephenson told the CHR board that he had inspected the bridge only a few hours before the accident; it was the first time he had seen it since the scaffolding had been removed. 'I confidently concluded that every part was firm and sufficient and if anything were wanting to justify such a conclusion I felt that the fact that the Traffic of the Chester and Shrewsbury Railway having been uninterruptedly carried on a curve; but as the radius was fully two miles the centri-made that the accident had occurred because the bridge was on a curve; but as the radius was fully two miles the centrifugal force was totally inadequate to derail a train.

The Railway Commissioners sent James Walker and Captain Simmons to Chester. Their report, dated 15 June 1847, was critical of the design of the bridge. They calculated that whereas Stephenson had taken the safe load on two adjacent girders as 180 tons it was in fact only 106, and 18 tons of stone, for protecting the woodwork from locomotive cinders, had further reduced this. To arrive at the figure of 180 Stephenson had taken into account the additional strength of the tension bars. Over a period, however, these had stretched; with a test load of a goods train weighing 48 tons both end suspension points moved towards each other by 7/8th inch. It was thought that, practically, the tension bars were of little use and that at the time of the accident the girders had been taking all the weight. Though the girder deflection was less when a train passed over at speed, the considerable shaking and oscillation had been a weakening factor. 'In addition to this is the tremulous motion of the beam (like the wire of a musical instrument) when the engine is going over. This tremor was so sensible that Captain Simmons could not distinctly see the edge of the beam'. The captain noted that during a test with the goods train, running at over 20mph over the intact spans, . . . 'I also certainly upon one occasion felt a sharp jerk as the girder was relieved of its weight', and, not surprisingly, 'none of these observations were taken at high velocities, as I did not feel myself warranted in further testing the structure'. Though connected, the girders did not move together laterally, so that the tie rods became weakened. With the line on a curve and the girders being on the skew, the load did not bear uniformly and produced a rocking motion. Also, the load being on one side only of the bottom flange of the girders, there was an outward thrust at the bottom which drew the two tops together by as much as 2 inches for 48 tons, imparting a twisting motion or torsional strain to the girders and tie rods. It was considered that the first fracture took place in the middle of the girder, not at the abutment end as Stephenson had suggested.

We may adduce, as a corroboration of this last view, the circumstance of an addition of 18 tons of stone having been made to the permanent weight of the bridge immediately before the accident; and the *fact* that, when a weight, partly permanent and partly pressing, but together forming a *very* considerable proportion of the breaking weight of the girder, is in continuous operation, flat girders of cast iron suffer injury, and their strength becomes reduced; and that if, when this has taken place, the momentum of the passing weight be increased by any irregularity in the rails, or in the motion of the engine, to which the best made and managed railways are subject, a fracture is likely to be the consequence.

The two inspectors felt that perhaps they could be accused of being unnecessarily cautious in their objection to the bridge design, 'but as we entertain these opinions very decidedly, it is our duty (by no means an agreeable one) to express them'. One cannot help wondering at this point whether the stone was not so much to protect the woodwork, as claimed, as to steady the structure, bearing in mind previous reports of vibration and that Stephenson himself inspected the bridge on the afternoon that the stone was put down. If it was for maintenance purposes, such an operation would hardly call for the presence of the chief engineer. The resumed coroner's inquest came to its verdict on the day following publication of the report. The jurors unanimously found that the girder broke because it was of insufficient strength to bear the pressure of 'quick trains' passing over it. The other eleven girders were likewise condemned, and as there were upwards of a hundred other cast iron bridges, either built or contemplated on the railways in the country, a government inquiry was called for to reassure the public. On 29 June the Railway Commissioners issued two minutes: cast iron bridges were to be the subject of an inquiry; and inspecting officers generally were not to be held responsible for structural work when inspecting new lines prior to opening. In the last resort responsibility was to lie firmly with the engineer to the railway company. After this Stephenson must have been concerned for the future of his tubular bridges or at least his own freedom of action respecting them; on 7 July the CHR board decided to ask

Stephenson whether he would permit a full-time government inspector on the works. He refused and to its credit the board backed him.

In July the S & C was informed that the Dee Bridge was now supported by timber piles and that a single line was open over it. The S & C replied that it would not send passengers over that or the Ellesmere Canal Bridge (also being strengthened) until both had been inspected and passed by the Board of Trade. This was done by Captain Simmons on 20 July. He thought them now safe but recommended low speeds so as not to loosen the piles. Omnibuses had been operated by the S & C since the accident, between Saltney and Chester. S & C trains started using the bridge again from Monday 26 July.[25] There followed a lengthy wrangle over compensation. The S & C sought exoneration from the accident but the CHR would not agree. In September 1847 the CHR undertook to meet all reasonable claims while not admitting liability. Compensation paid by the company totalled £12,727.

On 14 August 1847 the CHR directors recorded that 'they have every confidence that the sad event, in whatever way occasioned, will have the effect of leading the capable Engineer of the Company to increase, if possible, that care and watchfulness for the public safety, for which he has always been so highly distinguished'. What was more important, they affirmed their confidence in the tubular bridges. It was, therefore, both annoying and embarrassing to Stephenson to have to report to the board on 8 September that while experimenting on the spans of the Dee Bridge, his instructions had been disobeyed in that one of the girders was tested to destruction. It had fractured at a less weight to that which it ought to have carried. But, said Stephenson, 'I attach no importance to the result of the experiment, it does not in any way alter the mode in which I had proposed to add to the strength of this Bridge which is now in progress and considerably advanced'.

Meanwhile, a government commission had been appointed in August 'to inquire into the Application of Iron to Railway Structures'. It reported in July 1849 and the Dee Bridge figured largely in the evidence. One of the points dealt with the torsional strain set up by the cross timbers on the inner lower flanges of the compound girders. Fairbairn was called as a witness and suggested that the decking should be supported from beneath the girders. Stephenson, however, thought the strain was 'not enough to be noticed'. He was questioned on this: 'You admit the fact that the torsion takes place, but you consider it too small to be of consequence, and you disregard it?'— 'Yes, I do'. As to the failure of the compound girder it was disquieting, to say the least, to recall that Stephenson had taken part in a discussion at the Institution of Civil Engineers in April 1847, a month before the Dee Bridge disaster, on the breaking of just such a compound cast iron beam in a Manchester cotton mill.[26] Did he then, perhaps, have a premonition of trouble ahead? If so he had not taken action and, indeed, had confidently described his Dee Bridge design to his fellow engineers. Now, however, when explaining to the inquiry how he had strengthened the bridge, he set the record straight: 'I have added three corresponding parts to the top, so as to correct what I admit to have been a certain degree of oversight'.

This method of strengthening with an additional row of castings shaped to fit above the existing ones was hurriedly applied to similar bridges throughout the railway system following publication of the commission's findings. The use of compound cast iron girders of the type discussed almost completely ceased thereafter, and during the following years such bridges were either further strengthened or reconstructed. It was not until the Norwood Junction accident on the Brighton line in 1891, however, that all remaining cast iron underline bridges were finally replaced. In the case of the Dee Bridge the structure was extensively rebuilt in brick and wrought iron in 1870–1, the iron being supplied and the work done by W. S. Woodall of Dudley. The work was underestimated and there was heavy overexpenditure reported in September 1871, by which time the works appear to have been completed. The bridge was widened in the early 1900s (volume 2).

Though one cannot say that Stephenson had come through the inquiry unscathed, his tubular bridge at Conway was by then an accomplished triumph. That and the Britannia, both of which were extensively reviewed at the inquiry, successfully overshadowed the Dee Bridge tragedy. His standing in the country had not suffered; the electors of Whitby confidently returned him as their MP on 30 July 1847, an office he was to hold, as a Conservative and Protectionist, until his death.

Captain Simmons reported on 23 April 1848 that the Dee Bridge was perfectly restored and that both lines were ready for use. He had tested it with heavy trains and in no case had there been a greater deflection than 3/16th inch.

### GENERAL PASLEY'S LETTER

In August 1847, in the midst of his Dee Bridge worries, Stephenson had a disagreement with General Pasley. The general had written to the *Railway Times* to the effect that the method of using chains to raise the tubes at the Britannia Bridge was dangerous. He ended his letter with 'The chances are that the first tube which he attempts to raise will find its way to the bottom of the Straits'. This was going too far, and Stephenson appended a broadside to his report to the CHR half-yearly meeting.

> I feel that you may perhaps expect some observations from me, respecting a letter which appeared in the 'Times' a few days ago, with the signature of General Sir Charles Pasley, objecting in strong and somewhat uncourteous language to the method proposed to be adopted in the erection of the tubes at the Conway and Britannia Bridges. The conclusions arrived at are so clearly based in ignorance of the proposed plans, that I abstain from making any comment theron; indeed, I am precluded from doing so, since he merely indulges in random predictions without offering even the semblance of a reason for them. For the satisfaction of the Directors, I think it right to add, that nothing has occurred in any way to shake my confidence in the plan which we are preparing to carry out.

The general, it appeared, had gleaned the erroneous information on which he based his letter, from Captain Moorsom, while the two of them were chatting in a railway carriage. Stephenson declared that nobody, including Moorsom, could be fully acquainted with his plans, and Moorsom admitted that he had envisaged something quite different from what Stephenson now intended. It was a silly misunderstanding, and annoying in that it hinted at further doubts on Stephenson's competence.

## THE CONWAY TUBULAR BRIDGE

The architecture of the Conway Tubular Bridge was designed by Francis Thompson to harmonise with the castle. It was originally intended that the tubes should have a continuous machicolated cornice and loopholes but these features were, perhaps fortunately, omitted to save expense.[27] The two towers, which give a barbican effect, are faced throughout with limestone from Penmon Point and the Great Orme. The masonry courses vary from 15 inches to 3 feet in thickness, and the stones weigh between 5 and 8 tons, the total quantity used amounting to 161,450cu ft.[28] The base of the towers, to the underside of the tubes, is quarry-faced with smooth angles, with the exception of the dressed stone recesses in which the tubes were raised. Above the base the exterior is of dressed ashlar, and the backing throughout is of Runcorn stone or brickwork, the latter being mainly employed in the upper part of the towers. The amount of Runcorn stone used was 191,255 cu ft. Details of the tubes will become apparent during discussion of their erection.

## FLOATING THE FIRST CONWAY TUBE

By November 1847 work at Conway was waiting on the first tube. That month saw the arrival by train at Birkenhead (whence they were shipped to Conway) of the chains and presses from London.[29] By mid December, after the men had worked day and night, the first Conway tube was ready. On

16 January 1848 the workmen started cutting away the timber platform beneath the tube, which was to be supported at each end on sandstone piers, built to within a short distance from its underside. As the tube sank on to the piers the crushed timbers had to be splintered out, so great was the compressive force. Clark mentions that the creaking and groaning woodwork, and the great mass of the tube above them, so unnerved the men that they had to be restrained from a precipitate retreat. The tube took its own weight on the piers on 25 January. The deflection was $7\frac{7}{8}$in which increased to $10\frac{15}{16}$in under a 300 ton test load of iron bars in wagons within the tube.[30]

Herepath noted on 22 January that Brunel had been inspecting the bridge. 'We wonder whether he drew any comparison in his mind between the merits of this (bridge) and those of his Atmospheric whim. If he did, we should much like to know what they were.' The sarcasm was unnecessary. Brunel's appearance had a two-fold motive: he could and did learn much which was to be of great use later in his own undertakings; but mainly, one must believe, it was pure friendship and altruism which had brought him to Conway. He and Stephenson had long been in friendly rivalry. Stephenson's cautious genius had often shied clear of some of Brunel's most upstart ideas, but this did not alter the fact the each had great respect for the other and they were to remain close friends until death. Most important on this occasion, Brunel brought with him Captain Christopher Claxton RN, a close friend since the early 1830s when Claxton was quay warden at Bristol and Brunel was planning the Great Western Railway. Claxton had ventured with Brunel into the saga of the Great Western Steamship Company. They had been together through the adventures of the *Great Western* steamship, and the *Great Britain*, and were to go on to that mammoth and ruinous marvel the *Great Eastern*. But now, in 1848, they both appeared at Conway. There, and later at Britannia, Claxton was to be in charge of the navigational problems of floating the tubes, and Brunel to offer advice and encouragement. With them came numerous sailors from the *Great Britain* to help with matters nautical.

*Herepath's Journal* followed events keenly, and on 12 February noted rather quaintly that 'Mr. Robert Stephenson, the Engineer, goes down to-day, for the purpose of not returning until the Conway Tubular Bridge is fixed in its place'. In fact Clark says that Stephenson took up residence at Conway on 20 February. Though the tide was suitable on that day all was not ready, and the floating was postponed until 6 March, the next favourable date, and incidentally the highest tide of the year. The delay was partly due to the fact that it had taken longer than anticipated to excavate under the tube for the insertion of the pontoons. This done, however, and having tested their buoyancy and ability to lift their burden, they were left in situ, with their valves open, alternately filling and emptying as the tides rose and fell.

On 3 March all personnel were in their places for a rehearsal during which Clark was unfortunate enough to lose part of his big toe, an event which kept him inactive during the floating three days later. At 11.15am on Monday 6 March, in beautiful weather, the rising tide lifted the pontoons and the tube started on its journey, snapping the ropes which held it, but securely guided by great chains which passed through the hawse holes of the two outside pontoons. Clark watched from a carriage on Telford's suspension bridge. All around him was a multitude of sightseers, in the town, in the fields along the river bank, on the castle ramparts, and on the suspension bridge. The *Railway Times* had a man there and he did a particularly good descriptive piece which is worth recording for its eye-witness appeal. Brunel and Stephenson were with Captain Claxton on the tube. The captain was armed with a speaking trumpet.

> We observed him using two figures, of large dimensions, No. 1 and 2—when the red side was shown on the former number, a capstan fixed on the road from Conway to the tube works, was hove upon; when the white side was shown the heaving stopped, and a similar operation with No. 2

BRIDGING THE CONWAY AND PREPARATIONS FOR MENAI 115

governed the operations of a powerful capstan (we were told, lent by the Admiralty) fixed on the railway on the Chester side, with its rope made fast to the inside of the tube, on that end. In the pontoons, three enormous masses of timber, we were informed, 95 feet long by 25 feet wide, and 8 deep, bound together, powerful crabs worked by 44 men, hove upon the chains, which had previously been tightened up by a large crab, at which a dozen or more men strained with their utmost efforts on either end on shore, one end of each chain being fixed at the piers of the suspension bridge, while the other ends were fast to the aforesaid crabs, on the opposite side of the river; on these chains the pontoons appeared to traverse.

Interrupting, it should be made clear that there were in fact six pontoons, made of deal and hardwood, three at each end. Clark says they were 98ft in length and that each could carry 460 tons. The weight of the tube as floated was 1,147 tons. To continue with the *Railway Times*:

The western, or Conway end, was pointed first, but did not come quite home afterwards. The eastern, or Chester end, was dropt [sic] in after, or while the ebb was making, but before it reached by about a dozen feet the exact berth, it took the mason work, and no effort could disengage it. Nevertheless it was over its bed sufficiently to be landed and bedded up with timber previously prepared from a lower bed, which had been provided in case the tide should fall before the upper bed could be reached. The most extraordinary efforts were made with screws and tackles, no less than four of which latter were at one time applied, besides the Chester side crab manned by 60 people, while the tide was falling, to overcome the obstacle; but they appeared to be ineffectual, and Capt. Claxton was heard to give orders for bedding up, which was speedily accomplished. The barges were then sunk a little, and the noble fabric rested very near the hydraulic presses which are to be used in raising it. Cheers were then given for the Conway Railway Bridge, for Mr. Stephenson, and for Capt. Claxton; and heartily responded to by the masses lining the suspension bridge and the castle walls. Three steamers were in attendance below the bridge, two full of company, and a great number of boats plied with their freight upon the river. A band of music, playing martial and enlivening airs, followed by a dense crowd, marched from one end to the other on the top of the tube, which was but slightly thinned before sunset.

According to Clark the trouble at the bridge was caused by one of the pontoons fouling the rock at the Conway, not the Chester, end of the tube. Attempts were made on 8 and 9 March to get the tube into its correct position. The pontoons were in danger at this time from the tides and Clark says that Stephenson 'quite despaired' of seeing the tube safely home. On 11 March, however, the great mass of iron, for the up line of the CHR, was successfully moved into its place at the base of the towers.[31]

The successful floating was reported to the board by Moorsom on 7 March. The directors minuted their congratulations to Stephenson and expressed 'their firm reliance on his skill, energy, and perseverance, in overcoming all other difficulties connected with the Tubular Bridges'. Considering that at that very moment the recipient was said to be apprehensive about the whole business and had yet to position the tube properly, this was a mite premature. At the half-yearly meeting on 8 March the eulogies continued. Stephenson had not submitted his usual report, however, and a shareholder asked whether, since they had been promised in August 1847 that the bridge would be complete within three months of that time, there had been any delay which was being concealed by the absence of the report. Moorsom defended Stephenson. He had, he said, 'really been so harassed that it was not at all surprising that he should be unable to write his Report just at the moment of his great triumph'. Moorsom told how, after the tube had been floated, he had taken Stephenson's arm, when both were standing on top of the tube . . . 'after all was found safe, Mr. Stephenson requested me to offer any explanation the meeting required, and said, "Now I shall go to bed" (Cheers). All those who had been engaged in similar undertakings would understand the expression (Cheers).'

### RAISING THE FIRST CONWAY TUBE

Now the tube was placed, the presses and raising machinery were got into the towers. Two single presses were used at Conway, of 20 inches internal diameter, the diameter of the ram being 18 inches. Each full stroke raised the tube by 6ft, the time taken by each lift being about 34 minutes. Each 412ft long, to span 400ft, the tubes were lengthened after raising by 6ft at each end which allowed a bearing of 12ft in each tower. The Conway ends were fixed while, for expansion purposes, the Chester ends were left free on rollers. When finally settled on their beds the tubes were 9ft apart and 17ft above high water.[32]

Raising of the first tube commenced on 8 April 1848 and was completed three days later; it was lowered on to its permanent bed on 16 April. The permanent way, ordinary flange rail with chairs, and incorporating an expansion rail, was quickly laid down and on 18 April Stephenson drove the first train over the bridge.[33] On the following day a special train carrying directors and officials passed through the tube en route for Holyhead, there to make arrangements for opening the still separated line on Anglesey.

### BOARD OF TRADE INSPECTION—FIRST CONWAY TUBE

The Conway Tubular Bridge up line tube and the railway thence to Bangor was inspected in late April by Captain Simmons of the Board of Trade (chapter 4). His detailed report, which included the bridge, was made on 14 June. He had tested the bridge on a day of showers and bright sunshine with trains of different speeds and weights. The alternate heating and wetting of the tube affected the readings somewhat but the results amply proved the strength of the structure: the tube expanded ½in for every 15 degrees change of temperature; there was scarcely any vibration; the riveting was of great precision and the captain did not think there would be any stresses of abnormal nature to alter 'the texture of materials'. Oxidisation remained the only likely adverse condition, particularly in view of the proximity of the sea. (The tubes were, in fact, well primed in lead and were finished in a buff colour.) The line being single over the bridge, points and signals were installed at either end and put under the charge of one man.

The opening of the bridge must have done something to ease Stephenson's grief at the death of his father on 12 June 1848; the old engineer had been spared long enough to know that the Britannia was now a certainty. Robert himself came near to death at this time: he was knocked nearly unconscious while in a loose railway carriage which was demolished by an express train at Conway, only a few yards from the bridge, on 30 August 1848. As will be seen (chapter 10), the CHR and its successor were more than once to leave vehicles in front of expresses. To leave their engineer in one was more than careless.

### COMPLETION OF THE CONWAY BRIDGE

The floating of the second tube took place on 12 October 1848, From 'lift-off' at 9.30am to 'touch-down' took just under an hour. It was a model performance, similar in technique to that of the first occasion, and again drew vast crowds of spectators.[34] The tube was raised without accident on 2 November.[35] Clark, however, mentions that during the lifting one of the presses threatened to fail. This incident, which could well have smashed the tube, and possibly the first tube too, led to a modification in the lifting procedure to be used at Britannia and to Stephenson adopting a method of building underneath the tubes after each small lift, unlike at Conway where this was done as one operation after each tube had been completely raised. In this sense the near accident at Conway was a boon; because of these altered methods a very serious accident was to be avoided at Britannia when one of the presses did fail.

The Conway second tube was lowered on to its permanent bed on 8 December,[36] and on 2 January 1849 Captain Simmons made his inspection. Apart from the usual tests and results, all favourable, the captain noted one interesting fact. In the first tube it was found that the method of placing the timbers for the permanent way had led to the collection of water within the tube, giving rise to anxiety over corrosion. This was remedied in the second tube where the rails were laid on longitudinal sleepers. The company decided to take all traffic through the second tube while the permanent way in the first was relaid. The junction points and signals at each end leading to the new single line remained only until the first tube was back in use.

In September and October 1899 both tubes were further supported on cylindrical columns placed at each end. The centenary of the bridge was celebrated by a pageant at Llandudno Junction in July 1948 organised by the station master, Mr Robert Jones, also then Mayor of Conway.

CHAPTER SIX

## Open Throughout—The Britannia Tubular Bridge

BOARD OF TRADE INSPECTION AND OPENING LLANFAIR TO HOLYHEAD

On 27 July 1848 Captain Simmons of the Board of Trade inspected and approved the Anglesey line. The permanent way was of double track and had a ruling gradient of 1 in 100 (now 1 in 97 until Holyhead where there is a later addition of 1 in 75 down to the present station). There were two tunnels, Bodorgan Nos 1 and 2, 413 and 115yd respectively, about a mile south of Bodorgan station. The summit of the CHR, 186ft above sea level, is at about 1½ miles south of Gaerwen, a later station; from there the line falls for 4¾ miles down Llangaffo Bank on a ruling gradient of 1 in 97 to a viaduct of nineteen arches over Malltraeth Marsh and the River Cefni. It crosses the Stanley Sands, ¾ mile wide, by means of a broadening out of Telford's Holyhead Road embankment, the railway being on the west side. (The Anglesey stations are described in chapters 9 and 10.) Llanfair to Holyhead was opened to traffic on Tuesday 1 August 1848.

Shortly afterwards Collett noted . . . 'I have recently been travelling five times over the line, and as I always travel on the locomotive engine, I was enabled to see everything worthy of observation, and the general appearance of the line was most gratifying'. Collett may have been lucky; footplate-riding figured in an early, tragic accident on Anglesey. One 'extremely cold and piercing' day in December 1848 a young railway labourer's wife received permission to travel, with her infant, on the engine tender to Holyhead. Because of the cold, however, she huddled close to the boiler. According to *Herepath's Journal* of 6 January 1849, when at Llanfaelog one of the boiler steam cocks burst and the girl and her baby were scalded to death.

### FINANCIAL DIFFICULTIES

In October 1848 Messrs Glyn, Hallifax, Mills & Co, bankers, asked the CHR for repayment of a loan of £75,000. This was a symptom of an increasingly unfortunate financial position due in part to over expenditure, and Stephenson was asked to report forthwith on works which might be postponed. One of the first casualties was the figure of Britannia, planned to top the centre tower of the bridge.[1] Moorsom, who had less to do now that most of the line was open, offered to take a cut in salary by one half to £500 per annum. He resided rent free at Gorphwysfa, a house immediately south of the railway midway between Bangor and the Britannia Bridge, which had been purchased so as to avoid a Parliamentary contest. He proposed to stay there to overlook completion of the bridge.

By November 1848 the company's cash in hand was £31,488, including bad debt money. £250,000 was required to complete the works and two courses appeared available: a loan from the LNWR, or money raised by shares or debentures. The CHR finance committee's view on the latter prospect was that 'It is perhaps needless to say that there is no probability of raising money upon the Debentures of the Company at present'. The committee's report accompanied a plea for help sent to the LNWR, to whom the CHR was already considerably in debt. An attempt to get a government loan at this time was unsuccessful. The LNWR, however, agreed to take preference shares at the market price or CHR debentures at a proportionate discount. The contractors on the Britannia Bridge were asked to take payment in debentures instead of cash. To cut expenses it was decided to reduce the number of directors from

18 to 12 and the necessary powers were obtained in the Chester & Holyhead Railway (Increase of Capital) Act of 26 June 1849 (12–13 Vic cap xli). The Act authorised the raising of £325,000 additional capital, with £200,000 on mortgage. Collett and Thomas resigned as chairman and deputy in January 1849. Laird also departed; his directorship was incompatible with that of repairer of the company's steamers.[2] In February, Alderman Thompson became chairman, and Moorsom his deputy, but a month later Thompson resigned and Moorsom took his place (Glyn had previously declined an offer of the chair on the grounds of ill health).

At his first half-yearly meeting as chairman, in March 1849, Moorsom spelt out the financial position of the CHR. It might very well be, he said, that they would have to lay up the steamers and even possibly close the line on Anglesey. If the government was so concerned about the London—Dublin communication, and wished to compete against the CHR steamers with its own boats, 'let them pay the Chester and Holyhead Company the £1,250,000, or thereabouts, which the Company had spent upon those works, and the Company would content themselves with a line from Chester to Bangor'. The government had spent millions getting London and Dublin within 36 hours of each other, and he wanted to know what rights the CHR had after reducing it to 14 hours. As will be seen in chapter 7 there was more behind this public outburst than at present meets the eye. Some slight saving was effected by moving the CHR's offices to Euston though, as will be seen, this could be viewed as enmeshing the company closer in the LNWR net. It was during the period just discussed, against such uncertain and unpromising a background, that Robert Stephenson commenced construction of his masterpiece over the Menai Straits.

### THE BRITANNIA TUBULAR BRIDGE

Francis Thompson's magnificent architectural achievement at the Menai Straits, in a combination of Egyptian and Grecian styles—the former for the mass and the latter for the detail—is perhaps one of the best examples of engineer and architect successfully working together to be found in the early Victorian Age.[3] The structure was simple but had great power, the rectangularity of the white Penmon masonry complementing that of the tubes. Writing in the present tense, before the tragic fire of May 1970, the bridge consists of a central tower, the 'Britannia', two side towers, two abutments, and two portals, carrying eight tubes, four to each line. The tubes are in two sizes: the four centre or water tubes are each 460ft in length and were floated and raised as at Conway, and the four side tubes, between the side towers and abutments, are each 230ft in length and were constructed in situ on timber platforms supported by scaffolding. The total length of each continuous side tube, including the joining additions on each tower, is 1,511ft and its weight 5,188 tons.[4]

The Britannia tower is 221ft 3in high, with a batter of 1 in 36 on all sides, and the base measures 60ft by 50ft 5in. The foundation stones are on a stepped bed blasted in the Britannia Rock. The stone courses vary from 3ft 3in to 1ft 8in in depth, none beneath the tubes being less than 2ft deep. The tower is not solid; the walls, which are 8ft to 10ft 6in thick, are in part filled with rubble masonry in mortar. The tubes rest on cast iron beams topped with putty. The tower contains 151,158cu ft of Anglesey limestone, 127,001cu ft of Runcorn sandstone, and 68,411cu ft of brickwork. With the iron and the bearing weight of the tubes the full load on the foundations is 29,600 tons. The Britannia tower was constructed with recesses to enable the tubes to be lifted and these are similarly provided on the water side of the side towers. On the landward side of the latter, however, and on the abutments, no recesses were necessary. The foundations for the side towers and abutments are all on solid rock and their masonry is similar to that of the Britannia tower. The height of the side towers is 18ft less, and that of the abutments 53ft less, than that of the Britannia tower.[5]

The abutments are uniform in plan. There is a sharp rise to

the Caernarvon side of the Menai where the approach embankment is taken close to the abutment, and the height of the masonry to the top of the abutment is 88ft. The height of the Anglesey abutment is 143ft. This rendered it necessary to stop the embankment short and to carry the railway through the abutment on brick arches supported on brick piers on the rock. Over each entrance to the tubes there is a massive lintel and on either side of the approaches are colossal lions couchant on pedestals. Carved in limestone, 35ft long, 12ft high, and weighing 30 tons, they are the work of John Thomas, then engaged on the sculpture work of the new Houses of Parliament. To accomplish construction of the bridge three steam engines and 26 travelling cranes raised the building materials to the towers and abutments, and 2,177 vessels brought the necessary stone, iron, wood, cement, and stores to the Straits. Some eighty neat, whitewashed cottages were erected for the workmen, with shops, a school, Sunday school and meeting house.

### TUBE CONSTRUCTION STARTED

By July 1847 the timber platform for the construction of the first of the large tubes was ready and the first rivet was inserted by Edwin Clark on 10 August. In April 1848, to save immediate expenses, Stephenson ordered that the second line of tubes be proceeded with slowly for the present, and that the side or land tubes' scaffolding should be for one line of way only so that it could afterwards be moved over and used for the other line. He thereby expected the scaffolding to be ready by July; all was now to be concentrated on getting one line of tubes open. Stephenson did not wish to trust the floating of the Britannia tubes to the same pontoons as had been used at Conway and received permission to order ten new pontoons, to be constructed in such a way as to enable them to be sold afterwards.

Despite the slowing of the work on the up line tubes, November 1848 saw all four water tubes nearly completed and a substantial start made in assembling the side tubes. According to

Moorsom, in December masonry work on the towers reached the unprecedented amount of 8,300cu ft weekly. Clark says that the side towers were completed by 22 February 1849; and the Britannia tower was reported to have attained a height of 26ft above the planned tube level by March. Though progress appeared good, it was not fast enough for the directors. In April 1849 they asked Stephenson to report on the preparations for raising the tubes and impressed upon him the importance of getting the bridge open by the next half-yearly meeting in August.

Construction of tube for Britannia Bridge

## FLOATING THE FIRST TUBE

After some four months had been spent in cutting away the rock base to take the pontoons, the platform was completely removed beneath the first tube to be floated—the large Anglesey span on the up line—by 4 May 1849.[6] Stephenson had constructed a relief model of the Straits to assist in his calculations and was thus able to establish beforehand the rope and chain lengths and the capstan positions for the floating. The tide at launching was estimated to run at 1.8mph and it was proposed to have the tube arrive at the piers at tide-turn. This gave a period of ten minutes of calm water after which the tide would flow in the reverse direction with increasing velocity. To control the tube during this critical period there was an elaborate system of guide lines, cables, and capstans, manned by sailors under the command of Captain Claxton. There was much the same preparation as at Conway but the Menai required more safety precautions. There were 105 hands on each pontoon, which was equipped with pumps, tools, spare rope, and ladders to get to the top of the tube. There, in command, stood Stephenson and Claxton with, during the first floating, Brunel, Locke, Clark, Mare and others, including Sir Francis Bond Head, of whom more later. The signalling was by means of large letters, corresponding to letters on the capstans, and flags in conjunction with the letters, by which means a number of variations of orders could be given.[7]

The time of the floating was fixed for the evening of 19 June. The day started wet and windy but by afternoon the wind had dropped and the sun appeared. Throughout the afternoon spectators took their seats and the last arrivals by train hurried to a place of vantage. Among those present were many members of the nobility, eminent railway personalities, and a number of Stephenson's civil engineering colleagues, including Vignoles and Bidder. These took their places on chairs on top of the other tubes still under construction, and the directors of the CHR and their guests sat in a special stand erected on the

## OPEN THROUGHOUT—THE BRITANNIA TUBULAR BRIDGE

Anglesey shore. To minister to the crowds came cake sellers, men with gambling games, and travelling amusements, mostly congregated near the Caernarvon pier. In the presence of these spectators, in this arena-like atmosphere, the first attempt at floating the tube was an anti-climax. Clark tells what happened.

> . . . every eminence was covered, and all waited with breathless anxiety for the order to start.
>
> As the tide rose, and the pontoons began to bear against the tube, the deflection was taken out of it, and it returned partly to the original camber, which it had lost when the supports were removed.
>
> The noise of the timber crushing beneath the rivet-heads, soon ceased, and at 6 P.M. it was announced that she was clear from the piers at each end, and the order was given by Mr. Stephenson to cut away the numerous land attachments by which the pontoons were secured in their places, and the 'hauling-out capstans' were set merrily to work. Before proceeding many yards, however, the capstan in the Carnarvon pontoon gave way from the too great strain put upon it by so many fresh hands full of excitement. The spindle proved too weak for the temporary purpose for which this capstan was employed.
>
> The accident deferred the operation, and orders were given by Mr. Stephenson to bring the tube home again, which was easily and rapidly effected, to the great disappointment of the numerous visitors now accumulated.

During the night following the abortive floating the wind got up but all was ready for another attempt at 7am the following morning. There were even some hardy spectators at that early hour but they were out of luck for the capstan failed once more. The next attempt, at 8pm that evening, was successful, though two boats conveying the tackle were sunk. To the accompaniment of cannon salutes and cheers from the now satisfied crowds, the floating was completed. On top of the tube Stephenson, Brunel, Locke, Captain Claxton and others toasted their success in champagne.[8] Clark recorded the evening floating of Wednesday 20 June.

The wind was rather brisk from the S.W., and the tide very strong, and as soon as the radius-chain was let loose from the interior, the tube fell back upon the guide-lines, which, in their turn, were dragged out of the water . . . On approaching the buoys, the greatest difficulty was experienced in getting the lines on board from the drifting of the tube too near to the Anglesey shore. The success of the operation depended mainly on properly striking the 'butt' beneath the Anglesey Tower, on which, as upon a centre, the tube was to be veered round into its position across the opening. This position was determined by a twelve-inch line, which was to be paid out to a fixed mark from the Llanfair capstan.

The coils of the rope unfortunately over-rode each other upon this capstan, so that it could not be paid out; in resisting the motion of the tube the capstan was bodily dragged out of the platform by the action of the palls, and the tube was in imminent danger of being carried away by the stream, or the pontoons crushed upon the rocks. The men at the capstan were all knocked down, and some of them thrown into the water, though they made every exertion to arrest the motion of the capstan-bars. In this dilemma Mr. Charles Rolfe, who had charge of the capstan, with great presence of mind, called the visitors on the shore to his assistance, and, handing out the spare coil of the 12-inch line into the field at the back of the capstan, it was carried with great rapidity up the field, and a crowd of people, men, women, and children, holding on to this huge cable, arrested the progress of the tube.

About two hours after the start of the floating the tube was brought safely against the butt, swung round, and secured in the correct position at the base of its two towers. There were some more anxious moments, however. The tide had become very violent in the opposite direction and as the pontoons were released, they surged and crashed about in the gathering dusk to the terror of their crews, some of the pontoons drifting down the Straits as much as two miles before they were stopped at Velin-heli.[9]

### RAISING THE UP LINE TUBES

On 22 June, Stephenson ceremonially laid the last stone of

the Britannia tower.¹⁰ During the following two months, while the first tube remained just above high water, the raising machinery was placed in the towers, the Britannia having the two Conway presses and the Anglesey side tower a new single press. This had an internal diameter of 22in, the diameter of the ram being 20in, and the length of the stroke 6ft. Its weight was 13 tons, 16cwt.¹¹ On 11 July Stephenson told the board that in order to guard against accidents in lifting the tube he proposed to fill up the recesses with brickwork as it was raised. This would involve an extra expense of about £5,000, and would occasion a delay of about a month. There were, however, other troublesome delays, as explained by Stephenson in a letter to Alexander Gifford, by that time the company's secretary.

24, Gt. George St, Westminster<br>7th August 1849

Dear Sir,

I regret to say that my letters from Bangor this morning are desponding. The leakage in the large Anglesea press continues to such an extent when the pressure is put in that no progress can be made. Mr. Amos is there and is adopting every remedy which his experience can suggest. I have sent such directions as have occurred to me. Another casting has been ordered from the Vulcan Foundry to supply the place of the faulty one in case we should not succeed in stopping the leakage. I fear this mishap may occasion a delay of six weeks or two months, for so large a casting is liable to many contingencies in the Foundry. I cannot express my disappointment at this disheartening incident. I must put off my Report to the latest moment in hopes of being able to communicate some more cheering intelligence.

Yours truly<br>Rob$^t$. Stephenson

The board asked whether two smaller cylinders might be used instead of the large one. Stephenson said that he would consider this but the board minutes make no further reference to the matter. Clark says, however, that for technical reasons Stephenson much preferred dealing with one cylinder only at each end of the tube. He had accepted the two Conway cylinders since they were already there.

The decision to build up under the tubes was wise. Leakage in the big press having apparently been cured, lifting started on 10 August; on the 17th, when the tube was 24ft up, and while raising the Angelsey end, the cylinder bottom parted company from the body and the tube fell nine inches on to the packing below. Clark, who was standing on the cross head, which descended 'with a fearful crash on to the top of the press', was thrown without injury into the interior of the tower. A sailor was killed, and Clark's brother and several men had miraculous escapes from being crushed to death. Though the brickwork and timber packing averted a major disaster, the roof of the tube was badly dented by the cylinder bottom falling upon it and a portion of the cellular interior was seriously damaged. A replacement cylinder arrived within six weeks. Meanwhile, the tube was repaired and 1 October saw lifting restarted, the height of 100ft being reached on 13 October. A weekend intervened and on the Monday there was a further slight lift. The bed plates were then adjusted beneath the tube and the junction pieces in the towers and to the land tubes were riveted on. The tube was lowered to its permanent bed on 10 November 1849.[12] Tuesday 20 November saw the wayward Anglesey cylinder being lowered for its move to the Caernarvon tower. The rope, insufficiently secured round the capstan, suddenly surged free of the men, the cylinder fell, the cathead in the tower broke, and the great casting crashed on to the masonry below and plummeted 60ft into the Straits. Again a sailor was killed and several men injured. When retrieved, the cylinder was found to be virtually undamaged.[13]

Stephenson arrived in November to supervise the floating of the second tube, constructed on a platform closer to the bridge than the first one. While at Britannia he penned the following concerning the Conway tubes:

> Chester and Holyhead Railway
> Engineer's Office
> Britannia Bridge, 28 Nov 1849
>
> Dear Sir,
> I have not time to go into the particulars of the roofing of the Conway Tube, but it was absolutely necessary to prevent much leakage into the upper cells— The cost was well considered and is certainly not unreasonable in amount. If water had been allowed access into the cells, the structure would have been permanently injured.
>
> Yours truly
> Rob. Stephenson
>
> A. G. Gifford Esq
>
> We are progressing very satisfactorily. All the tackle nearly ready and in first rate order— The tide will serve for Monday morning next 10 o'clock and we shall certainly float unless it blows a gale of wind. R.S.

Nearly a month later Stephenson intimated that though the Britannia tubes 'will I have no doubt require some covering ultimately', the high cost of the Conway roofing was unavoidable. 'It is exactly one of those jobs which if not carefully done for the sake of saving a few pounds, we may lose hundreds without effecting the end in view'.

On 2 December the tube was lowered to take early advantage of the tide. The following day saw an attempt at floating, but a line parted and operations were put back until the next day. On Tuesday 4 December, a day of alternate sun and sleet, the tube started to lift at 11am. After some anxious moments—a broken line which Clark thought had 'been cut mischievously by a sharp instrument', a 12 inch rope fouling its block, and some dexterous work on the capstans—the tube was brought safely home between the Britannia and Caernarvon towers, welcomed by a salute of 68-pounders. It was raised to its final height by 7 January 1850 and thereafter work proceeded day and night to join the four tubes together. By 4 March the junctions were complete.[14] Meanwhile, Clark had been concerned with the permanent way. In January he suggested rails of GWR pattern—known as bridge rails and requiring no chairs.

Stephenson was asked to arrange this with Brunel but the rails were ordered from the Coalbrookdale Iron Company.

OPENING THE UP LINE

The track was ready for the first train to cross the bridge on 5 March 1850. At 6.30am on what was to be a beautiful, fine day, with the sun lighting the snow covered mountains on the mainland, three flag-bedecked engines, the *Cambrian, St David,* and *Pegasus*, started from Bangor, with Stephenson on the first engine. Also on the train were Francis Trevithick (the LNWR's northern division locomotive superintendent), J. G. Appold (friend of Stephenson and an eminent inventor), Edwin Clark and his brother Latimer, Hedworth Lee and others. The train reached the bridge at 7am and Stephenson took it through the tube at 7mph, stopping in the centre of each span. The journey through and back occupied ten minutes. There followed various weight tests with a train of 21 wagons of Brymbo coal weighing altogether some 300 tons. At noon precisely, cannon fire and cheering announced the placing of the last rivet by Stephenson and Mare in the up line tube. At 12.11pm, to the strains of 'Rule Britannia' from a party of Liverpool seamen aloft in the towers, a huge train, as long as the complete tube span, hauled by three engines (presumably the same three), and composed of 45 coal wagons, thirty to forty carriages containing 700 persons, and weighing altogether 503 tons, crossed the bridge to Llanfair on Anglesey. There a stop was made, the coal wagons left behind, and the *Cambrian* conveyed the passengers on to Holyhead where Stephenson's party took dinner at the Royal Hotel.[15]

On the following morning the directors resolved to petition the Queen that the bridge be formally opened by the Prince of Wales. He was not yet nine years old, however, and apparently the suggestion was not entertained. There was, therefore, no formal opening. The bridge was inspected by Captain Simmons of the Board of Trade on Friday 15 March. He had no hesitation in permitting it to be opened, together with the

Page 133

(above) *Britannia Bridge conference of engineers* (see p 142). *Engraving at Penrhyn Castle from a painting by Lucas;* (below) *Britannia Bridge from the Anglesey shore*

Page 134

(above) *Telford's suspension bridge and Robert Stephenson's tubular bridge at Conway*; (below) *Aerial view of Conway, late 1960s. The station is immediately beyond the castle. Conway quay in right foreground*

## OPEN THROUGHOUT—THE BRITANNIA TUBULAR BRIDGE 135

lengths of line to Bangor and Llanfair. There had already been so much coverage of the bridge in the press that the captain forbore to weary his superiors with a long description but his praise was fulsome . . . 'having full reliance in the care and skill displayed in constructing this *immense* tube, I feel assured that every confidence may be placed in the security of the structure'. There were points at Llanfair and at Bangor, connecting the double line of existing railway with the new single line over the bridge, and the trains were to be conducted through by pilotmen. The first public passenger train to use the bridge was the 2.30pm express from Holyhead on Monday 18 March which arrived at Euston at 11pm. Between Holyhead and Bangor 'a cheap pleasure train was attached to the express, and a numerous party from Holyhead availed themselves of it . . .'[16] That evening a dinner was given at the Royal Hotel, Holyhead, at which all the important CHR personalities were present. (The *Railway Magazine* for March 1914 gives the first public train through the bridge as being the 10.25pm mail out of Chester on 17 March.)

It might be thought that there would have been a note of jubilation at the CHR's half-yearly meeting in March 1850. Not so, however, for if anything Moorsom's remarks were sour. He did not know, he said, whether to condole with or congratulate the meeting. The bridge was open, thereby saving the government £60,000 a year on the concentration of the packet services at Holyhead in a harbour for which the company had been threatened into contributing £200,000. The proprietors had gained nothing. The Britannia Bridge had cost £674,000, three times the estimated cost of Stephenson's original design.

### FAIRBAIRN V STEPHENSON

During the months before the opening of the Britannia Bridge there had been ructions in scientific and engineering circles: Fairbairn was claiming the lion's share of the credit

I

*Britannia Tubular Bridge—entrance from the Bangor side March 1850*

for the design of the bridge. He had almost resigned in July 1847 but, Stephenson then told King, had withdrawn his resignation and expressed 'his willingness to continue his assistance in the construction'. On 7 June 1848, however, the board noted that Fairbairn had indeed resigned as assistant to Stephenson, whom they authorised to accept the resignation. A fortnight later Fairbairn wrote to the board saying his appointment was direct from them and not from Stephenson; he could not, therefore, accept that his resignation should be addressed to Stephenson. The board replied that Stephenson had appointed him, knew of his duties and abilities, and that his resignation had been thus accepted.

In the following month Stephenson called the board's attention to some mis-statements made by Fairbairn as to the nature of his employment. It seemed he had been putting it about that not only was he jointly responsible for the tubular bridges but that he, and he alone, had devised the final tubular principle. The matter was taken further by Sir Francis Bond Head, soldier, diplomat and author, who had attended the floating of the first Britannia tube. In 1849 he published an account of the tubular bridges, called *High-ways and Dry-ways*, part of a book about the LNWR called, in like vein, *Stokers and Pokers*. His account of the bridges gave unequivocal credit to Stephenson.

Fairbairn's son, Thomas, counter-attacked with a pamphlet entitled *Truths and Tubes*, the theme of which was that though Stephenson might have conceived the elliptical or circular-tubed bridge, William Fairbairn had alone carried out all the experiments which produced the cellular cum rectangular tube. For good measure he had also enabled the abandonment of supporting chains in the design and had prepared all the tube drawings in his own office. Back came Sir Francis. In letters to the railway press in January 1850 he published the results of recent inquiries to the CHR board for details of Fairbairn's appointment. He had been told of Stephenson's first suggestion for the tube bridge in April 1845, Fairbairn's appointment, as assistant to Stephenson, over a year later, and that the directors regarded Stephenson alone as being responsible to them. The railway press also published an extract from William Cubitt's inaugural address as President of the Institution of Civil Engineers on 8 January 1850, at which he tactfully inferred that Stephenson and Fairbairn should share the honour for the bridges.

Thomas Fairbairn was not satisfied. Next month he wrote to the *Railway Times* restating his argument in acid terms and adding, petulantly, that when giving evidence before the House of Commons committee in May 1845 Stephenson 'was totally ignorant of the principle of construction which has *since* been adopted'. With this the *Railway Times* hoped that the unpleasant wrangle was now finished. In the issue for 10 August, however, there was a report of a warm discussion on the affair at a meeting of the British Association in Edinburgh. This had been enlivened by a claim to originality for the tubular idea, in toto, from Monsieur Jules Guyot who, said the *Railway Times*, 'with characteristic nationality, charges British engineers with stealing the offspring of his brain'.

### COMPLETION OF THE BRIDGE

In April 1850, at the height of its financial crisis, the CHR board authorised Stephenson to proceed with the second line of tubes and in June Herepath noted that 250 extra men had been employed to prepare for floating the third tube. Despite past experience the floating on 10 June 1850 was accompanied by the fouling of lines and the awkward manoeuvrings of the tube and pontoons which had characterised the earlier occasions. The floating to the bridge took 50 minutes, and again Stephenson, Brunel and party, with Captain Claxton and his speaking trumpet and flags, were present. The tube was deposited on its bed on 11 July. The fourth and last tube was floated on 25 July in the presence of an immense crowd, and the last lift made to 'much acclamation' on Friday 16 August.[17] The job had taken four years and nineteen lives to complete. In *Herepath's Journal* on 31 August 1850 there appeared the following:

> Sir George Grey (Home Secretary) offered Mr. Robert Stephenson, at Newcastle, the honour of Knighthood, which however, Mr. Stephenson declined; probably, and, if so properly, considering that, to be ranked with some of those who bear the title, no honour.

### FINAL BOARD OF TRADE INSPECTION

As before, Captain Simmons inspected the down line tube. He arrived at the bridge on 19 October 1850 and noted that though the new line was connected with the main line on the

Anglesey side it was not so at the Caernarvon end. As the existing single line working seemed to him to be an unnecessary risk and hindrance he requested that the connection be made. This was done and the traffic sent through; Lee reported that he had allowed the express train of that day, 19 October, through the down tube. The captain's report ended with the thought that he might thus have been somewhat premature in anticipating the wishes of his superiors in Whitehall. It was not them he had to worry about; in November, Herepath criticised his experiments on the last inspection. On the matter of vibration the captain had previously said that a rapidly moving load caused a greater deflection than one standing still, and the *Journal* had then chided him that this was contrary to the laws of nature. But now . . .

> New experiments have been made under the Gallant Captain's eye, and the deflection, with a load in rapid motion through the tube, 'was *sensibly less* in the way of undulation than when the load was allowed to remain at rest in the tube'.
> 
> It is a pity but these Officers of the Railway Commissioners should return to school and learn a little of the ABC of Science, as their masters, the Commissioners, should a little commonsense and law.

According to the *Journal* the experiments were not properly conducted. Deflection had been measured by differing water levels in a pipe with raised ends which was fixed to the middle of the tube. Though acceptable for a stationary load, this was held as being useless in assessing the percussive effect of a rapidly moving train. Other strictures were made against the captain, who in time was to become a field-marshal and a knight. No doubt he was glad to be finished with the whole business. Captain Simmons' inspection took place on a Saturday; according to Herepath the public opening of the down line was on the following Monday, 21 October 1850.[18]

There remained but the clearing of the site. In September the scaffolding was taken down, and by the end of November the sale of surplus materials had realised £12,000. The hydraulic presses were purchased by their makers for showing in the Great Exhibition of 1851. With completion of the bridge, Edwin and Latimer Clark were shortly to leave the CHR. Edwin (born 1814) and Josiah Latimer (1822) both went to the Electric and International Telegraph Company as engineer and assistant engineer respectively in August 1850. Even then, they were still consulted by the CHR; in October 1850 Edwin's recommendation that the Britannia tubes be roofed over with 'wood and paper' in preference to galvanised iron was accepted by the directors. By the 1870s the covering was of tarred canvas and, with variations, it remained in that form, with disastrous results a century later.

Stephenson was not paid entirely in cash for his services to the CHR; on 11 June 1851 the board noted that he had taken 562 shares in discharge of the balance of money owed to him. The bridge had taken toll of him physically. Samuel Smiles, who has some masterly touches in his study of the two Stephensons concerning the building of the tubular bridges, brings out the strain Robert was under, particularly at the time of the floating of the first Britannia tube. The first at Conway had been bad enough.

> But the Britannia Bridge was a still more difficult enterprise, and cost him many a sleepless night. Afterwards describing his feelings to his friend Mr. Gooch, he said: 'It was a most anxious and harassing time with me. Often at night I would lie tossing about, seeking sleep in vain. The tubes filled my head. I went to bed with them and got up with them. In the grey of the morning, when I looked across the Square (No. 34, Gloucester Square, where he lived), it seemed an immense distance across to the houses on the opposite side. It was nearly the same length as the span of my tubular bridge!' When the first tube had been floated, a friend observed to him, 'This great work has made you ten years older.' 'I have not slept sound,' he replied, 'for three weeks.' Sir F. Head, however, relates, that when he revisited the spot on the following morning, he observed, sitting on a platform overlooking the suspended tube, a gentleman, reclining entirely by himself, smoking a cigar, and gazing, as if indolently,

at the aerial gallery beneath him. It was the engineer himself, contemplating his new-born child. He had strolled down from the neighbouring village, after his first sound and refreshing sleep for weeks, to behold [it] in sunshine and solitude. . . .

In August 1851 two events took place; a grand banquet was given to Stephenson at Bangor Ferry, and the aged Duke of Wellington was conducted by Lee over both tubular bridges. On 13 October 1852, while on a visit to Bangor, the Royal Family went via the Menai Suspension Bridge to Llanfair. 'There the railway was utilized, and Her Majesty's saloon was taken to the Anglesey end of the tube. The Queen walked part way into the tube, and then the carriage which she entered was drawn through the tube by the workmen; in the meantime, Prince Albert and the Prince of Wales walked over the tube, accompanied by Mr Robert Stephenson, who afterwards took the whole party to the shore to view the underside of the massive structure.' There, on the Caernarvon side, they inspected the damaged cylinder head of 1849, left mounted on a stone plinth as a monument to the near disaster.[19] At the time of writing it is still there, hidden among the trees.

In 1871 Hedworth Lee noted that during heavy gales spray from the Straits went right over the bridge and hung upon the rivets causing rust, though this was in small patches and inconsiderable in amount. At a conference of architects in 1878, however, a Mr Carroll opined that 'there was no doubt a process of rusting going on which must eventually, unless checked, have the effect of making the Bridge come down with a crash'. He 'believed tons upon tons of rust were extracted from the Tube every month'. His colleagues joined in the scaremongering. These statements, reported in the press, were immediately contradicted by the LNWR directors to the effect that both tubular bridges were practically free from rust, the edges of the plates being as sharp as when first placed in position. In fact considerable trouble had been taken to protect the bridges from corrosion; in February 1856 Moorsom had reported that the addition of sand to the paint had proved very effective. Of interest is that when the nearby statue of Nelson was erected on the Anglesey shore by Lord Clarence Paget in 1871, permission was given to the local harbour trust to place an obelisk on the railway embankment near the Anglesey end of the down tube. This was to act in conjunction with the statue to provide a landmark for sailors to certain rocks in the Straits.[20]

Stephenson went on to repeat his tubular design, over the St Lawrence at Montreal and in a modified form in two bridges across the Nile. He had less than a decade to live after completion of the Britannia Bridge, however; in the autumn of 1859 he sickened from an old liver complaint which developed complications leading to his death on 12 October, barely a month after the passing of his old friend and rival, Brunel. Robert Stephenson lies in Westminster Abbey, next to that other giant who bestrode the Menai, Telford. On p 133 is a reproduction from a painting by the Victorian artist John Lucas, portraying the chief characters in the building of the Britannia Bridge. Standing from left to right, are: Captain Moorsom, Latimer and Edwin Clark, Frank Forster, George Bidder, John Hemingway, Captain Claxton, a sailor, and Alexander Ross. Seated are Robert Stephenson, Charles Wild (assistant engineer during the tube floatings), Joseph Locke, and Isambard Kingdom Brunel. Notable absentees are Francis Thompson and William Fairbairn. The later history of the Britannia Bridge, its recent destruction by fire, and the rebuilding, is discussed in volume 2.

CHAPTER 7

## From Opening to Amalgamation

### STEAMER SERVICE AUTHORISED

In March 1846 two Royal Navy lieutenants, lately commanders of Admiralty mail packets at Holyhead, applied to the CHR board for command of the company's mail boats. They were informed that it was not then intended to operate a CHR packet service. Shortly afterwards the North Lancashire Steam Navigation Company made an offer to the CHR to establish a Holyhead—Dublin service, but the board minutes do not note the response. At the CHR half-yearly meeting next August, however, a shareholder complained that the government boats on the service were 'mere flea-bites' and that bigger vessels were essential. George Stephenson had always maintained that the company's welfare depended upon an efficient connecting packet service, worked in unison with the trains. The directors, however, were now unanimous that such an ideal arrangement with any existing packet company was impossible and accordingly, in September 1846, they formed a steam navigation committee and decided to seek Parliamentary powers to operate steamboats.

In October the committee recommended that an offer be made to the government to work the land and sea mail service for £40,000 per annum. When, in the following month, however, the Treasury was informed that contracts were about to be placed for steamers, and the government's view was sought as to whether the CHR would be required to take the mails, no price was mentioned. To their surprise and dismay, considering that there had always been an assumption that their company would operate the mail service between Holyhead and Ireland, the directors of the CHR were rebuffed by the Treasury reply in December: ' . . . it is the intention of Government, that the Packet Service between Holyhead and Kingstown shall be performed by Government Steam Vessels, which will also afford accommodation for the Passenger Traffic'.

Following this there were bitter complaints from shareholders at the CHR half-yearly meeting in February 1847 that the directors had ordered steamers prematurely, without waiting to learn of government intentions or receiving the shareholders' approval. Nevertheless, the directors were so convinced of their actions that they persuaded the meeting to vote in favour of the railway having its own steamer service. Such a vote was necessary for the continuance of the CHR Bill then before Parliament. Moorsom reported to the board in March that the Admiralty and the Treasury were still talking over the question. He thought that neither now had any objection to the CHR operating the service but it was understood that the City of Dublin Steam Packet Company meant to put in a tender. Also in March the steam navigation committee reported that it had made an offer to the Treasury to undertake a mail service of two passages each way daily for £35,000 per annum and, if successful to take over the Admiralty steamers. The Treasury had been told that the increased traffic expected from the CHR could mean an offer to work an additional daily steamer service once the line was open.

In June 1847, however, the CHR Bill, which included the steamer powers, ran into the combined opposition of the City of Dublin Steam Packet Company, which had by then offered to take the mail service and had been repulsed, the Steam Ship Owners' Association, and the General Steam Navigation Company. These last two were mainly against the principle of a railway company taking steamboat powers, and the latter had successfully opposed an earlier application for such powers involving the Eastern Counties Railway and a projected Harwich Steam Packet Company. Concurrent with the hearing of the CHR Bill, another committee which was hearing evidence on the government's own Holyhead Harbour Bill (chapter 9), said that it would report to the Commons against the CHR steamboat proposals. The CHR board considered this to be an infraction of an understanding already reached with the government, as set forth in a Treasury minute of April 1846, which concerned Holyhead harbour and the use of the Admiralty Pier by the railway. At this the Holyhead harbour committee undertook to hear all the CHR evidence afresh. Time for the CHR Bill was running out, however, and any further delay would put at risk clauses which dealt with the company's interest in Holyhead harbour and for which it had undertaken to seek powers, by agreement with the government. The steamboat clauses were therefore dropped for that session.

The situation had become farcical: steamers, financed privately by the directors since the company had as yet no powers for the purpose, were under construction; the Treasury had agreed to them using the Admiralty Pier; the CHR harbour powers were safely through Parliament; and yet technically the company was prevented from operating a packet service. Quite sure of eventual success because of government involvement, the directors promoted a new steamboat Bill for the session of 1848.

The new Admiralty steamers for the Holyhead service were ready early in 1848. Each of 350 horsepower, they were named *St Columba* (697 tons), *Banshee* (670 tons), *Caradoc* (662 tons) and *Llewellyn* (654 tons).[1] Herepath noted on 18 March that two of them would commence running from the following Monday between Liverpool and Kingstown, with the morning mail, so as to get the machinery run in by the time the railway was opened, when they would transfer to Holyhead.

Despite renewed opposition, the CHR steamer Bill for 1848 passed its second reading in the Commons on 27 March after George Hudson (in support), Glyn, Gladstone, and Labouchere had all had their say. The Board of Trade also supported the Bill, and when an appeal was made in May by its opposers to postpone the proceedings Peel and Labouchere dismissed it. They considered the rightful terminus of the railway to be Dublin; Holyhead was insignificant.[2] There was more vigorous opposition in the House of Lords but it was noted with gratification by the CHR board that, in the event of the Admiralty ceasing to operate the mail service, clauses had been inserted in the Bill as to conveyance of the mails by CHR steamers 'after notice'. Royal Assent came on 22 July 1848 when, by the Chester & Holyhead Railway Act (11–12 Vic cap lx), the company was authorised to raise additional capital of £250,000, with powers to the LNWR to subscribe £120,000, and to purchase, hire, and use steamboats for passengers, goods, and livestock, between Holyhead and Dublin. The powers were granted until 31 December 1862. After notice from the Postmaster General the company could be compelled to carry mails on agreed terms. It must have seemed to the CHR directors that the through mail service by their trains and steamers was now a foregone conclusion. But still the mail negotiations dragged on.

The CHR steamers are discussed in volume 2 but a note as to the main features and the matter of early ownership is not out of place here. In November 1846 the steam navigation committee recommended immediate contracts for four vessels, their sizes not to exceed those recently ordered by the Admiralty, 650 tons and 190ft in length, and their engines to be not less than 350 horsepower. Contracts were let in January 1847 and two steamers, built in London by Messrs Wigram and Messrs Ditchburn & Mare, were almost ready for service by the following December. One at Liverpool, built by Bury, Curtis & Kennedy, and the other, from Laird's of Birkenhead, were then said to be nearing completion. The CHR's finance committee reported that month that the two London vessels had been registered in the names of Collett and Thomas, the chairman and deputy chairman. In January 1848 the board considered operating the steamers from Beaumaris, pending

FROM OPENING TO AMALGAMATION 147

completion of the Anglesey line, but it was decided to await the successful outcome of the 1848 Bill in Parliament before commencing a steamer service. On 17 June 1848 the *Railway Times* noted that the steamer *Anglia*, from Ditchburn & Mare, was undergoing trials near Gravesend. On 12 July, with the Anglesey line nearing completion and the preamble of the Bill having been found proved in Parliament, the board decided to fit out and commission three of the steamers forthwith: *Cambria* at Liverpool, and *Anglia* and *Scotia* from London, the latter two to be furnished by Messrs Taylor of London who had equipped several stations on the railway. The fourth steamer, *Hibernia*, was not to be fitted out until the end of the year.

1847 WORKING AGREEMENT

Though at first the CHR had intended to operate its own rail traffic and had gone so far as to order locomotives, by September 1846 financial difficulties and the dependence on the LNWR were giving cause for second thoughts. Moorsom was also on the LNWR board and in October 1846 he and another LNWR director recommended that the LNWR should supply engines, carriages, and wagons, together with drivers, firemen, cleaners, and guards, the CHR providing clerks, porters, police, water stations, engine and carriage sheds and shops, and the necessary repair tools. CHR engines on order were to be taken over by the LNWR (chapter 8). Both companies set up committees to discuss the proposals. Partial agreement was reached in March 1847 and by June all but one point had been settled—responsibility in the case of accidents arising from defective stock. The main agreed provisions were as outlined. Though remaining in LNWR charge, that company's staff were to come under CHR byelaws. Payment by the CHR was to be as follows: each engine 13d per mile run by the trains, and first, second and third class carriages ¾d, ½d and ¼d per mile respectively. Freight was to be carried in the CHR's own wagons. Marshalling of goods trains by an engine was to be calculated as equal to five miles. No extra mileage was to be paid for pilot engines except when specifically required for loads above the maximum or when ordered out by the CHR. The contract was to commence from the date of opening the line. In August 1847 agreement was reached on the accident clause in favour of the LNWR, and the CHR half-yearly meeting that month was informed that the working agreement had been signed and sealed.

### FIRST IRISH MAIL TRAIN

The opening of the Anglesey line saw the commencement of the first through mail by the LNWR, the CHR, and the Admiralty steamers. Payment for the land service was agreed to be left for settlement later by arbitration. On 1 August 1848 the Admiralty packets were taken off the Liverpool run and the London night mail service via Holyhead was reinstated. At the same time the CHR started a day service with express trains in connection with its own steamers.

On the afternoon of Monday 31 July the Admiralty packets *Banshee* and *Llewellyn* and the CHR steamer *Cambria* arrived at Holyhead from Liverpool, and at 8.45pm the first down 'Irish Mail' train left Euston. At 3.45am on 1 August the train left the new Chester station, opened that day, and was scheduled to reach Bangor at 5.25. From there, in the early morning light, the passengers and mails were carried by coaches which rumbled over Telford's suspension bridge on the 3½ miles journey by road to Llanfair. The Holyhead train was due to leave Llanfair at 6am and reach the terminus at 6.45; the *North Wales Chronicle* of 8 August, however, reported that the first train did not reach Holyhead until about 9am where, as soon as passengers and mails had been got aboard, the *Banshee* sailed for Kingstown. A 3pm the *Caradoc* arrived at Holyhead and shortly afterwards an express train left for Chester and London, followed at 6.20 by the up mail. Next came the arrival of the down express train and the departure of the *Cambria* for Kingstown. In fact departure by the Admiralty packet from Holyhead was to take place as soon as possible after the 6.45am mail arrival, and the scheduled packet arrival time at Kingstown was 10.30am. The return journey for the mails was scheduled as follows: Kingstown dep 11.55 (London time), Holyhead dep 6.20pm, Bangor 7.50pm, Chester 9.25pm and Euston arr 4.45am. The LNWR and CHR day service was: London dep 9am, arr Holyhead 5.45 and Kingstown 10.30pm; and Kingstown dep 9am, connecting with the 2pm express from Holyhead due in London at 10.30pm.

### MAIL CONTRACT LOST

With proof of the CHR's ability to run a steamer service, the government became more conciliatory. On 10 August 1848 the CHR deputy chairman, accompanied by Moorsom, called at the Admiralty. They received a pleasant surprise. The secretary of the Admiralty told them that, mindful of the company's steamboat powers, and the fact that the Admiralty would be glad to be relieved of the mail service, the CHR might wish to make an offer to take it over. Such an offer, he said, could embrace the whole Admiralty establishment at Holyhead (chapter 9). Meanwhile, orders had been given to allow CHR vessels free access to the Admiralty Pier, and it was stated that two Admiralty boats could be made available should the CHR require them for the mail service. The CHR was naturally in favour of the idea and on 12 August the board set up a committee to treat with the Treasury on terms for taking over the whole packet service and the government establishment at Holyhead. At the same time it was decided that the steam navigation committee should be merged with the traffic committee, which latter would henceforth also be responsible for the maritime affairs of the company.

The CHR board, in the belief that it had now only to stretch out to take the mail contract, offered to take a 14-year lease on the government establishment at Holyhead, and to conduct a service of one mail crossing each way daily, for £20,000.

It was agreed to rent a coach-house next to the Royal Hotel at Holyhead to take the mail bags.[3] But now came a cold douche. On 22 September 1848 the Admiralty wrote saying that £20,000 was exorbitant, since the company would be taking passengers as well as mails. Also, the Admiralty vessels would have to be taken over, '... and they are the less inclined to waive this in the case of the Chester and Holyhead because they (the Admiralty) were not consulted in any way before the Packets built by that Company were ordered, although it was perfectly obvious that no adequate accommodation could be provided for them until the works in the new Harbour were completed'.

Surprised at this treatment, the CHR board replied that neither receipts nor expenses could be ascertained at present; and the vessels had been built only after a government promise that a new outer harbour would be ready in the course of the next year. Disabused of their expectations, for it now seemed that they might lose not only the mail contract but also right to use the Admiralty Pier, the directors decided to buy some land at Holyhead on the south side of the harbour in case they had to provide their own facilities.

By January 1849 the CHR boats were incurring serious losses. This was not surprising: distress in Ireland, and consequent drop in the number of passengers; government refusal to pay for the land mail service until the Britannia Bridge was open; inadequate accommodation at Holyhead; and the break in the line at Menai; all these contributed. Collett, writing from his sickbed, agreed that matters should be brought to a head: 'I would rather carry our threat of stopping the boats into immediate operation, than submit to our present state of uncertainty'.[4] This, of course, was at the time of the severe financial difficulties mentioned in chapter 6. Thus an ultimatum went to the Post Office: unless immediate arrangements were made with the company the CHR boats would be laid up and the Anglesey rail service withdrawn from 27 January.[5] Though there was an immediate and flurried response from the government, whereby talks were reopened

Page 151

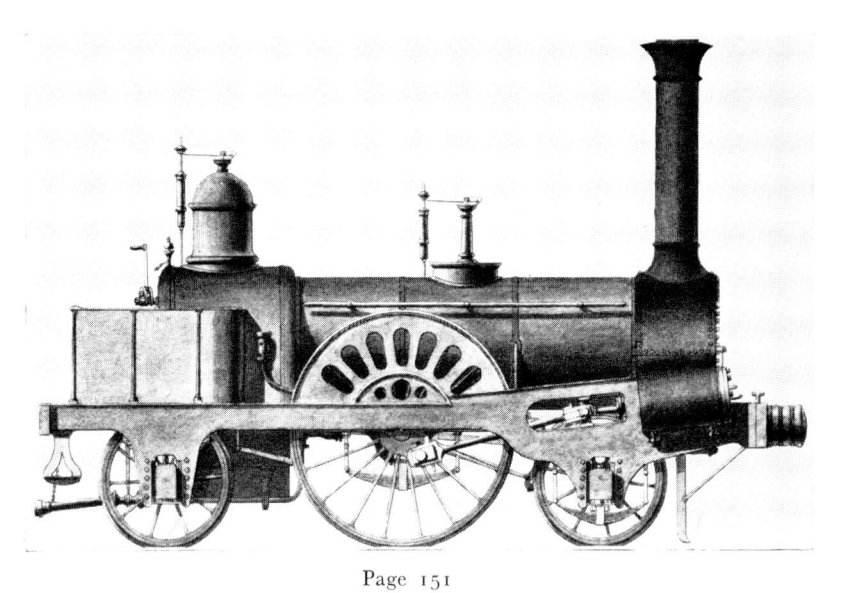

*Trevithick 2–2–2 'Crewe type'. From Lane's Volume of Locomotive Drawings, 1849*

*Trevithick 2–4–0 'Crewe type'*

Page 152

(above) *Interior of Chester joint station c 1860*; (below) *Down train entering Bangor station in the early 1850s*

and the threat of closure lifted, both sides were shortly to have the matter settled for them by a government decision to put all the mail services on to a contract system. For if the company steamers were not covering working charges, those of the Admiralty were having a far worse time. It had become obvious that the authorities were operating blindly and wastefully. Lord Auckland, First Lord of the Admiralty, decided that the ruinous costs should be transferred elsewhere. In April 1849 the CHR was informed that the from 20 June next the Admiralty mail services to Ireland from Liverpool, Milford, and Portpatrick were to be withdrawn, and that it was now recommended that a contract be made with the CHR for conveyance of two mails each way daily. This might be, but the Liverpool service was currently contracted to the City of Dublin Steam Packet Company which would therefore be on the prowl for a replacement job; its eyes were even then directed towards Holyhead. The CHR therefore asked whether the offer was to be solely to the railway company or whether it was to go to public tender.

While the CHR waited for a reply, the Post Office commenced the new service via Holyhead on 20 June 1849, with connecting trains leaving Euston at 5pm and 8.45pm, Admiralty steamer arrivals at Kingstown being at 6.15 and 11.45am respectively. Return workings left Kingstown at 12.30pm and 7.30pm, respectively reaching Euston at 4.50am and 1pm, the latter up train waiting nearly two hours at Chester for the up mail from the north.

Events now moved to a climax. On 1 July the government opted for public tender and again there was a warning from the CHR that if no agreement could be reached then the trains and steamers would be withdrawn, this time from 1 January 1850. A proposal in November from William Jackson, a director identified with the original CHR proprietors, to invite the LNWR and the Great Southern & Western Railway of Ireland to join in the loss inherent in taking on the mail service was defeated on a vote of the CHR board. This adverse vote gives a clue to what lay behind several otherwise out-of-

K

character decisions at this time. The CHR board was, in fact, a battleground between the directors appointed by the original CHR proprietors and those which dominated it and were appointed by the LNWR. During the events which now followed the two factions worked for different ends and, though in the process the mail contract was lost, the result was a temporary defeat for the pro-LNWR party and the election of an independent chairman.

It will be recalled that Collett, one of the first CHR directors representing local proprietors, had been succeeded by Captain Moorsom, a director of the LNWR, as chairman in March 1849. Since that time the CHR board had occasionally threatened withdrawal of the steamers and the closure of the Anglesey line, and many of Moorsom's public utterances appear with hindsight to have been at variance with his prime allegiance to Euston. The LNWR board instituted a 'stick and carrot' policy with respect to the CHR: by August 1849 the latter's financial position was desperate and the LNWR agreed to advance £100,000 on loan, of which £40,000 was made available. But then the LNWR solicitor pointed out to his directors that they had no powers to make the loan. In vain the CHR directors appealed for the remaining £60,000, telling Euston that they would be unable to pay the debenture interest due in January 1850. Though Moorsom offered his resignation to the CHR board in December 1849 this can only have been as a matter of form as he was urged to stay on, presumably at Euston's request. That month saw a decision by the CHR board to mortgage the steamers, though the company retained use of them. By this means £35,000 was raised from Messrs Glyn in January 1850, mostly to go towards completion of the Britannia Bridge. Meanwhile, the Post Office, sensing possible disruption of the Irish Mail service by an apparently rebellious CHR, agreed to pay £25,000 on account of the rail service already performed, subject to arbitration. In fact it had always been agreed that the Post Office payment would not commence until the Britannia Bridge was open. Of this amount, a windfall for the CHR and unexpected by the LNWR, £23,000 disappeared in January 1850 to the debenture holders. With the situation still desperate—the CHR had yet to find £200,000 towards the construction of Holyhead harbour (chapter 9)—the LNWR suggested in January that the steamers should be laid up and a single line of tubes completed as soon as possible over the bridge.

It was in this atmosphere of overt pressure from Euston to hinder the CHR's chances of operating its steamer service, that the Holyhead mail packet service was put to public tender. Moorsom's response was in character with LNWR policy. With the financial position of the CHR making a realistic offer for the mail contract impossible, he wrote to the Admiralty to that effect on 11 December 1849. Four days earlier William Watson, managing director of the City of Dublin Steam Packet Company, had also written to their Lordships offering to work the service for £55,000. The Admiralty thereupon commenced negotiations with the CDSPC. Meanwhile, unknown to Moorsom or his LNWR colleagues, William Jackson, on his own initiative, though on behalf of the original CHR proprietors, took action. Jackson, of Birkenhead and an MP, was the second largest shareholder on the CHR, having subscribed £81,000 in 1844. Knowing, as he explained later, that the directors of the LNWR who resided at Liverpool had 'made a vigorous attempt to compel' the entire withdrawal of the CHR steamers at Holyhead, he privately sought help from three personal friends and business associates. These were the eminent contractors Edward Ladd Betts, Thomas Brassey, and Samuel Morton Peto.

Of these three Peto was for the moment the driving force. A self-made man in the best Victorian tradition, Peto was one of the foremost contractors for public works, the firm of Grissell & Peto having built Hungerford Market, several famous London club houses and theatres, Nelson's Column, works on the Great Western and South Eastern Railways, and the Woolwich Graving Dock. In 1846, when Peto was thirty-seven, and at a time when they were together building the new Houses of Parliament, the partnership was dissolved:

Grissell kept the building contracts and Peto took over all the railway works. He then joined up with Betts who, incidentally, had married Peto's sister in 1843. The great partnership of Peto & Betts was to build much of the Eastern Counties, South Eastern and part of the London & South Western Railway works. Associated with them, but more particularly in the future, was Brassey, another great contractor. Most importantly for Jackson, all had money or a call on it.

Determined to be done with LNWR interference, Jackson induced the contractors to make an offer to lease the CHR for a term of 21 years, and to advance £200,000 to complete the works and pay interest on the debentures, in return for half the profits of the line. They agreed, providing the packet service was included. Jackson immediately approached the Admiralty and, after a meeting in the House of Commons library on the evening of 6 February 1850, at which Peto, Betts, and a member of the Board of Admiralty were present, it was agreed that Betts should put in a tender for the mail packet service on the following morning. He offered to work the service with five efficient steam vessels for £35,000 per annum, and to purchase two of the government vessels on the Holyhead run at valuation. This latter had by now become a condition laid down by the Admiralty. As surety for the tender, Peto was one of the guarantors.

By this time negotiations between the Admiralty and the CDSPC had reached a point where agreement seemed likely on a reduced figure of £45,000. Betts' last-minute intervention, however, effectively halted the CDSPC attempt and the Admiralty agreed that in the best interest of the public the mail service should again be put to public tender. Watson, baulked and annoyed, stormed into a meeting of the CHR directors, most of whom were frankly surprised to learn that, far from being out of the running for the mail service, effectively the CHR was again accepted by the Admiralty as a contender. They need not have worried, for they had in Watson an adversary even more determined to get the mail contract that Euston was not to do so. It was essential to the CDSPC, in order to survive, that the Holyhead mail service should be operated by its own boats.

Watson therefore put in two tenders. The first, for ten years at £30,000 per annum, included an undertaking to purchase the Admiralty's *St Columba* and *Llewellyn* steamers at agreed prices, and the second offered the same term of years at £25,000 but without taking the steamers. On the same day, 5 March, the CHR tendered at £30,000, with an offer to take the same two steamers at valuation. There were, therefore, now four tenders. On 8 March the Treasury approved Admiralty acceptance of the second CDSPC tender and the CHR and Betts were informed that their tenders had been declined.

The original CHR shareholders and their directors were embittered at losing the contract. They had counted on it and had sufficient support in Parliament to secure appointment of a select committee on the Holyhead mail service. Evidence heard by the committee detailed the events outlined above, during which Moorsom described the CHR as 'just staggering on the brink of bankruptcy'. He admitted that the LNWR was happy to reach agreement with a private company for the mail service as otherwise it would have had to operate the CHR steamers at a loss. More to the point, it became obvious from the evidence that had the CHR obtained the contract it would thereby have become a more viable concern, commanding a higher price and more respect from Euston.

*Herepath's Journal* of 23 March 1850 said that it was difficult to see how the CDSPC contract could pay, allowing for at least four steamers on the run, producing an average of £17 per trip, with the possibility of having to build new vessels, and all in competition with the CHR steamers. For the latter company had decided, in view of the current negotiations with the LNWR for leasing and working its railway, that the steamers should be kept on. In May 1850 the CHR commenced active competition for the sea traffic; fares were reduced and by the end of 1852 the CHR steamship account showed a small profit. The new contract started on 1 June 1850, the number of trains and sailings, and their timings, being not much altered from those commenced on the previous 20 June. To operate the service the CDSPC used an existing vessel, the 654 ton *Eblana*, purchased the *St Columba* and *Llewellyn* from the Admiralty, and also hired the *Banshee*. This last steamer came off the station in October 1850 and the CDSPC ordered a new vessel, *Prince Arthur*, which went into service in June 1851.

Jackson's attempt to get Peto, Brassey and Betts to lease and work the CHR had the inevitable result: though the CHR board rejected the proposal, Euston was forced in February 1850 into offering an advance of £250,000 to finish the works and pay off the CHR's debts in return for a lease of the railway. Negotiations resulted in a contract for seven years, based on the existing working agreement, the LNWR to guarantee four per cent per annum interest on the debentures. As security the CHR was to give mortgage bonds or preferences shares at the option of the North Western and such further security as might be available on the steamships and rolling stock, none of which were subject to the lease. Receipts, after payment of working expenses, maintenance, and interest on the bond debt, were to go towards payment of the dividend on the preference shares. There was to be joint control by seven directors, four from the LNWR and three from the CHR.

Despite considerable opposition from the floor at the CHR half-yearly meeting in March 1850, the directors nevertheless raised sufficient support to seek Parliamentary powers to lease the railway to the LNWR. That company itself was undergoing considerable soul-searching, with a sick Glyn struggling to keep afloat in a sea of recrimination over the LNWR's finances. The reverberations affected the temper of the CHR shareholders who were still smarting at the loss of the mail contract. Seemingly there was no end to the troubles: Great Western interests sought running powers over the CHR in the leasing Bill, the LNWR took two paces smartly backwards, and in August the Bill was abandoned.

## PETO IN THE CHAIR

With LNWR influence thus temporarily in eclipse the CHR was now offered a new lease of life. In July 1850 Jackson was asked by the CHR board to negotiate a loan of £10,500 in order to meet interest on debentures falling due that month. He approached the Chancellor of the Exchequer for a government guarantee for 21 years on the debenture debt and on a further sum of £550,000 required to cover debts, liabilities, and outstanding works, with the government appointing a receiver if thought necessary. The government would give no help, however, other than to release the company from its obligations to contribute £200,000 towards the construction of the new Holyhead harbour. Though this was accepted in August, a further attempt, this time for a direct government loan of £500,000, also failed. There was one man, however, who had already indicated his willingness to assist: Peto. The company was already in considerable debt to him for his construction of the Mold branch (volume 2). On 16 August 1850 Adam Duff, one of the original CHR proprietors, resigned from the board and Peto was elected in his place. In December 1850 Peto personally met debenture payments falling due, to the tune of £22,000, for which the board had been unable to find the money. He also persuaded Charles Mare, contractor on the Britannia Bridge, to postpone his outstanding claim for £80,000, instructed the CHR secretary to inform him of further payments falling due, and arranged for £10,000 to be made available to the company from Glyn's Bank. In that month, as will be seen, it was Peto to whom the CHR looked to negotiate with the LNWR on the proposed working agreement. He was chairman in all but name and now held £90,000 of the debenture stock on which there was more than two years' interest in arrears. With the company having liabilities outstanding of £350,000 the debenture holders were faced with a straight choice between foreclosure or allowing construction to continue with further possible loss but under new management.

They chose the second course, forcing the election of Peto as chairman on 12 February 1851. Moorsom relinquished the chair but remained a director.

Samuel Morton Peto 1851

Though his motive in providing much needed funds was not entirely selfless, Peto's character and position at the time were so unassailable that for most of his term of office the LNWR was unable totally to subjugate the CHR proprietors as its new chairman, Lord Chandos, and its general manager, Captain Mark Huish, would have wished. And when, at the end, Peto's sun waned and he saw the company into the LNWR constellation, the proprietors received a better deal than perhaps they would have done otherwise.

Peto was looked upon as being impartial and his arrival brought with it a surge of confidence. Herepath noted in April 1851 that new CHR preference stock had been wholly taken up, public demand being greater than the supply. In 1851 Peto was branching out. That year, with Betts and Brassey, he contracted for the Oslo—Bergen line in Norway. In 1852 they were to gain control of the London Tilbury & Southend Railway, and take on construction of the Grand Trunk Railway of Canada, with Stephenson as engineer and Peto and Jackson arranging the finances. Other British works were to follow, but with one foreign undertaking, the Royal Danish Railways (1853), another of their companies, the North European Steam Navigation Company, and the LTSR, they provided a new through service between Britain and Denmark. Peto also flourished in public life: he was a Baptist, noted for the humane treatment of his men, Liberal MP for Norwich, and had recently become well-placed in society by guaranteeing £50,000 towards the Great Exhibition of 1851, thereby being appointed as one of the exhibition commissioners.[6] In short, and one cannot do justice to his career in such a summary as this, he was, when he took the CHR chair possessed of considerable business experi-

Peto's signature

ence. Small wonder that the CHR shares flourished as never before and that the impoverished company, to him merely another investment with potential, should have received him without reservation. His first tasks were to arrange satisfactory terms with Euston for working the line and to reach agreement with the CDSPC.

### AGREEMENTS AND DISAGREEMENTS 1850–52

The lease of the CHR to the LNWR having been shelved in August 1850, the CHR sought revision of its working agreement with Euston. The CHR traffic committee met a deputation of the LNWR Crewe committee, which dealt with the working arrangements, at Chester on 20 September 1850. The original agreement, for a minimum term of three years commencing from May 1848, required eighteen months' notice of termination. The traffic committee told the LNWR representatives that the CHR still wished for its line to be worked by the North Western, even if the terms were somewhat higher than those for which an outside contractor would do the job. Nevertheless, the present terms were too high and the CHR was obtaining outside offers and would show the LNWR the results before further review of the agreement. October saw more positive action: formal notice of termination of the 1847 working agreement was made to the LNWR. In November the CHR proposed that the two companies should present a Bill to Parliament to affect an agreement but the LNWR countered that other arrangements might render this unnecessary. Thus encouraged, it was agreed in November that Peto should meet any LNWR director to settle the working agreement.

In the following month two important meetings were held: the LNWR, CHR, and CDSPC reached an understanding on the draft of a two-year traffic agreement for their joint benefit with the object of facilitating CHR traffic to and from Irish ports to which the CDSPC operated. Rates and charges for the sea crossing and mileage arrangements between the railway companies were agreed in outline. The Dublin company undertook to purchase the CHR steamers at valuation. The basis of the draft agreement was ratified by the CHR subject to any forthcoming arrangements with Euston. On 13 December a meeting was held at the CHR offices at Euston station, with Peto in the chair, at which it was agreed that the CHR line should be worked as an integral part of the LNWR. For this purpose the independent directors on the CHR board conceded that the company's LNWR directors should possess controlling power. In return the LNWR was to be invited to take £120,000 of the new CHR preference stock, thereby enabling the CHR to liquidate its debt to the LNWR of about £60,000 and pay off creditors with the balance. As to this latter, Peto believed that the large creditors would be prepared to take a third in cash and the remainder in preference shares. This done, he thought that the CHR could meet all its pecuniary difficulties. The CHR would, in fact, engage not to issue more than £300,000 of preference shares, £120,000 to the LNWR and £180,000 to the public. To all this the LNWR agreed.

A further meeting, held at Crewe by the LNWR on 27 December, at which the CHR was represented, laid down the principles for the working arrangement: the CHR was to pay 'the cost per mile run of working the Engines on the Northern Division of the London & N Western Railway—the expenses of the current half year to govern each succeeding half year on the Chester & Holyhead Line'. The CHR was to pay a 6 per cent annual charge upon the capital value of the locomotive stock employed or upon a fixed capital sum to be agreed. In the former case there would be an annual revaluation. The CHR line was to be regarded and worked as an integral part of the LNWR. Nothing in the agreement was to affect control by the CHR of the 'local traffic' arrangements, but the 'through traffic' was to be thrown on to the LNWR to the utmost extent.

In February 1851 the CHR board resolved that the CDSPC and LNWR traffic agreement should be approved, including the sale of one of the CHR vessels, the *Hibernia*, though in fact the vessel was not sold. In the following July, however, the CDSPC told the CHR that it understood that Euston would refuse to ratify the traffic agreement and Peto decided that, if necessary, the CHR should conclude a unilateral agreement with the Dublin company. At the same time, pending an agreement, facilities were introduced for through booking of passengers equally by CHR and CDSPC steamers (chapter 10). By October negotiations were in progress between the CHR, CDSPC and Irish railway companies for extension of the through booking. In November the LNWR put forward a proposal for a Bill whereby it would work and subscribe to the CHR, to which the latter agreed. Meanwhile, delays to the completion of the CDSPC agreement had resulted in serious loss of traffic, and in May 1852 the CHR board set up a sub-committee to arrange for the immediate commencement of the Irish goods, cattle, and mineral traffic so as to fall in with the arrangements of the CDSPC for that purpose. On 13 May, on a report that the current Bill, which included the LNWR working and subscribing powers, was unlikely to proceed, the directors decided to drop clauses which threatened the Bill's success and which related to acquisition and construction of new railways.

The committee negotiating with the CDSPC had met with no success, for the Dublin company responded that it could not enter into any agreement to work the goods traffic pending an agreement between the three companies. It furthermore threatened that if the CHR decided to place its own vessels on the station for a goods service this might throw difficulties in the way of a settlement. It was told in reply that the LNWR would not possibly agree to the management of the traffic via Holyhead being entirely in the hands of the CDSPC. The Dublin company was also asked upon what terms it would charter two goods vessels to the CHR to be operated in conjunction with the latter's *Hibernia* which had just been converted for freight traffic. On 29 May the CHR traffic committee resolved that if the CDSPC refused next to work the passenger traffic, thus throwing it entirely on to the CHR steamers, the *Hibernia* was to be added to the Holyhead—Kingstown service for that purpose. By June, however, the LNWR had agreed to arrangements for goods traffic by sea and in August to the agreement with the CDSPC as to English and Irish traffic. The disagreement had at last been brought to a conclusion by Braithwaite Poole, the LNWR's goods manager, into whose hands Moorsom and Peto had placed the whole of the arrangements for goods, cattle, and mineral traffic. The Irish goods traffic via Holyhead, at which place facilities to handle the trade had been waiting vainly for nearly a year, commenced on 27 September 1852.[7]

In an atmosphere of cooperation the three companies now set about consolidating their position. On the opening day of the goods service Captain Huish met representatives of the leading Irish railways and the Dublin Chamber of Commerce in the Irish capital. A committee was appointed, and two days later it met to consider an improved timetable and to formulate an approach to the government for an increased remuneration for the mail service. The committee considered that the boats were now inadequate for the expected increase in traffic and that if the government would allow a reasonable rate of return on the estimated cost of providing an improved communication, four new steamers should be provided by the CDSPC at an estimated cost of £300,000. These could give a reduced passage time of $3\frac{1}{2}$ hours, and two special trains each way daily could be provided by the LNWR for the Irish traffic, such as would reduce the time between London and Holyhead to $6\frac{3}{4}$ hours. Thus the total time between London and Dublin, inclusive of all delays, might be reduced to $11\frac{1}{2}$ hours. The LNWR would claim the actual cost of running the two daily expresses between London and Chester. All three companies agreed to the committee's proposals but as a safeguard against non-completion of an agreement, however, the LNWR and CHR agreed in November on a draft Bill for amalgamation of the two railway companies.

Nevertheless, despite meetings at which optimistic timetables were approved reducing the overall time to 11 hours, there was, by December 1852, another disagreement between the CHR and the Dublin company. The latter alleged that partiality was shown to the CHR boats by English booking clerks. In return, the railway companies complained of breach of agreement by the CDSPC.[8] On 6 April 1853 Peto told the CHR board that all the meetings with the CDSPC had been abortive; correspondence between them had reached a new low. Watson, of the CDSPC, had gone so far as to say that the Irish traffic was the property of his company and he justified its behaviour on those grounds. Heatedly, he was told in reply that the CDSPC had 'extraordinary pretensions respecting the Irish traffic'.

The argument which sparked off these sallies revolved around the division of the spoils from the traffic receipts. The CHR handled the CDSPC account at the Railway Clearing House and, possibly not being in too strong a position, refused to go to arbitration while stoutly defending its actions. On 8 June 1853, however, the board learned from the CDSPC that the LNWR was prepared to go to arbitration and the Dublin company now wished to know if the CHR would do likewise. On the same day the board read a letter from Peto, then in Brussels, requesting that no steps be taken with respect to the CDSPC during his absence. 'The London & NW Board', he said, 'must be prepared to undertake the entire responsibility of any change of policy if they force it on us.' He believed that Euston still really wished to sever connections with the CDSPC. The CHR board thereupon replied that the Dublin company had misunderstood the LNWR's intentions. Meanwhile, with no apparent hope that good relations could be restored, and fearing that CDSPC might well pull out of the goods service, the CHR board purchased two vessels in order, if necessary, to continue alone (volume 2). But now events overtook the three bickering companies, for the government stepped in.

### GOVERNMENT INTERVENTION

There had for some time been public complaints about the steamer services, and particularly of the late running of the mails and the conditions in which passengers had to travel. In 1853 a Commons Select Committee on Communications between London and Dublin inquired into all aspects of the service. The evidence heard was illuminating and disturbing. Captain Huish appeared first before the committee. He agreed that the mail trains could be run at an average of 40mph, but to avoid delays the Irish Mail must have its own special train; he had known mail trains kept thirty minutes at Tamworth for sorting of the branch post bags. The current two daily communications each way were as follows: a 5pm departure from Euston by the ordinary northern express as far as Crewe, and thence by another train to Holyhead due at 12.25am and Kingstown due 6am Dublin time. The second London departure was the 8.45pm mail train due Holyhead at 5.49am. The packet left at 6.14 and reached Kingstown at 11am. The return journeys were Kingstown dep 1.00pm Dublin time (1.25 London time), Holyhead 7pm, Euston arr 4.50am; and Kingstown dep 7.55pm, Euston arr 11am (the long Chester stop was reduced to five minutes in 1850). The CHR steamers also ran a daily service, Sundays excepted, for passengers only, in connection with the express trains, dep Euston 9.15am, arr Kingstown 10pm, and Kingstown dep 9.25am, arr Euston 11.25pm. Mail timings averaged 14 hours 25 minutes each way, though it came out that they were frequently up to two hours late. Huish thought, however, that the timing could be brought down to eleven hours.

Cusack Patrick Roney, much connected with Irish railways and later knighted, Irish traffic agent for the CHR, thought that its boats were too small. They became so overcrowded that some passengers would remain on deck in rough weather rather than be crammed below. He had known of over three hundred persons packed aboard one CHR vessel on a calm night on the eve of the Great Exhibition in 1851. Transhipment delays were rife: it took about an hour between the train arriving at Holyhead and the departure of the boat.

Moorsom, now a rear-admiral on the retired list, told the committee of his ideas to remedy the situation. To get sufficient speed and accommodation large vessels were required of from 1,800 to 2,000 tons. The railway companies would be willing to provide them. He thought the CDSPC could not possibly run the service for £25,000 when it was known that it had cost the government £50,781 in 1849. Because of this the Dublin company was economising: 'they must do, it is all they can do to make both ends meet'. (If anything could be, this was a case of the pot calling the kettle black!) The CHR, said Moorsom, operated two despatches six days of the week, while the Dublin company, with the same number of boats, took four. He thought this to be unsafe.

Watson, for the CDSPC, said that if the government was contemplating any new arrangements his company would not be willing to give up the mail contract. Despite losses, the company needed it to protect its Liverpool traffic. There had been tremendous competition for Liverpool during which the St George's Company had been ruined and the CDSPC unable to pay a dividend. He agreed that his company's four boats then on the Holyhead station, *Eblana*, *Prince Arthur*, *Llewellyn* and *St Columba* were slow and not entirely adapted to the service, but he had to laugh at a Huish witticism which had been getting about, that passengers on a Dublin company boat had been seen making a collection for coal in order to arrive sooner. As to trouble between his company and the CHR he instanced porters taking luggage to the railway boats but not to his. If the government gave sufficient subsidy, said Watson, the CDSPC would provide four new boats for the service.

Further details of the steamers came from Captain Hirste, CHR marine superintendent at Holyhead. He also agreed that the CHR vessels were small; there were no sleeping berths, only sofas, with room for thirty persons to lie down. In rough weather, however, everyone, including the ladies, lay down on the cabin floor in preference to balancing on the sofas. Only the stewardess could move about when they were down. There were also deckhouses with private cabins, and walking space on deck, 12 or 15ft wide abaft the deckhouse, the whole breadth of the ship, and 30 or 35ft between the forepart of the deckhouse and the paddle shaft. The CHR had two express boats, working alternate weeks, and connecting with the

5.30pm arrival from Chester. The steamer was due to leave at 6pm but in summer, as the train was often heavy and frequently late, departure could be as late as 7pm. There were also two boats for the goods trade.

The captain's evidence was amplified by Binger of the CHR. He described the cramped and inconvenient accommodation at Holyhead and the ridiculous business of drawing the train from station to pier by horses (chapter 9). The vessels were, he said, now slower than when first in service; it had been found too expensive to go racing across the Irish Sea. Machinery had been damaged, and twice he had been on board when deckhouses had been carried away from over the paddle frames. (He did not say whether or not they had been occupied.) The new deckhouses were fixed more securely on the quarter deck. So reduced was the number of steamers at one time by this buffeting that only one express boat was left in service. As it was normal practice, if a train was crowded, for Chester to telegraph ahead for a second boat, such a situation could cause considerable inconvenience to passengers. Binger countered Watson's proposed new steamers with his own company's offer of similar 300ft vessels and a passage time of $3\frac{1}{2}$ hours as suggested by Huish. Passengers were on the increase: 1850, 19,225; 1851, 26,308; and 1852, 27,252. There had all along been arguments with the CDSPC who had taken the contract on cheap terms when the CHR was not capable of competing. And the Dublin company had always opposed the whole Holyhead project.

Brunel and Claxton appeared before the committee with William Oliver Lang, master shipwright at Pembroke Dockyard. Lang, who had produced some of the fastest paddle steamers then afloat, had designed a 'monster' wooden paddler, 400ft long by 40ft in the beam (70ft over paddles), which would go at the rate of 25 statute miles per hour, cutting the sea passage to $2\frac{1}{2}$ hours. He preferred wood to iron as the vessel would thus be lighter and faster. Brunel and Claxton were then working on the much larger *Great Eastern* of some 700ft in length. Their *Great Britain* was by comparison a mere

L

322ft so they had no doubts on the practicability of Lang's steamer. Brunel too, said that he preferred paddles and wood for the Irish Sea.

The committee's report was outspoken. 'In a period when many advances have been made in the science of steam navigation, such as the Cunard to New York, and the Peninsular and Oriental Company's lines to the east have greatly improved, that with Ireland alone has deteriorated.' It was inferior in all respects to that before 1850. The report called for greater speed, larger ships, betterment of the rail service producing an 11-hour overall timing, and a morning express mail train picking up Lancashire mails. On 28 March 1854 the Commons referred the report to a new Committee on the Conveyance of Mails by Railway, recently set up, which reported in July 1854. This recommended a country-wide speed-up of mails, with the Post Office deciding train speeds, and the increased provision of apparatus for collecting mails from moving trains. As regards the Irish service, sorting offices were to be established either on the trains or the packets. The mail pick-up and travelling post office came into use on the Irish Mail in 1854, obviating stops at unimportant stations. The final difficulty as to train speeds, that of replenishing locomotive water en route, was to be overcome shortly afterwards (chapter 8).

As was to be expected, the CDSPC kept the mail contract, but the CHR withdrew through booking by Dublin company boats in December 1854. At the same time the CHR deposited a Bill for the session of 1855 which proposed among other things that it and the LWNR should purchase, hire, and work steam vessels. The LNWR was to be authorised to subscribe towards any portion of additional CHR capital required for these purposes, and the Holyhead extension (chapter 9), and to guarantee dividends. The Bill, safeguarding railway interests, was withdrawn when in January 1855 the two companies at last reached an agreement with the CDSPC.

The results of the government inquiry were embodied in the Improved Postal and Passenger Communication with Ireland Act of 23 July 1855, whereby the three partners could appoint a joint committee to operate steamers for mails and passengers between Holyhead and Kingstown or Howth, the two railway companies agreeing with the packet company to provide additional steamers as required. Steamer powers were to terminate on 31 December 1871. Rates and fares were to be charged equally whether passengers travelled by rail to Holyhead or not. Freight traffic was specifically ruled out; the joint steamers were to be for passengers, parcels, and mails only, including horses and carriages. If the companies were unable to agree with the Post Office by 1 May 1860 as to conveyance of the mails the powers in the Act would cease.

### THE LNWR TAKES OVER

Meanwhile, October 1852 had seen deferment of another amalgamation attempt between the two railways, and a new working agreement had taken effect from June 1854. Six months later the *Railway Times* charged the CHR with 'gross extravagance', for example on excessive and expensive stationery, printed circulars, etc, due, it was thought, to being part and parcel of the LWNR set-up. Peto also came under fire. In the Grand Trunk Railway he and his partners had lost nearly £1 million. To recoup and keep their labour force intact they had entered into ventures which were thought by some to be of dubious standing. There is no doubt that by this time Peto was regarded in some quarters as a 'fast operator' and the *Railway Times*, seeing itself as the self-appointed conscience of the railway world, attacked him with indignant vehemence on the slightest excuse. The paper's other pet abomination was Lord Chandos, and mud thrown at either of them tended also to stick to their undertakings. Nevertheless, general public opinion was on Peto's side. He was created a baronet early in 1855, in recognition of his construction with Brassey and Betts of the Balaclava Railway for the British Army in the Crimean War.

Traffic on the CHR was slowly on the increase and the half-year ending 31 December 1854 realised a profit which, after interest on the debentures, allowed a small dividend to be paid on the first preference shares. In March 1855, however, an erroneous report by the CHR's auditors concerning the company's financial relationship with the LNWR led to the creation of a committee of CHR shareholders to investigate the matter. The committee was composed of four CHR proprietors and seven from the LNWR. Although the committee considered the auditors' strictures to be unfounded, it reported to the CHR board that, having thoroughly examined the company's books, it was firmly of the opinion that there should be a closer identity between the two companies. Accordingly they were authorised, in conjunction with the proprietors' section of the CHR board, to negotiate with the LNWR for the latter to undertake the working of the line, to guarantee a minimum amount of traffic, and to develop the through and local traffic with such supervision on the part of the CHR board as might be agreed upon. The percentage of working expenses should be that of the LNWR itself for 1854. In May and June meetings took place but though Lord Chandos agreed to most of these points, he would not guarantee minimum traffic nor a reduction on the existing scale of working expenses. There was deadlock, and the discussions were postponed pending the fate of the Bill on communication with Ireland, the outcome of which would affect the issue.

With the Bill passed, however, it was Euston who, in July 1855, gave notice to the CHR of the termination of the current working agreement. In September the LNWR informed the CHR board that it would neither permit deferment of interest on sums advanced to the company, which the latter had suggested, nor would it concur in payments of dividends beyond the profits of the CHR up to June 1855. The CHR thereupon accepted terms agreed at recent further meetings between the special committee and Euston. These were that the LNWR, while still not guaranteeing a minimum traffic, should work the CHR as an integral part of its own system at 46 per cent for 1856, 44 per cent for 1857, and subsequently at one per cent above the current half-yearly rate per cent for working expenses incurred by the LNWR upon its own system. The LNWR would provide the plant and rolling stock but the CHR was to maintain the permanent way. The steamer service was to be operated on a separate account, losses being shared with the CHR, but all profits credited to that company. The LNWR undertook to develop the through and local traffic so as to give the CHR full benefit. The agreement was terminable by two years' notice. The *Railway Times* of 22 September 1855 thought that most of the agreement was illegal, since the LNWR had no authority to work the CHR or to take over its ships.

During early 1856 the CHR working stock and equipment, down to station furniture, was valued for transfer to the LNWR, and arrangements were made for the staff to be henceforth employed by Euston. The permanent way, though maintained by Lee, was to be under control of the LNWR's Chester & Holyhead committee, newly set up to administer Euston's acquisition from 1 July 1856, the date the working agreement commenced. Plant, wagons, and tools of the CHR's engineering department were purchased by the LNWR. By June 1857 the entire CHR 'office' staff consisted of the secretary, a senior clerk, an assistant, and a junior clerk. Binger, Comber, Hirste, and Lee all became employees of Euston as 'Holyhead District' officers, and the station and other staff went into LNWR uniforms. A list of CHR and Holyhead district officers is given in appendix 2.

It was now but a short step to complete take-over; the dependence of the CHR on the LNWR had gone beyond the point of no return. Peto was by now unable to exercise that influence he had wielded five years before. 'Spectator', writing in the *Railway Times* in February 1857, put the facts bluntly, pointing out that the £100 shares in the CHR were now worth only £36. Apart from this, Peto's other railway ventures had become running sores, held up to angry ridicule in the railway press. Nevertheless, the CHR board remained under his control. By the autumn of 1857, though there had been an increase in traffic since the start of the working agreement, receipts had remained stationary and, determined to wring a fair deal from the LNWR, the CHR directors gave Peto a free hand to arrange a 'closer alliance' with Euston by lease or exchange of stock. In December, Lord Chandos agreed to a merger of the two companies and at the same time agreement was reached on conditions for a new 14-year contract between the Post Office and the three operating companies, based on the provisions of the 1855 Act, to commence in midsummer 1859 when the existing CDSPC contract would be terminated. There were to be new mail boats and a faster service. Though the LNWR and Dublin companies had the option under the contract to be joint owners of the boats, the former decided to let its partner operate the steamer service, in return for relief from all liability. In 1857 the Holyhead steamboat interests were looking over their shoulders; the Great Western was operating through bookings from the Wellington district to Dublin via Liverpool, with screw-driven steamers at competitive fares.[9] It had also, in conjunction with the South Wales and Vale of Neath Railways, commenced a new improved steamer service from Milford to Southern Ireland.[10] In June 1857 the LNWR's Chester & Holyhead committee introduced the day express train and boat service to Kingstown called for by the government, but these were poorly patronised and were withdrawn after 15 October 1857.[11] Complaints of overcrowding of the CDSPC boats in 1859 led to consideration of reintroducing the day boat, but as this would compete with the CDSPC, and the loss in 1857 was £2,033, the idea was dropped.

Withdrawal of the day boat was followed by the LNWR's decision to drop its steamer interests. This led to the CHR board refusing to participate in or sanction the agreement with the Post Office. Under the existing Post Office contract for the rail service, due to expire in 1862, the CHR received a certain £30,000 per annum for two daily services each way at 35mph comprising a total mileage of 124,000 single miles per year. The service was operated clear of all penalties for late running and had the advantage of four stops in each direction for the local traffic. Under the proposed new contract with the Post Office, for payments to be settled by arbitration and therefore

FROM OPENING TO AMALGAMATION 175

likely to be less, the company was to be called upon to run an additional train each way, to increase the speed, give up the stops, come under heavy penalties, and perform other services in excess of the old contract. Besides this, the CDSPC was currently suspected of arranging new Liverpool—Dublin traffic at cheap rates, hostile to the CHR, and if, as was now suggested, the sea passenger traffic was to be concentrated in the mail vessels, the CHR boats would have to be relinquished at a heavy capital loss borne solely by that company. On the other hand, Euston would secure the best route to Ireland with an additional income to itself of about £20,000 for the rail service, and the CDSPC exclusive right to the sea crossing for which the CHR had for so long competed. Above all, while the working of the Post Office contract would be binding under the Act, the loosely worded LNWR working agreement was in fact technically illegal and could be overthrown at any time in the future leaving the CHR in an impossible position.[12]

The CHR board, on the casting vote of its chairman, considered that nothing could justify it in taking on so great a responsibility, and on 18 December 1857 further discussion of the Irish service was therefore postponed until amalgamation terms with the LNWR had been agreed. To strengthen the independent directors one of them retired in March 1858 to make way for Samuel Duckinfield Darbyshire, a Conway shareholder and member of the boards of the Birkenhead Lancashire & Cheshire Junction and Dublin & Drogheda Railways, the first being if anything at that moment pro-Great Western, and the other independent.

In May 1858 Peto informed Lord Chandos that the CDSPC was raising funds for the construction of new vessels on the assumption that the Post Office agreement was proceeding, but that until the LNWR had agreed amalgamation terms the CHR must protect the interests of its proprietors. Despite the fact that the CHR Bill for amalgamation was now before Parliament, Lord Chandos was still playing a double game; he intended to abandon the Bill if clauses for through booking and traffic facilities via Chester were kept in. He was, nevertheless, in a quandary; he had agreement with the CDSPC and Post Office as to the mail service but the vital link between the two operating companies was uncertain. And this was at a time when the MSLR, daggers drawn with Euston over Manchester traffic, had put on a Garston—Dublin steamer, said to be giving 'acute' competition.[13] By July, therefore, with the CHR still intransigent, Lord Chandos appeared to relent and the CHR and LNWR amalgamation Bill, with its solely permissive powers, was passed.

The Chester & Holyhead Railway Act of 23 July 1858 (21–22 Vic cap cxxx) authorised the CHR to raise £200,000 by preference shares bearing no more than 6 per cent interest, to form part of the general capital of the company, the money raised thereby to be applied to the general purposes of the undertaking. The LNWR was empowered to guarantee dividends not exceeding 5 per cent on these preference shares, and the two companies might agree that the LNWR should guarantee interest and dividends on stocks and shares not held by that company. The CHR could also raise by creation of non-voting 5 per cent debenture shares or stock a sum not exceeding £1,084,332, to be applied solely to paying off the company's mortgage debt. Power was given for the two companies to enter into a sub-contract, under the provisions of the 1855 England & Ireland Communication Act, as to the mail service. Powers for the sale of the CHR to the LNWR required there to be mutual agreement, based on three-fifths of the votes of the shareholders of both companies, and the CHR interest was safeguarded in that only original CHR proprietors, and not those of the LNWR, could vote. The Act provided, compulsorily and consequent upon the other provisions taking effect, that the LNWR should not enter into any agreement which would divert or obstruct traffic over the CHR to or from the most convenient and shortest route, but should afford facilities to any company whose line joined the CHR. The final six clauses of the Act empowered both companies to agree on conversion of the shares and stock of the CHR into ordinary LNWR stock, again subject to three-fifths majority of both companies and with safeguards to the CHR proprietors and the holders of that company's preference shares. At the same time, by the LNWR (Additional Works) Act 1858 (21-22 Vic cap cxxxi), the two railway companies and the CDSPC were empowered to enter into agreements for the Irish traffic.

Even now the LNWR would not play straight. In November 1858 Euston was still intent on having nothing to do with the traffic clauses in the CHR Act of 1858 whereby it would have to permit GWR and MSLR traffic on to the CHR. Such obligation was avoided by Euston simply electing not to exercise the permissive powers of the Act which thus became a dead letter. Now, at last, this latest volte face caused the CHR worm to turn. Determined to force the issue, if necessary even to a final break with Euston, the small company applied to Parliament in November for an Act to sanction working arrangements with any company which would furnish additional sources of income. Powers were sought to run over the LNWR's Chester and Crewe branch so that a new route would be opened up to the North Staffordshire, Midland, and Great Northern Railways, and to make arrangements with the LNWR, GWR, GNR, BL & CJ, Warrington & Stockport, Manchester South Junction & Altrincham, MSLR, and NSR companies as to supply of rolling stock, and interchange and transmission of traffic. It was a desperate throw but it succeeded; in December the LNWR agreed on full amalgamation with the CHR, based on the terms of the 1858 Act. It took effect from 1 January 1859. At a CHR meeting a few days beforehand, Peto said that it meant an ultimate guaranteed $2\frac{1}{2}$ per cent interest to the CHR proprietors. To objections that just as the line was beginning to show promise it had been handed over, he responded by saying that the Irish traffic was strongly competed for and, above all, the whole of the debts and liabilities were being taken over by the LNWR. At that company's meetings in January and February 1859 there was some dissent. A shareholder, asking why the CHR shareholders should have guaranteed dividends, was told that the CHR finances were greatly improved and that if the great bridges had not been so expensive the company might have been able to work its line itself. Another LNWR shareholder objected strongly that CHR shares had been increased in value by 33 per cent, at the cost of the LNWR. The next meeting of the CHR board, on 18 March 1859, with Peto in the chair, was the last, and the company's seal was attached to the deed of conveyance to the LNWR. With this last meeting Peto fades out of the story.

In the two years following the amalgamation there were many changes at Euston, both of personalities and policy. Captain Huish retired in February 1859, to be succeeded by William Cawkwell, formerly goods manager of the Lancashire & Yorkshire Railway, and in the following October hatchets were buried when the LNWR board agreed with the GNR and MSLR as to through rates and interchange of traffic, and with the GWR as to joint ownership of the Birkenhead Lancashire & Cheshire Junction. In 1861 Lord Chandos left the LNWR and the chair was taken for a short time by Admiral Moorsom. On the latter's death later that year Richard Moon (later Sir Richard), one of the most indefatigable of the board of directors, was elected chairman. The Chester & Holyhead Railway Company remained nominaly in existence until it was dissolved by the LNWR (Additional Powers) Act of 21 July 1879 (42-43 Vic cap cxlii). The amalgamation of 1859 included two branches of the CHR, the Mold and the Bangor & Carnarvon, discussed in volume 2.

### 1860 MAIL SERVICE

There was now nothing to hinder a new postal agreement, and on 3 January 1859 a 14-year contract was executed between the Post Office, the CDSPC, the LNWR, and the CHR. The two railways were nominally responsible jointly for the train service and, together with the CDSPC, for the steamers. The LNWR received £75,000 per annum for the train services, subject to certain conditions, as well as the allowance of £30,000 per annum originally granted to the CHR and due to expire in 1862. This latter payment was stated by the Postmaster General as being partly for the postal service and partly a government grant to increase the general facilities for communication with Ireland. The CDSPC was to receive £85,900 per annum less half of the passenger receipts earned over and above the normal receipts for the traffic, estimated at £35,000—again, in fact, a government subsidy. On the same day the Dublin company sub-contracted with the railway companies whereby the latter, in reality the LNWR, made a loan to the former to enable it to purchase four new vessels for the mail service, the LNWR having virtual control under the contract of the receipts to the CDSPC (chapter 10). The Post Office contract reduced the overall timing to eleven hours as follows: London to Holyhead 6 hours 40 minutes, transfer at Holyhead 35 minutes, and the sea passage 3 hours 45 minutes. A penalty was fixed of £1 14s (£1.70), payable to the Post Office for every minute over the contract time, though in fact it was not levied due to the government's slow progress with the works at Holyhead and was relinquished for some time as a 'quid pro quo' for the loss of benefit of those works to the operating companies when the government abandoned them (chapter 9). The LNWR (ex-CHR) passenger steamers were transferred to the company's recently opened cargo route between Holyhead and Dublin (North Wall). Being at that time a tidal service, the North Wall steamers did not appreciably affect the mail route though there was later to be severe competition when the harbour was improved, and the LNWR commenced a day express service in 1876 (chapter 10).

Four new steamers each of 2,000 tons were ordered for the new CDSPC service of 1860. They were a considerable improvement on the old steamers, had a greater speed (15 knots), and increased passenger accommodation. A new feature was a sorting office on board for the mails. The steamers were the four-funnelled *Leinster* and *Connaught* and the two-funnelled *Munster* and *Ulster*. The vessels were 334ft long with 35ft beam and 21ft depth. The first to operate, on the old schedule, was the *Leinster* in August 1860. During the time of their building, an Act was passed whereby the Post Office took over the Admiralty functions as to the packets, though as they were now operated by contractors this did not make any significant difference. To facilitate the reduction in the overall timing, a new jetty—known as the 'Carlisle Pier'—had been brought into use at Kingstown on 23 December 1859, enabling Dublin trains to connect direct with the steamers.[14]

On Monday 1 October 1860 the new contract commenced with timings as follows: Euston dep 7.30am, Chester 11.58, Holyhead arr 2.5pm and Kingstown arr 6.5pm (Dublin time); and Euston 8.30pm, Chester 12.58am, Holyhead arr 3.5 and Kingstown arr 7.5. On the up journey: Kingstown dep 6.50am, Holyhead 11.40, Chester arr 1.45pm and Euston 6.25; and Kingstown 7.45pm, Holyhead 11.55, Chester arr 2.5am and Euston 6.45am. The 84½ miles between Chester and Holyhead were accomplished non-stop in new record times of 2 hours 7 minutes down, and 2 hours 5 minutes up. Sorting offices on the trains effected further gain in time for the mails, morning letters from either capital being delivered on the same evening. The average rail speed for the whole journey was 42mph, and the mail bag exchange apparatus was further extended to cover the new service, the mails being collected and dropped without stopping at fifteen pick-up points en route.[15] The *Railway Times* reported on the first train on the new service. Consisting of three passenger carriages, two large Post Office sorting vans and two brake vans, it was under the personal supervision for such an important occasion of Edward Page, the Inspector General of Mails. Calling only at Rugby, Stafford, and Chester, it reached the Holyhead ticket platform at 2.1pm, and the packet pier eight minutes later. The *Leinster*'s paddles started turning at 2.16 and, after a perfect run in beautiful weather, she reached Kingstown at 5.44pm.[16]

CHAPTER 8

# Locomotives and Rolling Stock 1848-1880s

The early locomotive history of the CHR has for some time been the subject of controversy. From time to time assertions have appeared in the railway press from two opposing factions—those who claimed the company had its own locomotives and those who flatly stated it did not. It is pleasing to be able to record that in a sense both were right; for a very short time the CHR was technically the owner of at least six known engines.

### FIRST CHR LOCOMOTIVE ORDERS

At the beginning the CHR directors intended to work their own railway and in July 1845 they set up a locomotive committee. A month later Robert Stephenson advised that about thirty passenger and ten goods engines would be required to work the line, all on six wheels with 15x24in cylinders. Passenger engines were to have 6ft diameter driving wheels and the goods 4ft 6in wheels, the latter all coupled. The committee decided to seek tenders at once for twenty-four passenger and six goods engines and these were accepted as follows: from Bury, Curtis & Kennedy, six passenger engines at £2,000 each, for delivery by March 1847; Jones & Potts similarly; Nasmyth & Co, six engines at £1,650 each, delivery during the course of the next year; Robert Stephenson & Co, six goods engines at £2,100, to be completed in January 1848; and Tayleur & Co, six passenger engines at £2,000, delivery dates being the earliest so far—two in each of July, August, and September 1846.

In January 1846 Stephenson recommended ordering a further six passenger and fourteen goods engines, making totals respectively of thirty and twenty of each type. The Haigh Foundry, Hawthorn, Kitson, Jones & Potts, Stephenson & Co, and Tayleur, were all asked to tender, delivery to be on or before 1 March 1848. Despite this, events now compelled the CHR, as noted in chapter 7, to ask the LNWR to work the line, and as part of the resulting agreement the latter company was to take over the CHR engines on order. A letter from Captain Moorsom, written in September 1846 and headed simply 'Engines' is of interest:

> The engines on Mr. Stephenson's specification supplied to this Co. by Messrs. Tayleur & Co., Longridge & Co., & Potts Jones & Co. are not working altogether satisfactorily and on Mr. Stephenson's return an investigation will be made into the causes with a view to remedy the defects in the engines or that specification yet to be delivered. Will you let me know the state of the 50 engines under contract for the Chester & HH Co. in order that if necessary the manufacturers may be communicated with.

The above is among a collection of Moorsom letters, most of which are addressed to King, the CHR secretary, concerning that company's affairs. As it was not until October 1847 that an 'experimental train' was worked over part of the unfinished CHR (chapter 4), Moorsom must have been speaking of recent deliveries to the LNWR from the builders mentioned. Though there is no note in the minutes, however, he confirms the CHR order for twenty additional engines. The letter had its effect: in January 1847 the CHR board minuted that Stephenson be 'requested to report what alteration has been made or is proposed to be made in the specification of the Locomotive Engines, and when they will be ready for delivery'.

Meanwhile negotiations on the working of the CHR by the LNWR resulted in agreement in June 1847 as to the locomotives and carriage stock. Both were to be supplied by the LNWR and were to be similiar to those employed on the London—Liverpool services. Spare locomotives and carriages were to be made available at the terminal stations as required by the CHR, together with breakdown appliances. The maximum number of carriages of all descriptions drawn by one engine was to be twelve, and the maximum load for one goods engine 150 tons. Extra engines were to be supplied at the discretion of the LNWR. Mail train speeds were to be the same as those on the North Western main line, and penalties were fixed for timekeeping infringements by LNWR engines. A fortnight's notice was required by Euston of an intention by the CHR to vary the number of regular daily trains.

### MOTIVE POWER SHORTAGE ON THE LNWR

Euston's acceptance of CHR engines in 1846–7 becomes understandable if the doings of the LNWR's locomotive establishment are investigated. In December 1846 Edward Bury, locomotive superintendent of the southern division at Wolverton, latterly the locomotive headquarters of the London & Birmingham Railway, gave notice of resignation. In February 1847 J. E. McConnell of the Birmingham & Gloucester Railway accepted the appointment of 'principal superintendent of the Locomotive Department at Wolverton'. His opposite number on the northern division at Crewe, the Grand Junction establishment until July 1846, was Francis Trevithick, son of the famed Richard. Since the opening of the London & Birmingham, Bury's small locomotives had performed sterling work with ever increasing train loads, but they were now underpowered and McConnell saw their replacement as his first task. In March 1847 he suggested that all the 'old small luggage engines' should be sold off or broken up and that new, more powerful, engines should be ordered. This was not so easy; locomotives generally were at a premium at this time, due to the rapid expansion of the railway systems of the country, and approaches made to several locomotive builders for twenty engines to be delivered in 1847 were mainly unsuccessful. Only Bury, Curtis & Kennedy, and Nasmyth offered any hope, the former for six engines and the latter for four, but not to be delivered until the end of 1847. The offers were accepted, the engines to be built to the pattern of Engine No 117, except for two which were to be of the Bury four-wheeled design. No 117 was one of two Bury 0–4–2 5ft goods engines built in 1846. In March 1847, however, Bury, Curtis & Kennedy said that if the CHR would postpone taking delivery of its six engines then due, the firm would be prepared to supply the LNWR with eight 'luggage' engines. Six goods engines to the pattern of No 117 were delivered to the southern division in 1848, together with six 6ft 6in singles which, allowing for the bigger driving wheels, were possibly the CHR order.

### CHR ENGINES GO TO WOLVERTON

Between March and May 1847 correspondence passed between King of the CHR, McConnell, and Tayleur of the Vulcan Foundry.[1] It shows what happened to the earliest of the CHR orders. The first letter, from Edward Tayleur to King, was dated 6 March. It appears that the CHR had been playing for time.

Sir,
  The first Engine for your Line is complete; we are sorry to trouble you so much about it, but if it remains here, it will be a serious inconvenience to us, & we shall be glad to know your intentions, as soon as possible that we may arrange accordingly.
  P.S. There will be another ready every week.

As the CHR was nowhere complete, other than for the S & C from Saltney, this postscript must have led to a minor panic. But the LNWR wanted engines, and within a fortnight King received a letter from McConnell.

My Dear Sir,
  I beg to inform you that Captain Moorsom has intimated his desire that some Locomotive Engines now ready at Messrs Tayleurs Vulcan Foundry Warrington for the Chester & Holyhead Railway should be sent to Wolverton.
  Mr. Heathcote from Messrs. Tayleur has been here and

appears anxious to forward them. Of course we cannot interfere in the matter and I have requested him to see you or Captain Moorsom in order to have arrangements made for the transfer of Engines and I assure you we shall be very happy to see them on this Line being very short of power at present.

The next missive from the Vulcan Foundry was despatched to King on 27 March.

Sir,
We are in rec$^t$ of your esteem'd favor of yesterday instructing us to forward the Engines that are now ready to the Wolverton Station, & we have this day in accordance sent off the three of which we have handed you Invoices; we shall be glad to recieve your instructions as to the remaining three of the Engines, the first of which will be ready the day after tomorrow & the second in the course of the week.

We are obliged for your promise of a cheque for £3,000 & as the Engines have been ready for some time shall be glad to receive the Balance at your earliest convenience.

According to McConnell the first three arrived at Wolverton on 29 March, and the fourth, with a defective wheel, on 2 April.[2] King duly paid the firm £6,135 after which Tayleur sent off the other two. These arrived at Wolverton by 21 April. The six were allocated southern division numbers 176–181. On 3 May, King told the CHR finance committee that he had applied to the LNWR to pay the CHR the entire value of the engines, £12,270. Two days later the LNWR southern division finance committee authorised such payment to be made. King also told his committee that he had deferred asking the LNWR for the amount (not stated) paid to Hawthorn & Co until the working arrangement with the LNWR was concluded. Hawthorn's records merely show order Nos 520–25 allocated to the CHR but with no running numbers given. The firm delivered six 5ft 0–6–0 Stephenson long-boilered locomotives to Wolverton in 1848 which could fit the description, except that this implies payment in advance—an unlikely circumstance.

On 25 May 1847 McConnell informed King that one six-wheeled passenger engine had arrived at Wolverton from Jones & Potts and had been put to work, as No 182. Eight more engines went to Wolverton from Jones & Potts and were numbered 183-190. According to Ahrons they were rear-drive long-boilered engines with outside cylinders. Four had 6ft 3in driving wheels and the last five 6ft 6in wheels, the cylinders all being 15x24in.[3] The firm also supplied the southern division with No 175, similar to the others, though not apparently of the CHR order.

The records of Robert Stephenson & Co (Order Book No 10) show four engines, not six, marked for delivery to the CHR in 1847, works Nos 621-4. They then had 15x24in cylinders, and 4ft 9in coupled driving wheels. The engines are later shown repeated but with 'Chester & Holyhead' deleted and 'London & North Western' written in. Cylinders had been altered to 18x24in and the wheels, all coupled, to 5ft diameter. Tender capacity had increased from 1,200 to 1,500 gallons. Thomas Pattinson's notebook of engines finished by the firm (at one time in the Stephenson archives) gives the following delivery dates: 621 May, 622 June, and 623-4 July, of 1848. Additional orders, presumably from Wolverton (or two of the original CHR six plus eight of a later order), were given as 625-6 September, 627 October, 628-9 November, and 630-31/34 December, all of 1848; and 633 February and 632 March, both 1849.[4]

The lists of Nasmyth and Kitson are inconclusive. The first shows order Nos 47-50 for 5ft 6in 2-2-2 locomotives for the CHR, sublet by Stephenson's. The only Nasmyth engines delivered to Wolverton which might conceivably fit this situation were six, not four, 6ft 6in 2-2-2s. These arrived in 1848, were given Nos 191-6, but apparently were transferred shortly afterwards to the LNWR's Yorkshire lines.[5] Kitson's order book shows six blanks at the appropriate time; and any other evidence has been elusive.

The fragmentary information here summarised would seem to indicate that of those engines which were actually constructed to the CHR order, probably all went originally to the

LOCOMOTIVES AND ROLLING STOCK 1848–1880s 187

southern division of the LNWR. As mentioned earlier, however, the CHR were actual owners of the six Tayleur engines for a short time. Legend has it that when made they bore suitable Welsh names but that on arrival at Wolverton these were removed.[6]

PREPARATIONS FOR WORKING THE LINE

In October 1847 Moorsom chaired a meeting of the LNWR general locomotive committee at which was discussed the proposed opening of the CHR, then fixed for 1 November as far as Conway. It was agreed that as the Lancaster & Carlisle Railway had taken thirty engines from Crewe to work its traffic instead of sixteen originally contemplated, and as the working of the new Trent Valley Line had recenty been assigned to the northern division at Crewe, the latter would be unable to work the CHR unless some of that company's engines were returned from Wolverton. Moorsom thought that six would suffice for the opening. Rather than take them from Wolverton, however, the committee agreed that such of the engines of the Huddersfield and Manchester and Leeds and Dewsbury branches, as might be ready but not immediately required, could be transferred to work the CHR.

Trevithick, however, had other ideas. He preferred using Crewe engines and undertook, if necessary, to find power for four trains each way between Chester and Conway from 1 March, the latest then anticipated opening date. After further postponement he asked for a firm date and was told, with instructions to have the engines ready, that it would be on 1 May. Meanwhile, a special boiler, described as 'absolutely requisite', was ordered for making grease for the stock working over the CHR. At first engines were supplied with LNWR fuel but shortly after the opening a contract was made for a supply of Brymbo coke.[7] In the early years coaling of engines took place at the main intermediate stops, as required, between Chester and Holyhead but in 1860 it was decided to concentrate coaling at Holywell, as being the station nearest the

Mold district from which the fuel was drawn, and at which nearly all the through trains still stopped.[8]

In June 1848 Binger told the CHR traffic committee that it was imperative that engines be sent to Anglesey and the LNWR was informed that five would be required for that purpose in a month or six weeks' time. This presupposed a planned service of three trains daily in each direction on the island—two mails and an intermediate slow. In April, Moorsom informed the CHR board that an engine had gone from Wolverton and across the Conway to work on Jackson's No 9 contract. 'Mr. Creed will communicate to Mr King as to the charge for the Engine, which being 2-wheeled coupled of 14in cyl. may be usefully employed in Anglesey when the Line is open'. It appears that it was in fact sold by auction while still on contract 9 in November 1850.[9] The LNWR also sent an engine to Conway to convey plant for floating the tubes there.[10]

As the Anglesey engines would be too heavy for the Menai Suspension Bridge Trevithick decided that they should go by sea from Liverpool to Holyhead. On 1 August 1848 he wrote to the Crewe locomotive committee from Anglesey where the railway was opened that day. Two engines and tenders had, he said, arrived by sea on Anglesey and had been put on the line. He hoped they would be sufficient for a short time. The carriage went over by the suspension bridge.

EARLY LOCOMOTIVES

The CHR traffic on the main line soon increased and required additional engines. April 1849 saw three further engines supplied, two for an additional train and one in lieu of an old ballast engine on which the CHR had cast aspersions. From 16 June two more engines were needed for a further train. In November 1849 the Crewe committee asked whether, since trains were very light in winter, a smaller class of engine might be employed, and the CHR was urged to extend the time allowed for working the Chester to Bangor journey

LOCOMOTIVES AND ROLLING STOCK 1848–1880s 189

by twenty minutes. The CHR replied, however, that competition with the GWR for the Irish traffic necessitated a high rate of speed. The heavier engines therefore stayed on. The LNWR works committee thereupon decided to relay or strengthen the Crewe—Chester line, the condition of which had been partly behind the suggestion for lighter engines. With the onset of long, dark evenings Trevithick supplied Binger with twelve white and six green buffer lights for the engines on the CHR.[11]

The first three engines to cross over the Britannia Tubular Bridge (chapter 6) were *Pegasus*, the leading engine (old 5ft 6in Grand Junction No 31, and also LNWR No 31, built by Tayleur in 1838), and *Cambrian* (LNWR No 249) and *St David* (No 205), both mentioned below. Perhaps sentiment suggested that the old veteran *Pegasus* should be honoured as first over the bridge. LNWR engines working the CHR in the early years were Trevithick 6ft 2–2–2 singles or 5ft 2–4–0 goods of the 'Crewe type', a series developed from an early Grand Junction design of that company's locomotive superintendent, William B. Buddicom.[12] These first 'Crewe type' engines by Trevithick were nearly all named, the allocation of which, coincidental with CHR opening dates, probably indicates which locomotives first worked the line. There was a preponderance of appropriate Welsh names for the 1848 2–4–0 engines, when the line was opened to Bangor: 205 *St David*, 206 *Menai*, 207 *Conway*, 208 *St Patrick* (to please the Hibernians), 225 *Llewellyn*, and 227 *Snowdon*. In 1849 came 239 *Powis*, 245 *Ellesmere*, and 249 *Cambrian*, and in the following year, again appropriately 257 *Stanley* (honouring the great Anglesey family), and 260 *Anglesea*. The engine *Penmaenmawr*, No 295, appeared in 1852 but five years later found itself—somewhat out of place for such a name—with the Lancaster & Carlisle Railway. If additional engines were required there was always a number with classical names which would not offend Welsh nationality. Welsh names were rare on the Trevithick singles. Not until 1852, when nearly a hundred of the type had been built, did No 280 *Glendower* and 291 *Prince of Wales* appear.

In September 1850 the CHR asked for revision of the working agreement and a reduction in the charges paid to the LNWR. There were complaints of insufficient motive power and wagons which delayed traffic, especially coal. On Trevithick seeking redress from the CHR in December 1850 for some damage done to engine 247 *Mammoth*, a Trevithick 2–4–0, he was promptly told that the claim would be admitted as a credit against a counter claim for loss of traffic. Shortly afterwards he sent to the CHR the 7ft 2–2–2 experimental passenger engine No 187 *Velocipede*, built at Crewe in October 1847, and another rare 'one-off' type, the 7ft rear-drive 2–2–2 Crampton engine No 176 *Courier*, built at Crewe in November 1847. To meet the terms of the mail contract speed and reliability were essential. Both engines were singled out in an acid minute of the CHR traffic committee on 28 September 1854.

> A statement of failures of *Courier* and *Velocipede* Engines having been laid before the Committee. Resolved that the London & North Western Company be requested to supply competent Engines in their place, and also one in lieu of No 10 (the old *Pegasus*) which is not fit to assist trains.

*Courier* in fact came off the CHR duty at about this time. *Velocipede*, however, had found favour at Crewe and was a prototype of the 'Raven' class of 1854, 2–2–2s with 7ft 0½in diameter driving wheels and 3ft 7½in carrying wheels. Another prototype of this class, into which it and *Velocipede* were assimilated, was the 2–2–2 7ft passenger engine No 290 *Rocket*, built at Crewe in August 1852. *Pegasus*, referred to in the minute, must in fact have by then lost its name as both this, and the No 31, had been allocated by February 1854 to one of the new 'Raven' class. Finally, another of the class, No 18 *Cerberus*, built in July 1857, should be noted. This engine, and the new *Pegasus*, were stationed at Holyhead, and the *Velocipede* and *Rocket* at Chester, the four engines together working the Irish mail traffic until the advent of the 'Lady of the Lake' class, mentioned later.[18]

In 1857 there were yet more complaints of late running of the mail and express trains which were still considered to be underpowered. On other occasions the opposite claim was made; in November 1857 the Hon. W. O. Stanley, one of the CHR directors, called attention to the dangerous speed of the express trains through the Britannia tubes and down the Malltraeth incline. John Ramsbottom, who had succeeded Trevithick at Crewe in the previous August, ordered that drivers were to shut off steam on the approach curves to the bridge. The permanent way was also suspect; Binger earlier reported that an engine had become derailed on one of the approach curves and had run a short distance off the rails.

### RAMSBOTTOM, THE 'LADIES', AND WATER TROUGHS

In February 1859 Ramsbottom was ordered by the locomotive committee to lay down two passenger engines of a larger type and in May the number was increased to six. In the following November, Crewe turned out the first of the sixty famous 'Problem' or 'Lady of the Lake' class, 7ft 6in singles which worked the CHR mail trains until the 1880s. To them were entrusted the new timings called for by the Post Office agreement of 1860 (chapter 7). The old Crewe types which they had replaced lasted generally into the 1880s. Some went through many changes after leaving CHR metals: No 206 *Menai* and 245 *Ellesmere*, for instance, were converted into side tank engines and, with three others similarly treated, went to the North London Railway late in 1859 or early in 1860 where they dropped their names and took the NLR numbers 36 and 35. The name *Menai* was transferred to a Trevithick 2-2-2, built in 1847 as No 169 *Huskisson*, which had become Lancaster & Carlisle No 37 in January 1857 and, returned to the Crewe fold in December 1859, took the No 500 and its new name. It would appear that No 500 retained the name for only a short time for in April 1860 it graced a new DX goods, No 206. The name *Ellesmere* was transferred to a new DX goods No 245 in November 1859. Returning to the

North London engines, No 36 became LNWR No 45 *Sybil* in 1861, No 1840 in 1881 and was cut up in May 1886, while No 35 became LNWR No 141 *Pheasant* in 1861, No 1945 in 1881, and was sold out of service in 1882. As to the four mail engines, it would appear from the 'Trent' run mentioned later, that *Cerberus* at least was still at Holyhead in 1862.

The new mail timings required that trains should be able to run non-stop from Chester to Holyhead. One of the main difficulties to this was that of providing enough water for the engines. From the very first there had been water tanks at the express stopping places at Holywell, Rhyl, Conway, and Bangor. The Holywell water early became contaminated by the sea and a special reservoir was built. Similar troubles at Rhyl in 1849 necessitated water being taken from the River Foryd. A year later the locomotive people were still complaining of the poor water, especially at Holywell and Holyhead. Lee reported to the CHR traffic committee in September 1850 that he had been obliged to erect a tank at Bodorgan and sink a well at Holyhead; owing to the persistently poor water at Holywell and Rhyl an intermediate tank had been put up at Prestatyn. In 1853 two water pumping engines were installed at Bangor and Holyhead to take the place of twelve men who manned the pumps. Three years later a reservoir was constructed at Conway and from 1 June 1857 this became the only water stop for the down expresses. By October of that year, however, this supply, which also served the town of Conway, was found to be insufficient at certain times and land was taken for an enlarged reservoir.

Meanwhile, Ramsbottom worked on a solution. In the summer of 1860 he patented a design for water troughs whereby engines could be replenished without stopping. On 12 July 1860 Richard Moon, chairman of the LNWR general stores and locomotive expenditiure committee, reported that he had authorised the trial of Ramsbottom's water trough on the Holyhead line. On 9 August orders were given for Lee to carry out the necessary work. The site chosen was on the down line at

Mochdre between Colwyn and Conway. Experiments on 23 October, at which LNWR directors attended, worked well and on 8 November Ramsbottom recommended that a trough should also be laid on the up line. The locomotive committee approved of this and the works committee asked Lee to sound out the local landowner, Lord Mostyn, on terms for the use of the Mochdre stream for the supply. A rent of £10 per annum was agreed in July 1861.[14] The total length of the Mochdre troughs—the first to be used in the world—was 473 yards and the cost £1,030.[15] So successful were they that they were soon followed by others, at Parkside on the Liverpool and Manchester line (removed to Eccles in 1876), and at Tamworth, and in the following years many more were to be installed. On 23 September 1869 Ramsbottom reported to the locomotive committee that in consequence of the scarcity of water at Mochdre he proposed moving the troughs to a site about a mile on the Chester side of Aber station, where there was a very plentiful supply of water of excellent quality. Three months later the committee approved this proposal and it was agreed that the move should take place in the spring of 1870.[16] This did not happen, however; in March 1871 Ramsbottom reported that as Lord Penrhyn would grant only a five-year lease for taking water from the River Aber, leaving him free after that time to impose his own terms, it would not be desirable to move the troughs from Mochdre. In April the question was referred to the LNWR chairman to try to reach agreement with Lord Penrhyn. This was at last done by a lease dated 9 February 1872, whereby for a term of 40 years commencing from 25 March 1871, and in exchange for granting access for Lord Penrhyn's tenants at Glan-y-Mor to the southerly platform at Aber station, the LNWR obtained the right to take water from the River Aber (which runs immediately beneath the station) to supply the locomotive troughs a mile to the east. The rent was £10 per annum and though Lord Penrhyn could after five years give six months' notice of termination, compensation would then be payable to the LNWR on the capital outlay on the troughs.

In fact the agreement ran its full term, was renewed from time to time, and was finally cancelled in March 1968.[17] The site of the reservoirs for the Mochdre troughs could be seen until quite recently in fields adjoining the down side of the line immediately to the south of Mochdre & Pabo station, but apparently all traces were ploughed out in 1958.[18] Note of later CHR water troughs is made in volume 2.

## THE 'TRENT' RUN

Installation of the first water troughs was amply vindicated in 1862 when there took place the epic run of No 229 *Watt*, a 'Lady of the Lake' class, on a special three coach train carrying the 'Trent' despatches. An excellent account of the event was given in *The Locomotive Magazine* for December 1905 and January 1906. Locomotives had been kept in readiness at Holyhead for several days in anticipation of a fast run to London with the despatches, on the contents of which perhaps hung peace or war with the United States. The mail steamer carrying the despatches arrived at Holyhead at about 8.15am on 7 January 1862. The Queen's Messenger and the mails were transferred to a saloon and van already waiting at the Admiralty Pier and then the 7ft engine No 18 *Cerberus* pulled them along the pier railway to Holyhead station. There they were coupled to *Watt* and another van and a start was made for Euston at about 8.28. Bangor was passed at 8.57. Thereafter strong winds along the coast slowed the special somewhat but, with water taken at Mochdre troughs, Chester was nevertheless reached at 10.05½, and Crewe at 10.28. The 25 miles on to Stafford were covered in 24 minutes. At Stafford, by that time the boundary between the northern and southern divisions, a McConnell engine, No 372, continued the journey non-stop to Euston, arriving at 1.13pm. The average speed for the Holyhead—Stafford leg worked out at 54.6mph. The run was generally regarded as an excellent achievement at the time and was a deserved piece of publicity for the LNWR and especialy for the 'Lady of the Lake' class. Ahrons throws some light on the class toward the end of their career on the Irish Mail (1878–80).[19]

The Stafford No. 1 link had two turns to London. With the first of these they left Stafford with the up Irish Mail at 3.23 a.m., due at Euston 6.45 a.m. and came down with a train at 9.15 a.m. to Rugby. They reached Stafford at 2.58 p.m.—rather a long day's work. The second turn was the 3.8 p.m., due at Euston 6.25 p.m., and they returned with the down Irish Mail at 8.25 p.m., due at Stafford 11.40 p.m. Here another Stafford engine of the same class took the train through to Holyhead (due 3.5 a.m.). On this turn they returned with the up day express from Holyhead and reached Stafford at 3.5 p.m. The down day Irish Mail (7.15 a.m. from Euston) left Stafford at 10 a.m. for Holyhead and the engine returned with the night mail due at Stafford 3.20 a.m. They also worked a train to Chester and back. From the above it will be seen that the whole of the Irish Mails—except the 7.15 a.m. from Euston to Stafford—were in the hands of the Stafford "Ladies" from end to end. They could not work the down 7.15 a.m., as they reached Euston on the up train at 6.45 a.m., and had not time to turn and get ready.

But I regret to say that the Irish Mails of those days were trains that jogged along in the consciousness of a reputation only, without deeds in the way of speed to suit. Their real speeds were poor, and their running average (exclusive of stops) was only 42 miles per hour. Yet they were sometimes referred to as the "Wild Irishmen"!

At the end of 1881 or beginning of 1882, Crew "Precedents" ousted the Stafford "Ladies" from the Irish Mails between Crewe and London, and, as previously mentioned, the up train was handed over to the first of Mr. Webb's compounds.

As to the remark concerning speed, Neele mentions that in the interests of economy the chairman, Richard Moon, attempted to persuade the Post Office to allow a reduction in the speed of the mail trains. Apparently he had little success.[20] Calls for economy from the chairman were an almost everyday event at this time, and had much to do with the policy of providing small engines to run the LNWR services. Ramsbottom retired in September 1871 and Francis W. Webb was appointed locomotive superintendent in the following month. Until then North Western northern division engines were in green livery while those of the southern division were resplendent in vermilion. Two years after the coming of Webb the well-known 'blackberry' was adopted instead throughout the system.

Another locomotive type, designed by Ramsbottom and which was in use on the CHR expresses during this period, was the 6ft 7½in 2–4–0 'Newton' class, the first of which appeared early in 1866. These engines had, at first, 16in diameter cylinders and 24in stroke but were later rebuilt by Webb with 17in cylinders and to a pattern closely resembling the later 'Precedent' class (volume 2). The 'Newtons' were originally designed specifically for the Crewe—Carlisle expresses,[21] but were soon put on the Crewe—Manchester, Manchester—Leeds, and Holyhead services, for the last of which several of the class were stationed at Chester and Llandudno. Their success on the LCR and CHR led to over a hundred of the class being built.[22]

The small tank engines, for working the pier railway at Holyhead, are discussed in chapter 9. Finally, a word on the enginemen: in April 1867 the locomotive committee stipulated that footplate staff were expected to work a 60-hour week before overtime became payable.

CHR ROLLING STOCK

In February 1846 the CHR half-yearly meeting was informed that the directors were considering arrangements with the London & Birmingham and Grand Junction companies for the supply of carriage and wagon stock. Later that month, however, the board considered a list of proposed rolling stock prepared by Moorsom, 'reduced from one I had drawn out after conferring with Mr King'.

Proposed Carriage & Wagon Stock

| | | | | |
|---|---|---|---|---|
| 50 | Carriages | 1st Class | 4 | Parcels vans |
| 30 | — do — | Composite | 2 | Bullion vans |
| 50 | — do — | 2nd Class | 400 | Goods wagons |
| 60 | — do — | 3rd Class | 6 | Timber wagons |
| 30 | Horse boxes | | 20 | Iron wagons |
| 20 | Carriage trucks | | 50 | Cattle wagons |
| 10 | Dummies for luggage | | 20 | Sheep wagons |
| 5/6 | Post Office vans | | 30 | Pig wagons |
| 3 | Post Office tenders | | 6 | Brake vans |

Despite this, the original proposal as to the rolling stock was upheld and carriages were supplied and worked through by the LNWR from the first. The carriages, at least in the first class, were lit by oil from May 1848 but footwarmers did not appear until January 1856, these being supplied by the CHR.

As to freight wagons, the LNWR apparently proved incapable of maintaining a sufficient supply and the CHR was forced to order its own vehicles, some coming from Crewe. In 1848 eight luggage vans were constructed at Crewe for the CHR, and 31 iron hopper wagons and 60 wood flat wagons came from private builders. Coal and slate wagons, cattle vans and horse boxes were ordered in 1849. In the same year 100 CHR wagons were built at Crewe and 200 hired. The CHR traffic committee summarised the position in October 1850 when a report from Comber listed the stock of wagons then required for working the main line and the Mold branch, with the estimated cost. Altogther 797 vehicles were listed at a total cost of £45,555. At first brake vans were borrowed from the Shrewsbury & Chester Railway but by 1850 these had been replaced by two brake vans built specially at Crewe.[23]

There was a continual shortage of wagon stock. In April 1851 the LNWR was unable to supply sufficient cattle and mineral wagons and the CHR traffic committee decided to order 375 mineral, 25 hopper, 200 cattle and 30 timber wagons, and eight brake vans. These were in addition to existing stock and what might be supplied by the coalowners. Tenders were accepted in July 1851 from private builders. Timber wagons cost £25, cattle wagons £64, and brake vans £73. Even then the shortage persisted. Comber complained in December 1852 that he had about 850 mineral wagons and the use of 100 privately owned wagons. He needed 1,025. This was irrespective of coal traffic from the Shrewsbury and Chester line, conveyed up to that time in that company's wagons and which were now to be refused to the CHR. There was also a delay of up to 36 hours in transferring goods at Chester.

A return of CHR rolling stock in 1853 showed the company as then owning 200 cattle wagons, each carrying seven animals, and 878 goods and other wagons averaging 6 tons' capacity each.[24] By September 1853 the loss on slate traffic alone for lack of wagons was 700 tons a week.[25] It was impossible to hire wagons unless promise was made of eventual purchase, and insufficient capital was available for the latter purpose. An appeal was made to the LNWR, and sufficient money was made available for tenders to be accepted in September from private builders for 288 mineral wagons at £68 each, 100 goods wagons at £78, 100 cattle vans at £84, and 12 brake vans at £125. The financial position became so desperate, however, that in November 1853, when the CHR tried to pledge its rolling stock to the LNWR for a loan of £25,000, the latter thought it best to purchase the existing wagons and accept a transfer of the contract for the additional stock ordered. The LNWR agreed to let the wagon stock remain in CHR livery and for it to be appropriated solely to CHR traffic. The stock was transferred to the LNWR early in 1854. In June 1856 the LNWR decided that all the CHR wagons were to be used in common with those of its own stock and that all distinctive marks should be obliterated.[26] In August, however, Binger pointed out the difficulty there would be in obtaining suitable wagons for the coal and slate traffic if the 'C&H' mark was obliterated, and the LNWR was asked to consider whether the 'Prince of Wales feather' might remain. They were kept

LOCOMOTIVES AND ROLLING STOCK 1848–1880s 199

until September 1860 when the LNWR locomotive committee ordered their discontinuance. The CHR engineering wagons had been taken over by the LNWR in 1857.

GAS LIGHTING, BRAKES, AND ROLLING STOCK FAILURES

The Irish Mail train was the first on the LNWR to be lit by gas. On 24 April 1861 the locomotive committee ordered that one of the trains be fitted up experimentally for gas lighting, and a year later the apparatus for supplying gas was erected at Stafford, Chester, and Holyhead, and also at Liverpool for the 'Rainhill train'. In October 1862, however, though kept for the local Liverpool and Manchester service, gas lighting was discontinued on the Irish Mail except for the Post Office vehicles, the other carriages returning to the old oil system. In May 1864 the 'Boilers, meters, fittings, &c.' at Stafford, Chester, and Holyhead, were ordered to be removed.[27] Because of an explosion in one of the Rainhill trains early in 1870 gas lighting on local trains was also ordered to be discontinued.[28] On 3 July 1874, however, the locomotive committee noted that Pintsch's patent gas apparatus had been fitted to one of the composite carriages running between Euston and Holyhead and that two of the first class compartments were lit from it. The reservoir for the system as fitted contained about 40 cu ft of gas when compressed, which was sufficient for outward and return journeys. The apparatus at Euston consisted of a fire basket, with two wrought iron tubes passing through it acting as retorts, a small purifier, accumulator, and force pump. The gas was manufactured chiefly from dirty oil from the lamp room. In 1875 it was arranged for LNWR officers to visit Berlin to examine and report further on the Pintsch gas lighting system on the Prussian railways. Meanwhile, other British companies had been installing gas lighting and both Pintsch's and Pope's systems came into regular use on the LNWR.

On 4 December 1861 the locomotive committee noted an application from Mr Newall to fit his patent brake to the Irish Mail train, which he was then fitting up for gas lighting. This was agreed to as it would give an opportunity to compare it with Fay's brake, 'which is now at work on one of these trains'. The results favoured Fay's system; in October 1862 it was noted as being more simple and effective that that of Newall and negotiations to purchase the patent right of Fay's brake were commenced. In the following December instructions were given to apply Fay's brake to the carriage stock without delay. Nevertheless, by July 1863 the brake had been fitted to only four trains, one being one of the Irish Mails, and to forty vehicles of the west coast joint stock of the LNWR and Caledonian Railways. In December 1864 it was ordered that all the Irish Mail trains should be so fitted, together with all branch line trains.[29]

Both Newall's and Fay's brakes were based on a central revolving shaft, connected by universal joints between the carriages, acting on wooden brake blocks to all the carriage wheels, and controlled from a wheel in the guards' vans. The Fay brake was in use on the Irish Mails until the mid 1870s when Webb modified John Clark's chain brake (not Latimer Clark who was then busy with a pneumatic brake) for use on the LNWR. By March 1875 there were 230 carriages and brake vans so fitted and to ensure smooth working of the complicated arrangements inherent in the Clark-Webb sytem skilled mechanics were stationed at key points on the LNWR, including Euston, Stafford, Crewe, Chester, and Holyhead.[30]

In November 1875, despite setbacks and some indifferent performances at the Newark brake trials in the previous June, orders were given to fit the Clark-Webb chain brake to Post Office vans and tenders, and family carriages, at a cost of £18 each. By July 1876, 562 vehicles had been fitted with the brake, and Richard Bore, in charge of the carriage works at Wolverton, was ordered to continue the work until a third of the total carriage stock was so treated. All vehicles not fitted were to have the chain installed so that they might be run in otherwise fitted trains. In March 1879 Bore reported that he was 'putting the breaks (sic) in the carriages as fast as possible'. Neele mentions that 'the system completely failed

Page 201
(above) *Flint station from the west, 1970;* (below) *The first Prestatyn station from the west, 1970*

Page 202

(above) *Penmaenmawr station from the east, 1970;* (centre) *Llanfairfechan station from the west, 1970;* (below) *The closed station at Aber from the west, 1970*

to comply with the Board of Trade requirements, promulgated in 1876, viz., that the brake should be applicable to all vehicles on the train; that its control should primarily be in the hands of the driver; that the guards should also be able to apply it; and that it should act automatically on the vehicles in case of a break-away'. Neele also says that by the end of June 1879, near the end of the time covered by this volume, no less than 2,812 vehicles were fitted, and by July 1880, 'the whole of the main line trains out of Euston were thoroughly fitted with the Chain Brake, but still sectional, and not in any way automatic. As an instance, the 9.0am out of Euston had two engines and seventeen vehicles behind them, the brake in three parts, seven vehicles for Liverpool, six for Holyhead, and three for Birmingham, each section with separate brake communication, but all of no service as a continuous brake.'

This naturally leads on to the question of communication between the driver and the guard, the former being required to signal by whistle to the latter for application of the Clark-Webb brake. As early as February 1861, the locomotive committee noted that engines working the Irish and Scotch mails were being fitted with whistles for just that purpose. Various experiments were tried but by the 1880s there was on the LNWR still no fool-proof brake nor driver-guard communication acceptable to the Board of Trade. This was during a period when, with embarrassing frequency, faults in the rolling stock led to accidents.

The fracture of wheel tyres, for instance, was a common occurrence. On 1 October 1861 there was just such an accident at Ty Croes on Anglesey, made that much more unfortunate since similar mishaps had recently overtaken trains at Pinner and Tring, and the Board of Trade was thus enabled to pass scathing public condemnation on the LNWR directorate. The 9pm down Irish Mail from Euston on that day, composed of engine, tender, a guard's van, composite carriage, a Post Office vehicle and a parcels van, had earlier collided with a goods train near Rugby. Though thus nearly three hours late by the time it reached Anglesey, it was nevertheless dawdling at a mere 38mph near Ty Croes when the near trailing tyre on the composite carriage broke, throwing it and the last two vehicles off the road. The Board of Trade report noted that the wheels were of inferior description; they were composed of cast iron bosses with short round wrought iron spokes resting in cast iron shoes fitting upon wooden felloes $5\frac{3}{8}$in thick. They were remarked upon as being unsuitable for fast trains. The rails were not connected with fish plates, and on the morning in question the railway was in the grip of a hard frost and was not resilient. The train had no working brake van at its tail and was without communication between driver and guard. Captain Tyler of the Board of Trade included the following in his report:

> It seems almost hopeless to recommend the latter precaution [driver-guard communication] to a body of Directors who are so little alive to their own responsibilities, and to the interests of their Shareholders, as to permit their fastest trains to travel without a working break-van behind them, and without a means of communication between such a van and the engine—trains are run, some of them, daily and nightly, at the highest speed, for 83 miles without stopping; and when they allow these simple means to be neglected year after year, whilst other companies have them in constant use.

The captain suggested that the Post Office, which required high speeds, should ensure that all trains carrying mails should have both continuous brakes and driver-guard communication. These would benefit the company and the travelling public . . . 'and the so-called limited mail trains, in which too many passengers were now afraid to travel, would again become favourite means of conveyance'. Though no deaths had resulted from the Ty Croes accident, a plain warning was given that legal action might follow a future accident caused by such working and which resulted in death to a passenger. In April 1863 thirty-two head of cattle perished in an accident near Abergele when a broken tyre resulted in a wreck heaped to a height of 40ft.[31]

LOCOMOTIVES AND ROLLING STOCK 1848-1880s 205

To deal with accidents or breakdowns on the CHR, Ramsbottom recommended in December 1870 'that a ten-ton travelling crane and two old covered vans, one to be cut off to suit the jib of the crane while travelling, be provided and stationed at Bangor', at an estimated cost of £280. This was ordered to be done. In September 1873 the locomotive committee ordered that the engine *Dwarf*, then at Crewe and used for inspection purposes south of Stafford, should be replaced by an old Grand Junction engine and transferred to the Holyhead division. *Dwarf* was at Bangor until November 1877 when it was replaced by 2-2-2 No 1868 (old No 49 *Columbine* built at Crewe in 1845). No 1868, renamed *Engineer Bangor*, was to stay on its special North Wales duties until 1902.[32]

SLEEPING CARRIAGES

Sleeping carriages, albeit primitive compared with present-day standards, were introduced on the Irish Mail on 1 March 1875, after having been first put on the west coast route in October 1873. The vehicles were six-wheelers, based on the design of the popular family carriage. They comprised one compartment for ladies, with day seats and roof 'hammock' beds which made up into four sleeping berths in all, and two similar but intercommunicating compartments for gentlemen. There was a lavatory at each end of the coach. Passengers were charged an additional 5s (25p), and seats were bookable on application at Euston and Holyhead. Until that time passengers 'in the know' had bridged the space between opposite seats in ordinary carriages with special twin sticks and a cushion provided, for a 'fee', by the guard.[33]

EARLY ENGINE AND CARRIAGE SHEDS

On undertaking to work the CHR, the LNWR insisted that there should be adequate engine and carriage sheds. In January 1848 orders were given for a shed for two engines at Colwyn, and in August for two temporary sheds, at Llanfair for two engines, and at Holyhead for four. In the latter case, however, a shed is clearly shown on a plan as early as November 1846 though at that time it could only have been as an intention. The Holyhead shed was erected in 1848 and measured approximately 105ft by 65ft. After the opening of the Britannia Bridge the Llanfair shed became redundant and was removed early in 1851.[34] Complaints from Trevithick in 1854 of lack of repairing facilities at Holyhead led to a tripling of the size of the engine shop—not the shed—in the following year, but at a cost of only £120, so that the work done must have been minimal.[35] In 1860 a new steam shed for twelve engines was ordered to be placed on the north side of the main line at Holyhead, opposite to the existing shed which was handed over to the wagon department.

Details of the early CHR engine shed accommodation at Chester are elusive. In April and June 1848 discussions took place between the CHR and the LNWR as to erection of a joint shed. In February 1852 the CHR board noted that this had been made larger than necessary for working the Holyhead line in order to accommodate the engines working the Chester and Crewe line. The position of this structure is uncertain, however, and the first definite information appears in September 1860 when the LNWR agreed with the Great Western Railway as to equal division of the existing shed accommodation at the station. In April 1867 Ramsbottom reported on additional shed room needed at Chester and recommended a building similar to that at Ordsall Lane (near Manchester), capable of holding forty engines, to be erected in the fork between the Chester—Crewe and Chester—Warrington lines. The GWR agreed, and in February 1870 the tender of Messrs Warburton Bros of Manchester was accepted at a price of £6,070. The shed was built with eight roads and was some 475ft in length.

Though there was probably an engine shed at Bangor in the early years, the first reference appears in June 1879 when the LNWR permanent way, works, and estate committee noted, while arranging land purchases at the station, that Webb was to prepare a plan for removing the existing shed to another site. Likewise, at Rhyl there was an early shed but details are elusive. In April 1870 plans were prepared for an enlargement of the Rhyl shed during which it was suggested that it be made 'wide enough for three engines abreast'. In May 1870 the tender of H. C. Chester of Prestatyn was accepted at a price of £1,233. The shed at Llandudno Junction, constructed consequent upon the extension of the Conway Valley line to Festiniog and the widening of the Llandudno branch in the late 1870s, is noted in volume 2, as is the later shed at Mold Junction, and those on the branch lines.

In April 1848 carriage sheds were ordered for the first class stations, each to hold three vehicles. This was none too soon for in the following month, immediately after the line was opened to Bangor, the LNWR complained that its carriages were being left out in the open and were being damaged by the salt air. The sheds were soon erected but were apparently none too substantial; in September 1849 Lee reported that the Bangor carriage shed had been blown down. In August 1848 plans were prepared for a 100ft long carriage shed at Holyhead, just west of the town station. In May 1864 a new carriage shed was ordered for Holyhead at an estimated cost of £2,500.[36]

As to turntables, again the evidence is scanty. In 1849 two engine turntables were ordered, one for Mostyn and the other for Rhyl. A 36ft turntable went in at Bangor in 1852-3 (the first mention of any engine facility there in the records). In 1859 the tables at Bangor and Holyhead were lengthened two feet at each end, and in 1860 orders were given for a new 40ft turntable at Holyhead, presumably making two, though two years later Lee was instructed to remove the 'spare' engine turntable there to the London Road station, Manchester. In 1862 a 40ft turntable was ordered for Rhyl for the joint use of main line trains and those from the Vale of Clwyd line.

CHAPTER 9

## *Holyhead up to the 1880s*

By the early nineteenth century the small harbour at Holyhead had become incapable of providing shelter adequate for the increase of coastal shipping. Movements of vessels were restricted; at low tide the depth of water alongside Rennie's 1824 Admiralty Pier at the south east tip of Salt Island diminished to 10ft, leaving navigable only a small space near the harbour entrance. At low tide most of the inner harbour went dry, and the inhabitants frequently held races across the mud between the low surrounding cliffs. There were, however, distinct possibilities of improvement both for refuge purposes and as a packet station. For such works . . . 'We have ascertained that stone may be had at a convenient distance from the port, and may be readily conveyed thither by railroad'. Thus spoke the naval committee in January 1840 (chapter 3), their generally favourable opinion of Holyhead being confirmed by further government inquiries during the next three years. James Walker reported to the Admiralty, for instance, that though the existing harbour was nothing to boast of, it had nevertheless sheltered some four hundred vessels during the first three months of 1843. He produced plans for an improvement based on a breakwater from Salt Island. The passing of the CHR Act in 1844 emphasised the need for action; it became essential to provide a suitable harbour of refuge so as to leave the Admiralty Pier free for the mail packets to operate unhindered. Of the several schemes suggested, that of James Meadows Rendel was accepted in December 1845. Rendel had trained under Telford and was an acknowledged authority on harbours. His works had included Par, Bude, Brixham, Torquay, Plymouth, Newhaven, and Littlehampton harbours, railway, canal and bridge construction, and latterly the Birkenhead Docks.[1]

PROPOSED REFUGE AND PACKET HARBOUR

Meanwhile, the railway side of the question had been developing. There had been objections to any idea that railway locomotives should run through the town to the Admiralty Pier, and in March 1844 George Stephenson informed the provisional committee of the CHR that the difficulty might be overcome by making the station at the entrance to the town and working thence to the pier by horse power. Though this was what eventually happened, an alternative route was considered first. At the CHR half-yearly meeting in February 1845 it was noted that Sir Robert Peel hoped for a speedy introduction of a government Bill for harbour works. By August 1845 Parliament had voted a provisional grant and in January 1846 Rendel met Moorsom and Robert Stephenson to discuss an integrated harbour and railway scheme. Rendel proposed a new harbour of refuge with a north and an east breakwater, and including an inner steam packet pier, 920ft in length, on to which the railway was to run direct, via the back of the town (map p 210). It was expected that the CHR would pay for the pier. Rendel hoped to obtain powers to allow the two breakwaters to be so far constructed as to afford shelter for vessels within three years. This, as it turned out, was a wildly optimistic aspiration. On completion, the harbour as then planned was to extend to 316 acres, holding up to a thousand vessels.

The estimate for the harbour of refuge came to £700,000 and the Treasury asked the CHR how much it would be prepared to contribute in view of the benefit the works would bring to the railway. The CHR directors, fearful that unless they participated other parties might come forward, recommended to their shareholders that the company should

# DEVELOPMENT AT HOLYHEAD
## 1846 – 1880

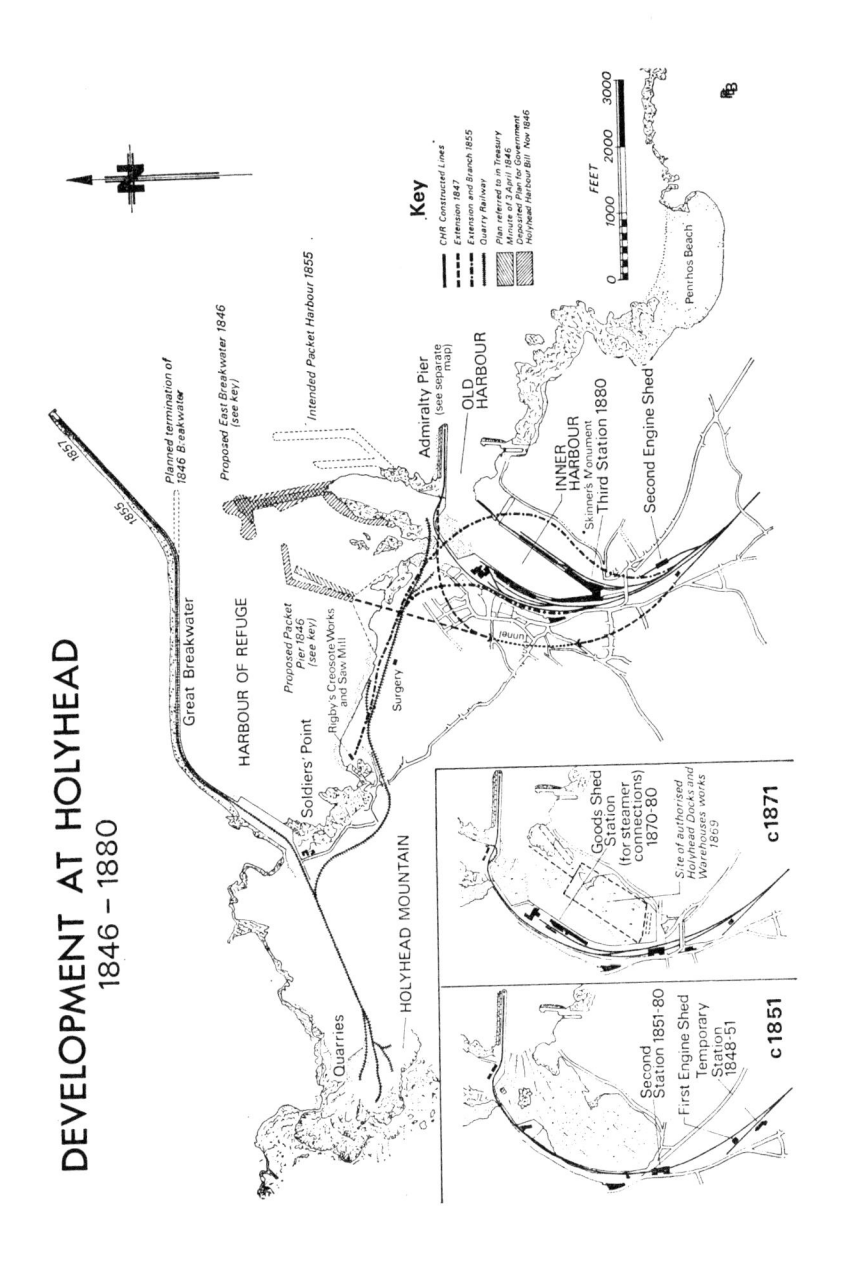

contribute in the proportion of £25,000 to every £100,000 from the government until the total outlay reached £700,000. Robert Stephenson, however, had doubts about Rendel's estimate, saying that the works would require employment of up to 5,000 men for four or five years and that wages alone would amount to £600,000.[2]

At the CHR half-yearly meeting in February 1846 the shareholders warned the directors against involvement in the harbour of refuge. Collett, however, replied that if the company did contribute, the harbour would be started immediately, including the packet facilities, whereas otherwise it might not be made for some time to come. In March the Treasury asked for an amount of £200,000, payable in instalments. The company replied that this must be the maximum figure, and asked that if agreement was reached work on Rendel's scheme should proceed forthwith. Also, the inner pier should unequivocally be appropriated to railway use, and land should be made available at the base of the pier for a station. While the work progressed, the present harbour should be deepened to take a larger class of steamer, and the company should be permitted to lay a temporary railway to the Admiralty Pier. To these requirements the Treasury largely agreed in a minute of 3 April 1846, with the proviso that on completion of the new harbour works and transfer to them of railway traffic, the temporary railway would be taken over for government use. At a special meeting on 8 April the CHR shareholders voted in favour of the £200,000 contribution. To complaints that the London & Birmingham Railway was not bearing some of the cost, Glyn told the meeting that his company had 21,000 shares in the CHR and that in any event the Holyhead harbour works were against the LBR's Liverpool interests.

In August 1846 Rendel reported that the works in the existing, or 'old', harbour, including dredging and additional timber jetties to the Admiralty Pier, were ready for contract but that a more detailed survey was necessary for the refuge harbour. This was carried out by diving bell and, by September,

Rendel was satisfied with the plans.[3] At this point a misunderstanding arose: Rendel believed that the railway company would be building the packet pier. Hasty interviews with the Treasury assured the CHR directors that their contribution covered construction of the pier and Rendel had to admit that he had not provided for it in his estimates. During the bitter weather of January 1847 Collett inspected the works progressing in the old harbour and was pleased with what he saw. 'From a question which he took the liberty of putting to the Secretary of the Admiralty in the House of Commons . . . he was enabled to say that the Government were about to proceed vigorously in forming the harbour of refuge.'[4]

## PROPOSED EXTENSION LINE 1847

In May 1847, with dredging still in progress in the old harbour, the CHR Bill in Parliament for the extension railway at Holyhead and other works was threatened with delay until an Admiralty commission had arrived at a decision concerning Rendel's plans and the government's harbour Bill. On 22 June the Admiralty reported itself satisfied and the CHR Holyhead Extension Bill then underwent some heavy opposition in Parliament on the grounds that it conferred a monopoly on the railway company. King, the CHR secretary, did much to put his company's case in a good light and, with clauses written in which guaranteed against undue preference or privilege towards the railway, the Bill passed its third reading in the Commons on 24 June. That it was ever truly in danger of failing was unthinkable; official backing saw to that. The government's Holyhead Harbour Act and the Chester & Holyhead Railway, Holyhead Extension and Amendment Act both received the Royal Assent on 22 July 1847.

The CHR Act (10–11 Vic cap ccxxxviii) empowered the CHR to construct an extension railway, 1 mile and 23 chains in length, commencing from a junction with the authorised main line about 900 yards south of the latter's termination, and ending at the base of the proposed packet pier, which was to be 100ft wide and carry five lines of rail. At the base of the pier there was to be a station on seven acres of land with a frontage to the packet harbour of 1,200ft.[5] The railway, on a ruling downward gradient of 1 in 264 towards the harbour, would pass through the high land at the back of the town by a tunnel 24ft wide and 490ft in length. Just north of the tunnel a branch, 5 furlongs and 4 chains in length, was to curve to the east to terminate at the Admiralty Pier.[6] The company was authorisied to raise additional capital of £150,000 for its own works, and £200,000 for the contribution to the government harbour.

Of interest is that the CHR had a second string in reserve: in November 1846, when the refuge harbour and therefore also the packet pier were unknown quantities, plans were prepared for a 'Holyhead Railway or Tramway', from just south of the authorised termination of the CHR and along the west side of the old harbour to the Admiralty Pier. Hedworth Lee was the engineer, and although it appears from later evidence that the scheme was promoted by a nominally independent company, it is obvious that the CHR was behind it. The Bill was not presented to Parliament but as will be seen the same plans were brought out again in 1850.[7]

### CONSTRUCTION STARTS ON HARBOUR OF REFUGE

The works for the first stage of the refuge harbour were let to Messrs Rigby, of Holywell Street, Westminster, who entered into a contract with the Admiralty on 24 December 1847.[8] They were to construct, within eighteen months beginning in January 1848, sea walls around Soldiers Point and Salt Island Point to which were to be laid railways to a gauge of 7ft from the quarries in Holyhead Mountain. The broad gauge was adopted to enable large stones to be carried. Facing and coping stones were to be of Anglesey limestone or granite, and the backing of sandstone. Filling behind the walls was to be of local rock. Rendel's specifications for the second contract, signed by Rigby on 16 August 1848, detailed the works to be done on the breakwaters. There was to be a north breakwater, 5,360ft in length from Soldiers Point and terminating about 200 yards north-west from the Platters Buoy, an east breakwater, 2,000ft in length from Salt Island Point, terminating some 120 yards south-west of the Platters Buoy, and a steam packet pier, 1,570ft long from South Shore at Rectory Rock, carried in a north-east direction, and ending at an angle in an east-north-east direction.[9] The pier, to be of timber with a nucleus of rubble stone deposit, would, with the east breakwater, have afforded some 3,000ft of quay space.[10]

Within a year events combined to lead to the withdrawal of the CHR from the harbour works. As early as September 1848 the company decided, in view of the apparently long-term nature of the government works, to postpone construction of the 1847 extension railway. It also seemed to the company that it was to be indebted to the tune of £200,000 in a period when it was already borrowing £100,000 from the LNWR and paying out heavily, and more than had been anticipated, on the principal engineering works on the main line. Appeals for government aid failed, and in August 1850 the Treasury decided to continue the harbour works alone, no contribution from the CHR having so far been made. *Herepath's Journal* commented on 10 August:

> We are glad to find that the Chancellor of the Exchequer has leave to bring in a Bill to relieve that hardly dealt with and sorely pressed line, the Chester and Holyhead, from contributing £200,000 towards Holyhead harbour. It is the first symptom of justice manifested towards the Company, and we hope it will be followed by others. No line as a public benefit deserves it more, and not one of the English railway companies needs it more.

The government's Holyhead Harbour Act of 15 August 1850 (13-14 Vic cap lll) relieved the CHR of contributing towards the harbour and of its powers in relation thereto. Now a dead letter, the CHR Holyhead Extension Act of 1847 was repealed but provision was made for the government to authorise certain specific CHR works at Holyhead in the future.

In 1852 and 1854 two government Acts successively transferred responsibility for the harbours at Holyhead from the Commissioners of Woods and Forests to the Commissioners of Works and Public Buildings, and then to the Admiralty. The second Act authorised the Admiralty to appoint a harbour master and other officers for the harbour of refuge, and from time to time to permit the railway company to construct works at the port. By the Harbours Transfer Act of 1862 the Admiralty powers passed to the Board of Trade.

By mid 1853 about 100,000 tons of rubble had been deposited on the line of the east breakwater, but it was found that the works were so exposed to heavy seas that it was decided to concentrate on the north breakwater until the latter could afford sufficient protection.[11] Rendel, giving evidence to the Committee on London—Dublin Communication in June 1853, six years after the passing of the Holyhead Harbour Act, said that he did not wish to proceed with the packet pier until it had been decided what class of vessel would use it, and that it might prove necessary to enlarge the packet harbour. In the meantime he thought a landing pier at Soldiers Point would suffice for large vessels and that there were good facilities for running trains down to the Point.

PROPOSED RAILWAY EXTENSIONS 1855

To this end a Bill was deposited for the session of 1855 to authorise the CHR to make a deviation of a short length of the main line at the existing railway terminus, and an extension and branch, both of which were to terminate at South Shore (map p 210). The deviation, to allow the extension to by-pass the terminus, was 3 furlongs and $3\frac{1}{2}$ chains in length and was to commence at the Pont Penllech—Nest level crossing (later replaced by an overbridge) and continue thence to the terminus. The extension, 1 mile 3 furlongs and $3\frac{1}{2}$ chains, was to commence at the level crossing, then parallel the deviation past the terminus whence it was to continue on a different level but nearly the same course as the existing tramway (p 231) until it turned north and west to run along South Shore. It was to terminate at the west end of Newry Beach near the Rigby's saw mill and creosote works. The branch—presumably an alternative to the extension, and thus offering a better chance of getting the Bill passed should one of the routes be objected to—was 1 mile 4 furlongs and 6½ chains in length. It also was to commence at the level crossing but was then to turn eastwards across the Shrewsbury turnpike, after which it turned westwards to cross the inner harbour and join the same route as the South Shore extension line with similar termination. Powers were sought to authorise the LNWR to pay the whole cost of the works, £134,000, which the CHR would construct. As the Bill also contained clauses relating to steamboats, already covered by the provisions of the Improved Postal and Passenger Communication with Ireland Bill of the same session (chapter 7), and thus ran contrary to current LNWR policy, it was withdrawn.

### FURTHER SCHEMES IN REFUGE HARBOUR

Meanwhile, it had been decided to enlarge the refuge harbour. As the 1847 north breakwater neared completion the harbour was so frequently filled with wind-bound vessels that in February 1854 the harbour master complained to the Admiralty. The breakwater was obviously of insufficient length and Rendel prepared plans for an extension of 2,000ft in a north-easterly direction. Messrs Rigby, meanwhile, had claimed against the Admiralty for loss of work on the 1847 packet pier and east breakwater. They were, therefore, given the extension to the north breakwater, and the construction of 2,500ft of the superstructure. The contract, dated 1 January 1855, formally abandoned the packet pier. As to the 1847 east breakwater, on which a small amount of work had been done, it was deemed to be abandoned if no instructions to proceed had been given by June 1856.

In February 1856 Rendel confirmed abandonment of the east breakwater by proposing a new structure, from the same

HOLYHEAD UP TO THE 1880s 217

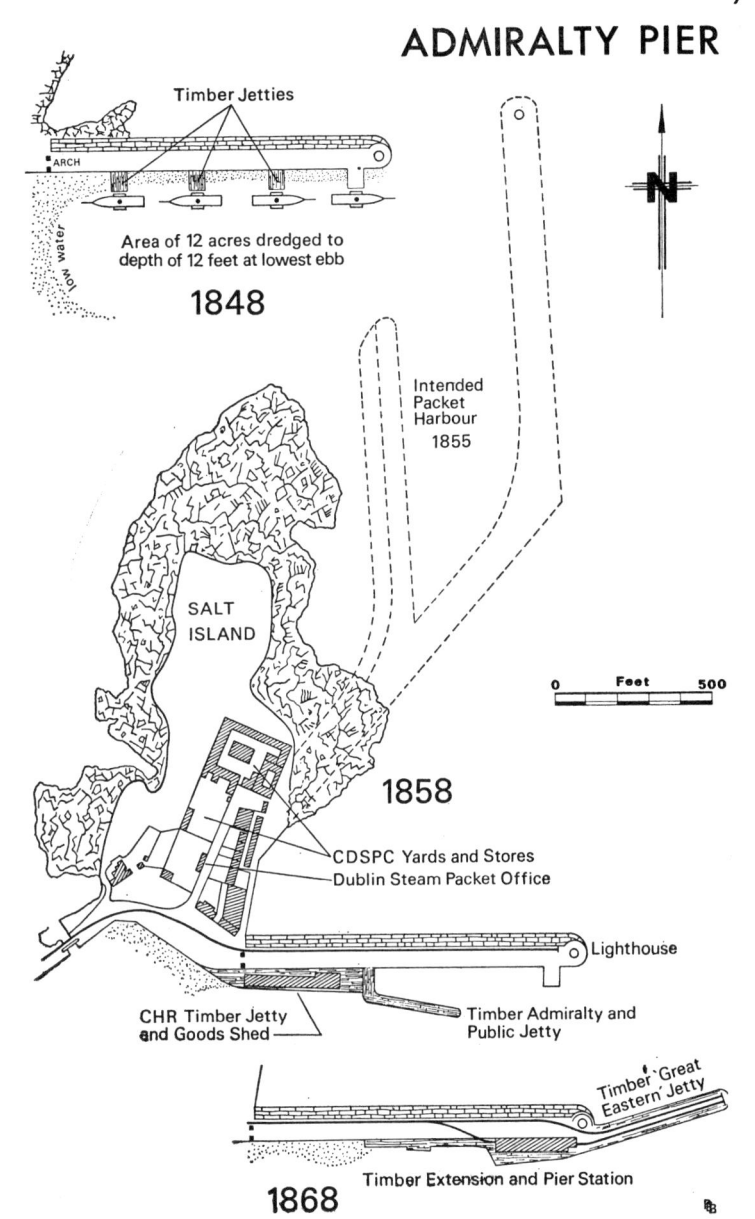

# ADMIRALTY PIER

Timber Jetties

Area of 12 acres dredged to depth of 12 feet at lowest ebb

**1848**

Intended Packet Harbour 1855

SALT ISLAND

**1858**

CDSPC Yards and Stores
Dublin Steam Packet Office

Lighthouse

CHR Timber Jetty and Goods Shed

Timber Admiralty and Public Jetty

Timber Great Eastern Jetty

Timber Extension and Pier Station

**1868**

base on the shore, to cover the Platters and Skinners Rocks. From this there was to be a floating wooden landing stage at right angles on the west side. The plans were objected to by the CHR and the City of Dublin Steam Packet Company: access would be inconvenient for large steamers sweeping into the harbour, and it was considered that the landing stage would be too small and would give poor access to the railway. Something had to be done soon, however, if the provisions of the Communication with Ireland Act of 1855 were to prove workable, for otherwise the existing packet facilities would be insufficient. In July and August 1856, therefore, directors and chief officers of the LNWR, CHR and CDSPC, met Rendel at Holyhead, when it was agreed that a new packet station should be built based on Salt Island. That autumn Rendel was engaged in preparing the plans but in late October or early November he caught a cold. His condition worsened, leading to his death on the night of 21 November 1856, from 'intermittent fever' which had lasted 25 days. He was 56 years old, and his obituary in *Herepath's Journal* described him as amiable and kind in private life and a 'brilliant ornament' of his profession. Like his illustrious contemporaries, Brunel, Locke, and Stephenson, he contributed some of the greatest engineering works of the nineteenth century and, like them, so soon to follow, a tireless dedication to his profession was tragically cut short by early death.

The harbour works passed into the hands of John (later Sir John) Hawkshaw, the famous civil engineer. From discussions with the CHR and CDSPC, he learned that the larger steamers, which were to be put on the packet service, required close contact with the trains for ease of loading. Hawkshaw first considered lengthening the Admiralty Pier by some 2,000ft but it was found that even then the water was so shallow that the pier would still terminate in only three fathoms, a depth useless for transatlantic liners, which it was envisaged might use the harbour. He therefore proposed an entirely new packet harbour on the east side of Salt Island, consisting of an outer stone pier 1,200ft in length and 120ft wide, and an inner stone

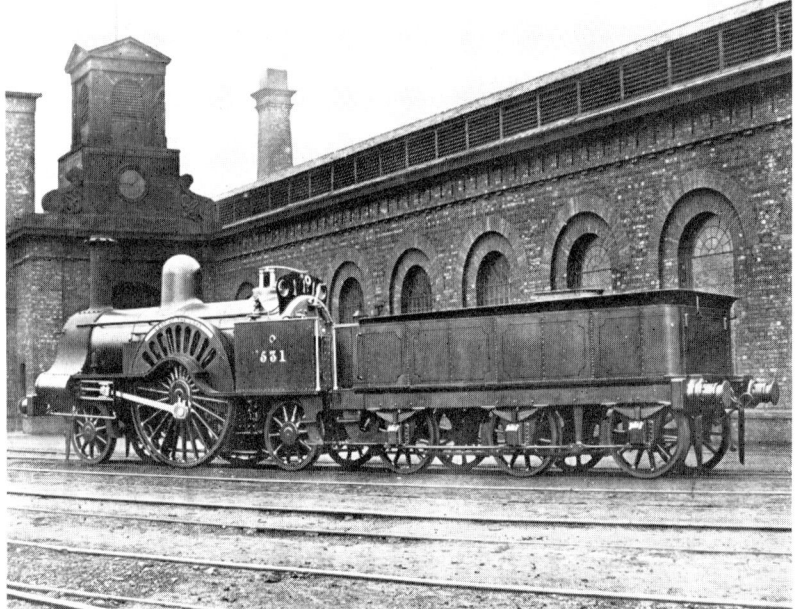

Page 219
*Drawing of the 2–2–2 experimental locomotive No 187* Velocipede, *1847*
Ramsbottom *2–2–2 locomotive No 531* Lady of the Lake *at Crewe, 1862*

Page 220

(above) *Gaerwen station from the west, 1965;* (centre) *Valley station from the south, 1970;* (below) *Admiralty Pier station, Holyhead*

pier 900ft by 50ft. These would provide adequate depth of water and would permit of further extension. The outer pier was to take a railway station with platforms, two double tracks, and a refreshment room. As an interim measure, to provide for the new but still comparatively shallow-draught steamers which were to operate the new postal contract then being negotiated, the Admiralty Pier was to be extended by a timber structure. All these works, which met the requirements of the CHR and CDSPC, were estimated to cost £445,000, and were approved by the Admiralty and Treasury in February 1858.[12]

THE GREAT BREAKWATER

Despite the authorised 1855 extension to the north breakwater—by now known as the 'Great Breakwater'—it became apparent within a year that Rendel's plans were still insufficient. By a contract dated 23 April 1857 Messrs Rigby undertook to lengthen it by a further 500ft, the works to be completed by 1 January 1860.[13] The final basic breakwater was thus to be 7,860ft in length. With this decided, Hawkshaw prepared plans for altering and extending the existing superstructure, for which Messrs Rigby contracted on 30 November 1857. These works included a parapet walk and roadway and, within the thickness of the parapet, stores, sheds, and privies.

For construction of the Great Breakwater, stone was blasted out of the Holyhead Mountain at up to 50,000 tons at a time by charges of gunpowder expended at an average of 10 tons weekly, the explosions being fired by galvanic battery. Fifty mobile cranes, some being steam powered, then attacked the stone and loaded it on to the broad gauge railway on which were employed 250 large iron tilting tip wagons. The railway ran out over the line of the breakwater on five tracks on staging of Quebec yellow pine, 17ft above high water, 150ft wide, and supported on 8oft piles. By this means the trains could deposit up to 5,000 tons of stone daily direct into the sea—a method of construction employed by Rendel in 1838 when building Mill Bay Pier near Plymouth. All the while, cranes at the end of the staging, aided by a small screw steamer, manoeuvred new piling into position so that it was kept just in advance of the stone deposits. The stone was tipped in layers 15 to 20ft thick, lower levels being of stone as quarried, whereas in later ones the proportion of large stones was increased, with some of the blocks weighing up to 15 tons. The rubble was levelled to a depth of 30ft below low water of spring tides, enclosing the piling as it progressed, and on it was superimposed outer stone block walling 18ft thick up to the low water line. The breakwater was formed 250ft wide at low water, with a basic height of 38ft 9in above low water. On the inner, harbour side, at a level of 27ft above low water, a 40ft wide terrace or quay was formed. The breakwater head, in massive square-hewn stones, was formed 150ft long and 50ft wide, the blocks diminishing in thickness of outer walling from 18ft to 8ft at the top. They were likewise backed with rubble stone from the mountain and South Shore.[14] Limestone was also brought to the works by the CHR from Crockford's quarries at Holywell.[15]

In September 1853 the Royal Family had visited Holyhead on their way to Ireland. Accompanied by Rendel and one of the Rigbys, they inspected the harbour works and quarries where a particularly spectacular explosion was arranged for their benefit. By that time the Great Breakwater was over 4,000ft into the bay. In September 1857 Hawkshaw noted that it had reached 7,700ft, $6\frac{1}{4}$ million tons of stone had been tipped, and 1,200 feet of the superstructure had been built up to the level of high water at spring tides.[16]

In 1863 a report was presented to Parliament on the state of the works, and Hawkshaw was questioned as to the other uses to which the breakwater might be put. It was agreed, however, that it should serve only as a defence against the sea, and proposals for packet piers or jetties to be built on to it were scotched. The report noted that at that time, the breakwater head being unfinished, a lightship was kept moored there. Soon afterwards work started on construction of the lighthouse on the head.

During the years of construction, everywhere around the harbour there was tremendous bustle and noise: the hammer of pile drivers, detonations from the mountain, the hiss and rumble of the stone trains and the giant cranes in the quarries, and the roar of tipping in the bay. And overall, an army of some 1,400 workmen swarmed, with an admixture of Victorian tourists dutifully taking in one of the marvels of the age. At times there were days of a different nature, when howling winds from the north-west whipped the sea into a crashing fury against the breakwater. Time and again the staging suffered: in July 1856 a two-day storm wrought terrible damage and the roadstead was strewn with heavy timbers dangerous to shipping. Early in 1858 some 70,000ft of timber was torn from the staging and carried along the coast near Penrhos. At such times the works stopped. Men went unpaid, and soup kitchens were set up in Holyhead.[17]

Though the elements did thus occasionally retard progress it slowly became obvious that there were more serious reasons for the delays to completion. Life for some people at Holyhead was too cosy; Rigby had no inducement to bring the contract to a speedy conclusion. A report to the Board of Trade in 1869 noted that he occupied rent free 'a large and handsome residence and garden upon the Government land'; this was the house with castellated turrets at Soldiers Point which he had built under a government contract in 1849 for residences and workshops for himself and his staff. Rigby also had the run of surplus government land along the shore which he let as gardens to persons who had nothing to do with the harbour. Finally, it was hinted that his men, and perhaps himself, were engaged in other profitable sidelines unconnected with the breakwater but more with the produce of the sea. There appears to have been an absence of whip-cracking on the part of the resident engineer, sixty-seven years old George Clarrise Dobson. He had been assistant to Rendel since 1831 and while at Plymouth both men had married sisters from the same family. At Holyhead, Dobson lived in the other residence nearby to Soldiers Point, named 'Government House', and likewise built by Rigby. He was credited by Rigby as being the brain behind the novel stone-tipping method of breakwater construction. The two were firm friends. There was, therefore, something of a cold shock when the 1869 report recommended that Hawkshaw should 'insist peremptorily' that Rigby got on with the job.[18]

Nevertheless, it was not until 30 June 1873 that Hawkshaw was able to inform the Board of Trade that Holyhead New Harbour had been completed and that his duties as superintending engineer had ended that day. The Great Breakwater now sheltered a roadstead of 400 acres of deep water, in addition to 267 acres in the refuge harbour itself. Hawkshaw reported that expenditure so far, including works on the packet facilities in the old harbour, had amounted to £1,479,538, of which £1,285,000 had gone on the Great Breakwater, equivalent to £163 10s (£163.50) per foot run. On average, some 3,500 vessels sought refuge in the harbour in the course of a year.

On Saturday 16 August 1873 a squadron of Ironclads arrived at Holyhead with numerous dignitaries aboard, and on the following Tuesday the royal yacht brought the Prince of Wales and the Duke of Edinburgh. That afternoon they travelled on the quarry railway, hauled by the broad gauge locomotive *Prince Albert*, to the breakwater head and there ceremonially opened the harbour of refuge. From sunset that evening the red revolving light first shone out from the new lighthouse. His work done, Dobson died in 1874, and Government House thereafter became the home of successive harbour masters.

BROAD GAUGE LOCOMOTIVES

It is uncertain how many locomotives were employed on the quarry railway. The *Illustrated London News* for 3 September

1853 noted eight at work, either in the quarry or on the staging. It is known that on completion of the breakwater three engines, named *London, Holyhead, Cambria,* and possibly a fourth, *Queen,* were sold by Rigby to William Boulton of Ashton-under-Lyne.[19] Another was disposed of to the harbour authorities at Punta Delgada in the Azores, while a sixth, *Prince Albert,* so called after it had hauled its namesake at the time of the royal visit in 1853, remained at Holyhead until the twentieth century. It was used for constant tipping of stone to arrest erosion by the sea of the foundations of the Great Breakwater. The quarry locomotives appeared very utilitarian in design. They were constructed by R. B. Longridge & Co of Bedlington in 1852 as 0–4–0 well-tanks with 3ft 2in wheels, $10\frac{1}{4} \times 18$in cylinders, and a working pressure when new of 112lb.[20] In November 1856 one of the Rigby engines fouled an overbridge while being conveyed over the Chester and Crewe line by the LNWR. The authorities at Crewe were rebuked for lacking a proper loading gauge, so the fact that it was bound for Holyhead might indicate that it was a new locomotive.[21]

STEAMSHIP 'GREAT EASTERN' AT HOLYHEAD

In June 1857 there arrived at Holyhead, Captain Harrison, commander of the newly-built *Great Eastern,* Brunel's most awe-inspiring and costly maritime achievement. With Harrison came officers of the Great Eastern Steamship Company, bent on discovering whether the new harbour was sufficiently advanced to serve as a port of departure for the great vessel on her first transatlantic crossing. The harbour was found to be satisfactory, and arrangements were made for rail fare reductions of one third to through passengers by the steamer. Terrible things happened to the *Great Eastern* before she arrived at Holyhead, however, things which mortally wounded the sick Brunel. By the time she arrived from repairs at Weymouth, in October 1859, it was considered to be too late in the year for the transatlantic voyage and it was decided that she should spend the winter at Southampton. Nevertheless all was brightness and welcome at Holyhead. The LNWR directors wined and dined their opposites of the steamship company at the Royal Hotel. In Holyhead at this time was the Royal Family, and Prince Albert and the French Prince Napoleon took the opportunity to inspect the vessel. Crowds swarmed to all vantage points to see the arrival and departure of the ship and fifteen excursion trains arrived in one day with wide-eyed trippers.[22] All the junketing and high hopes at Holyhead, and in the board room at Euston, were to be disappointed, however, for the *Great Eastern* never returned.

### ABANDONMENT OF GOVERNMENT PACKET HARBOUR

On 16 June 1858 Messrs Rigby entered into a contract with the Admiralty to construct the temporary wooden extension to the existing packet pier, mentioned earlier, on to which rails were to be laid, and which would be used for the packet services until Hawkshaw's 1857 proposed stone piers were ready. The extension was known henceforth as the 'Great Eastern Jetty' and was presumably that at which passengers from the great ship were landed in 1859. On 23 May 1860 Messrs Rigby contracted to make yet a further wooden extension to the Admiralty Pier. In the following month, to the disgust of the LNWR and the CDSPC, the Treasury decided not to proceed with Hawkshaw's expensive 1857 scheme for a separate packet station and harbour, and it was agreed that the new mail contract, due to start in the following month, should be postponed to 1 August. Both the LNWR and CDSPC immediately complained that the first timber extension, that of 1858, was quite inadequate to hold vessels securely in heavy gales. The CDSPC's *Llewellyn*, for instance, had a particularly hair-raising escape on 27 May 1860 when heavy seas washed through the timber piling and threatened to tear her lose. The LNWR wrote with barely restrained fury that all along it had been agreed that the timber extensions were a temporary expedient only, and as late as 13 August 1859 the government inspector, in reporting upon the extension railway to the pier, had stated the same view:

> Its object is understood to be a temporary one, another site having been selected in the Harbour for permanent service of the mail packets.
> The new Pier has not been designed with reference to the special accommodation of Passengers: it is in an exposed situation, and I would suggest the addition of a covered way round the extension to the light house, to afford shelter to the servants of the Company on duty at the Pier and perhaps occasionally to passengers; and that provision should, so far as possible, be made for the safety of females and children embarking and disembarking in dark nights and bad weather by means of double chains bounding the Pier and by ample means of lighting it.

Such a state of affairs, said the LNWR, was not right. In a letter to Hawkshaw dated 6 July 1860 the company was pessimistic. 'We shall be ready to run the trains, and have assured the government that we will use every exertion; but the commencement of the service, with the proposed appliances, must prove a failure.' It was in this atmosphere that on 1 October 1860 the new mail service began, and the Post Office recognised the situation by not inflicting penalties for the late working of the mails. In 1862, for instance, the mails were late no less than 874 times, and the uncharged penalties amounted to £24,549. The CDSPC addressed remonstrances concerning the accommodation to all concerned, and some ameliorative work was carried out by Rigby, by contract dated 23 May 1862, to the extent of piling and other measures to reduce the wash of the sea and force of the wind through the Great Eastern Jetty.

Eventually, the situation was the subject of yet another Commons' committee, which heard evidence in the summer of 1863. The committee examined a plan of Hawkshaw's to make a new breakwater, running east-west from Salt Island, parallel to and on the north side of the Admiralty Pier and its extension. Another plan proposed taking away the Great

Eastern Jetty and altering the accommodation at the Admiralty Pier so as to allow the packets to come alongside more readily. Watson, however, said that the CDSPC would still require the use of the Great Eastern Jetty and it was decided to leave it be and improve the existing structure. Rigby got the contract on 27 January 1864 and work was commenced in the following month. The first train shed and the old Admiralty jetty, on the south side of the Admiralty Pier, were cleared away; the outer angle of the latter with Great Eastern Jetty was emphasised or built outwards so as to afford an increase of sheltered water for the arrival and departure of the packets; a shed with refreshment room was erected immediately to the south of the old lighthouse, at the angle mentioned above; and a screen wall of planking was fixed beneath the floor of the Great Eastern Jetty, and screen walls on the Admiralty Pier. All this might have to suit the CDSPC, but the railway company decided to become more independent of the Admiralty Pier. It embarked on a series of improvements to the inner harbour so as to provide proper facilities for the LNWR trains and ships. Before discussing this, however, it is necessary to trace the early railway development at Holyhead.

### FIRST RAILWAY STATION

In March 1848, with the postponement of the 1847 extension line, the CHR board decided to develop the existing harbour works to enable transfer between the trains and their new steamers then building. These facilities were supposed to last only until the new packet harbour was ready. In the following July, Betts was given the contract to build a 'temporary' station at Holyhead at a cost of about £800, 'to be finished in a month or six weeks', and the first station master, a Mr Massingberd, was appointed.[23] The station, of wood, was erected during July when the main line was inspected by Captain Simmons of the Board of Trade (map p 229). He considered the station to be incomplete and the accommodation

## FIRST STATIONS AT HOLYHEAD

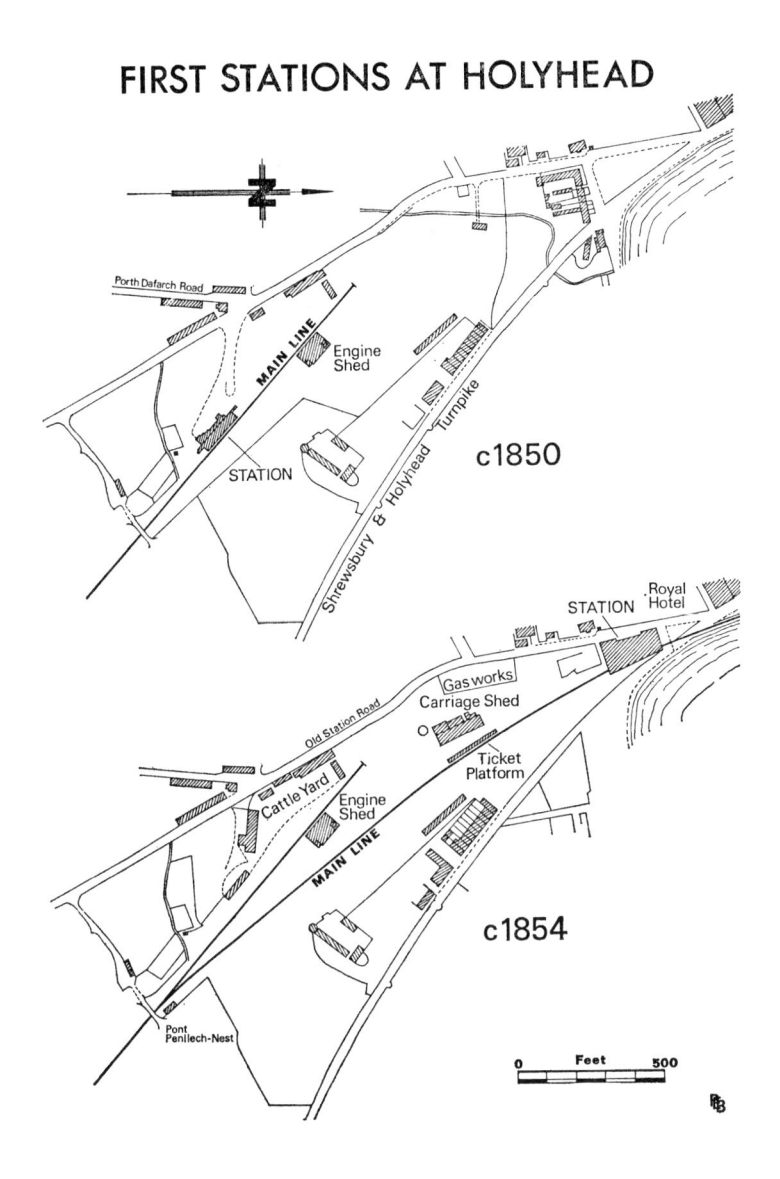

indifferent, but let it pass. Moorsom reported to the traffic committee in August 1848 that he had given instructions for plans to be prepared for laying down rails suitable for a locomotive engine between the station and the Admiralty Pier, with a curve into the government timber yard on Salt Island. He was also examining the eastern shore of the inner harbour for a suitable place for a wharf for goods and cattle traffic. At that time Roberts' omnibus operated between the trains at the temporary station and the packets at the Admiralty Pier. Moorsom thought the arrangements bad: 'The packets leave passengers at a naked pier at Holyhead, where they suffer every inconvenience and annoyance, which the Company cannot remedy, so that I wonder at there being so large a traffic by our route'. His comparison was, of course, with Liverpool.

There was also a lack of creature comforts which was highlighted in a letter in October 1849 from James Boothby, a director lately resigned from the company:

... a small refreshment room would be a great comfort to passengers when the boat arrives too late (as is frequently the case) to permit a stoppage at the town, and especially after a rough passage, travellers are greatly exhausted, and often unable to proceed further on their journey without some refreshment. This has happened twice to myself and I have heard it much complained of.

The other day we were not allowed to get out of the Coaches, being told there was not a moment to spare, yet when we got to the Station nearly twenty minutes were consumed in getting out the Tickets, Luggage, etc. during which a simple cup of Tea or a Sandwich and Glass of Wine would have been invaluable to most of the Passengers. Two Ladies were so exhausted when they reached Chester as to be unable to stand on their feet, and Mrs Johnston, of the Royal Hotel, told me similar complaints were frequent. Pray bring this matter before the Committee, it is a great drawback to the route, and of easy remedy. Roberts, I have no doubt, would be glad to do it, for the Refreshment he provides at the Inn are frequently (for want of time) left untouched.

Boothby was on the board of the Great Southern & Western Railway of Ireland at this time, and was busy negotiating arrangements for the Cork traffic via Holyhead. He ended his letter to the CHR board with 'we open on the 22nd to Cork and wish to advertise the through Fares to London'. Hence his strictures on the Holyhead service. Shamefacedly, an immediate order was given to spend £50 on extending the waiting room at the station so as to provide refreshments.

### EXTENSION RAILWAY AND SECOND STATION

Plans for the extension to the Admiralty Pier were already to hand for the session of 1850-1 (p 213) but the advent of Morton Peto and his 'fixing' ability seems to have made Parliamentary powers unnecessary. On 6 November 1850 the CHR board noted that Peto had been having discussions with the Commissioners of Woods and Forests, owners of most of the lands between the station and the pier. The Bill, entitled as its 1846-47 predecessor, was drafted to incorporate a private company, or to name an individual, for the purpose of making the railway, the CHR to have the use of it when constructed. The Bill was withdrawn, and the commissioners deputed Rendel to act for them in matters concerning the extension line. In December orders were given for its construction 'so that the Irish Traffic be carried over the Extension Line previous to the opening of the 1851 Exhibition'. The cost was estimated at £28,000, and the contractor was George Giles. Early in 1851 it was decided to construct a permanent town station with adequate refreshroom rooms and, in April, Peto reported that the extension works were proceeding satisfactorily and that the line would be opened for passenger traffic on 15 May. It was in fact brought into use on Tuesday 20 May.[24]

The extension works involved a cutting a third of a mile in length and from 10 to 15 feet deep, demolition of some ten houses, and filling and levelling space for the new station. The line, on which the railway carriages were to be drawn by horses, passed on a half-mile timber viaduct alongside the harbour cliffs, then over a timber drawbridge (replaced by an iron structure in 1881), to Salt Island, whence it continued as a tramway on one side of the Admiralty Pier. As to the new station, *Herepath's Journal* of 26 April 1851 noted that 'the refreshments were to be presided over by one, who, in her way, is as great as the redoubted Soyer—the famous Mrs Hibbert. We are surprised to learn she deserts the great cradle of her fame—Wolverton—for the classic retirement of Holyhead harbour . . .' In fact Herepath had it all wrong; Leonora Hibbert, who had made Wolverton refreshment room a by-word, saw this as a promotion, and the fact that she had been specially brought to Holyhead by the LNWR emphasised the importance placed by the railway company on passenger comforts. After all, this was an opportunity to impress the large number of influential passengers coming to England for the Great Exhibition, and anything which put the CHR and LNWR in a good light, as opposed to the CDSPC's arrangements, was a bonus. Mrs Hibbert agreed to the move in May, and the LNWR took charge of the Royal Hotel, formerly the Eagle and Child, on 24 June.[25]

The opening of the extension line was not an immediate success. Binger reported that the curves were so sharp that it took four horses to draw six of the LNWR's diminutive coaches at 4mph. He thought that if locomotive power could not be used—and to this the sanction of the railway commissioners had been withheld—very great delay and inconvenience would be experienced during the winter months; it would be almost impossible to work the extension during a gale. As boat and train arrivals were almost simultaneous, sidings at the timber yard and on the pier were absolutely necessary. Peto agreed and demanded action; the curves were eased and sidings laid. The estimated costs of the various works were: £6,852 for land, including possession of the Royal Hotel; £19,793 for the pier works and sidings; and £2,800 for the station, apparently designed by Charles Reed.[26]

It would appear that the station was not opened until the week commencing 14 September 1851.[27] Situated approximately opposite but a little to the south of the line of the present Holborn Road, in the corner then made by the junction of the Shrewsbury turnpike with what is now Old Station Road, the station was described, rather fulsomely, in 1853, as being 'an extensive and commodious one, connected with which are Refreshment Rooms, with Waiting and Dressing Rooms attached, Telegraph Office and a well furnished Book Room, the whole fitted up on a most splendid scale, well arranged and in excellent order, and plentifully supplied with luxurious food'.[28] The eatables were, of course, under the care of Mrs Hibbert. At the Royal Hotel, where Mr Hibbert lent a hand, the same account noted that there had been some renovations. 'It is fitted up in a style of elegance which renders it one of the most complete establishments of the kind in the kingdom, and in every way suited for visitors of the highest grade of society . . . Here are hot, cold and shower baths; carriages, cars, post horses, etc, omnibuses to and from the Railway Station and steam packets for the convenience of parties, frequenting this hotel, gratis'. That is if they did not take the horse-drawn trains along the extension line, squealing on the curves and buffeted by the wind across the open harbour. The trains were a source of delight and danger to local children, for passengers would throw money out to them as they kept pace alongside. As early as August 1852 a child was run over by a train on the extension but it was not until June 1855 that bills were posted requesting passengers to restrain their impulses, and the police were ordered to keep the children away.[29] It would seem that the hotel omnibus was kept in operation at least until after horses were replaced by engines on the extension railway: in October 1861 the LNWR locomotive committee agreed that 'Mrs Hibbert's omnibus may be repaired and repainted at Saltley, at her cost'

In August 1851 Lee was instructed to erect a gas works, and in October a 25ft gasometer was to be completed forthwith. This supplied the government lighting on the Admiralty Pier. The gasworks were sold to the Holyhead Gas Company in 1855, and in January 1856 part of the town was first lit from the supply.[30] In 1851–2 a jetty, cattle shed and yard, and a goods shed were erected, together with a turntable on the

The Queen at the Admiralty Pier, Holyhead 1853

Admiralty Pier, in time for the commencement of the goods traffic (chapter 7).

An outline of the proposed railway extensions to the new harbour between 1847 and 1855 has already been given. Hawkshaw's proposed Salt Island packet harbour led to a renewed CHR application to run locomotives over the extension line. To this the Board of Trade consented, and Hawkshaw was told to make the necessary arrangements. In November 1857 he instructed Lee as to the strengthening works required. These were put in hand but it was not until the Chester & Holyhead Railway at Holyhead Act of 13 August 1859 (22-23 Vic cap 60), and after the new postal contract had been entered into, that permission was received to use locomotives over the extension and on to the Admiralty Pier. Retrospectively, the Act empowered the extension line improvements, and also construction of a branch to Hawkshaw's two proposed piers. The branch, of course, proved unnecessary.

On 10 August 1859 Captain Ross of the Board of Trade met Lord Chandos at Holyhead and together they inspected the extension line and the additional structure to the Admiralty Pier. The captain's comments on the latter have been noted. The extension was described as being a 72-chain single line, of sufficient strength to carry locomotives. The timber viaduct appeared to be 'well bolted up', but a single span timber bridge between the town and the Custom House required some repairs. Additional fencing was needed, especially where the line ran near to the turnpike and the public quay. Several level crossings, over the turnpike, and between the quay and the town, required keepers, and points needed to be locked where two tramways and several sidings joined the line. On 11 August, Lee was ordered to carry out the fencing and to erect such signals as the Board of Trade might require.

HOLYHEAD TANK ENGINES

Because of these requirements, and the condition generally of the extension railway, particularly 'an awkward S curve of small radius near the Custom House', the captain recommended that speed along the line should nowhere exceed 8mph. Finally, Lord Chandos, said the captain, 'informed me that he was preprepared to give an undertaking that the Single Line should be worked by Tank Engines on the Train Staff System and that the Tank Engines should be to a description suited to the S Curve'. There were, by 1859, several existing tank engines, both side and saddle, in stock, mostly converted from the early Trevithick locomotives. Presumably these were too heavy, for on 11 August, on hearing from Lord Chandos of his undertaking to Captain Ross, the locomotive committee ordered Ramsbottom to 'alter 2 of the old Liverpool and Manchester Engines to Tanks to work the curve at Holyhead, as quickly as possible; Mr Ramsbottom stated they are in hand but cannot be ready by 1st proxo'. The precise date for the initiation of steam haulage on the extension railway does not seem to have been recorded, though allowing Ramsbottom a further month to get the engines ready, it could well have been a full year before the 1860 mail service commenced. (A minute of the committee of 1 October 1859 referring to a tank engine made for the CHR being still unemployed relates to the working of the Llandudno branch and not Holyhead.) On 13 October, however, the committee read a letter from Lord Chandos to Richard Moon, the committee's chairman, 'as to use of coke by Engines using the Tramway at Holyhead (another name for the extension line) and which was referred to Mr Ramsbottom to be strictly adhered to'. On 2 February 1860 Binger reported to the committee that following the use of locomotives at Holyhead there were seven horses not required. In the next month five of these, noted as being too light for goods shunting, were sold, and the remaining two were transferred to Liverpool.

The first tank engines did not last long: on 19 December 1861 Ramsbottom told the locomotive committee that the two converted L & M engines were so nearly worn out that it was difficult to keep them running. He recommended that drawings should be prepared of a small shunting tank engine, 'somewhat similar to the one employed at Chester Station, to be used in several parts of the Line where Shunting has to be done over Sharpish Curves'. Ramsbottom was ordered in December 1861 to prepare such drawings, but the easing of the curves at Holyhead in 1862, at the time of the Board of Trade improvement works to the Admiralty Pier, probably accounts for the fact that the first evidence of submission of a tracing for a shunting tank engine to the committee does not appear until 18 June 1863. In the meantime, as noted in chapter 7, and despite the earlier undertaking, it was one of the more reliable Holyhead mail engines, No 18 *Cerberus*, which was employed on the extension line for the 'Trent' special in 1862.

Five 0–4–0 saddle tanks with 4ft diameter wheels were completed at Crewe in December 1863, and one in January 1864. These were replacement engines and carried the running numbers 835, 839, 844, 685, 687, and 846 up to 1885–86 when they were renumbered. Between 1864 and 1870 thirty more of the type were built. On 12 May 1871 Ramsbottom reported that all thirty-six were profitably employed and recommended that ten more should be built. Further engines to this design were built under the Webb regime at Crewe. One of these engines, No 1439, built in 1865, lasted on the LNWR until sold out of service in 1919.[31] It was presented by its owners, for preservation, to the British Transport Commission in 1954.

## INNER HARBOUR WORKS 1860s to 1880

With the final abandonment of government schemes for a packet harbour, and with the LNWR now in sole command of the railway facilities at Holyhead, the authorities at Euston reached the only possible decision. They had so to extend and improve the inner harbour as to provide a sufficiently impressive establishment that would eventually gain the mail contract from the CDSPC. Twenty years' work followed, in two main stages, bringing the port to a position which has remained almost unaltered until recent times.

By the LNWR (Chester & Holyhead) Act of 11 July 1861 (24-25 Vic cap cxxiii) the company was authorised to purchase additional lands at Holyhead, and the powers relating to steamers, obtained by the CHR Act of 1848, were renewed for a period of nine years from 31 December 1862. The LNWR (Additional Powers) Act of 7 August 1862 (25-26 Vic cap ccviii) authorised construction within five years of an embankment on the north-west side of the inner harbour for the eventual replacement of the timber staging of the extension line, the deepening and improvement of the harbour alongside the embankment, an enlargement of the station with a new footbridge at its south end, and a diversion of the Shrewsbury and Holyhead Road whereby the existing level crossing at the north-west end of the station was to be discontinued and the road taken over the railway. By a 99-year lease in May 1863, between the Board of Trade and the LNWR, the latter took possession of certain lands on the west side of the inner harbour. Permission was received, in the LNWR (New Works and Additional Powers) Act of 12 July 1869 (32-33 Vic cap cxv), for the company to purchase the freehold of lands leased from the crown at Holyhead. The 1863 lease provided for the company to make a coffer dam across the harbour. It was then to dredge out a channel to the nearby newly-acquired land on which was to be constructed a goods shed 750ft long and 41ft wide, with offices 350ft by 17ft, together with railway lines, a public quay and road, and berthing facilities. The contract was let to the ubiquitous Messrs Rigby in May 1863, and to facilitate the work a third rail was laid from Rigby's establishment to the new works providing mixed gauge for Rigby's broad gauge wagons.

The dredging work was completed and the water let in on 1 July 1865, the quay having been finished and the goods shed nearly so.[32] The new inner harbour and works, providing a greatly enhanced facility for the LNWR, and replacing the old goods shed on the Admiralty Pier (map p 217), came into use on 1 January 1866, and a new road to the cattle pens ten days later.[33] In the following month work commenced on dredging a widened channel between the old harbour and the goods shed, increasing the width from 66ft to 140ft.[34] In

1868 an electric gong communication was installed between the station and the Admiralty Pier to advise of train movements. Also in that year the marine department reported that new steamer repair facilities at Holyhead had turned out the first replacement boilers for the company's vessels.[35] Finally, these works in the 1860s saw the diversion of the mail train line to a route to the west of the new goods shed. In June 1870 the company decided to enlarge the goods shed and put in a new platform and waiting room for the steamer passengers. This is most probably what Neele refers to as having been constructed outside the goods shed wall on the west side and which was connected by stairs and a gallery within the shed to the quay on the other side.[36] Steamers berthing at the quay were, of course, those of the North Western; the mail train passengers continued their journey from the Admiralty Pier via the CDSPC boats.

Late in 1870 the Board of Trade approved the construction, from land near Pelham Quay, of a fish jetty. This was required by Captain Dent, the company's marine superintendent (appointed in 1866), who complained of fishing boats, not under his jurisdiction, taking up valuable quay space.[37] Neele remarks that the trade decreased soon after the jetty came into use, and that in later years it was more often used as a stand-by pier for LNWR steamers waiting to go into traffic. Nevertheless, in October 1877, the LNWR permanent way, works, and estate committee ordered that the jetty be put in permanent repair, using cast iron piles.

The initiative for new harbour works appears to have passed from the LNWR when, by an Act of 2 August 1869, a new company was formed, apparently unconnected with the railway world, to develop the inner harbour. With a share capital of £450,000 and powers to borrow £150,000, the Holyhead Docks & Warehouses Company was authorised to make docks, piers, new channels, warehouses, tramways, and sidings, with rail connection to the LNWR. Provision was made for agreements between the new company and the LNWR as to leasing facilities, working agreements and tolls. When the Holyhead

Docks & Warehouses Bill had come before Parliament it was opposed by the LNWR but by the time it was to go to committee, in April 1869, agreement had been reached between the two companies whereby numerous clauses favourable to the railway had been inserted, and the Bill, now unopposed, passed without a fight. In the Act, however, there was specific provision that unless the whole capital had been subscribed within three years of the Act, half of which should have been paid up, and the works commenced, the LNWR was to be free to apply to Parliament for powers to construct its own harbour works. As the North Western was in none too happy a financial state in 1869, due to diminished country-wide trade, and recent heavy expenditure on its own works, both of which had caused the half-yearly dividend to drop, the Holyhead Docks & Warehouses Company seems to have provided a useful breathing space, particularly as the Act gave the LNWR almost unlimited powers to use the works had they been made.

By the early 1870s the potential additional traffic from the new Greenore service (chapter 10), necessitated expansion of the harbour. The docks company having failed to proceed, further important works were therefore authorised by the LNWR (Holyhead Old Harbour) Act of 5 August 1873 (36-37 Vic cap ccxxv). These included more dredging of the inner harbour and of the shallow, shelving, east shore, where a sea wall was to be constructed. As the existing government graving dock was frequently occupied when required by the LNWR, and in any case would be too small for the company's newest steamers, it was decided to construct a new graving dock with a length and width of 410ft and 70ft respectively. There were also to be new roads and other works, including a public quay on the east side of the inner harbour to replace the existing one which was situated on the south-west side.[38] The works were let in November 1874 to Messrs Scott & Edwards of Lytham for £151,912. The resident engineer was William Adams.

By the LNWR (New Lines and Additional Powers) Act of 19 July 1875 (38-39 Vic cap clii) a road was to be made giving more direct access from the Shrewsbury Road to Turkey Shore Road and thus to the public quay. Between 1874 and 1876 more land was leased on the east side of the inner harbour for these purposes. The position of the proposed public quay, however, was found to be unsuitable, as vessels using it would constantly have to pass and repass the company's steamers lying in the harbour. The LNWR (New Lines and Additional Powers) Act of 24 July 1876 (39-40 Vic cap clxxx), therefore, repealed the relevant sections of the 1873 Act and authorised construction of a substitute quay, not less than 300ft long and 50ft wide, near the entrance to the old harbour on the west side of Parry's Island. Access was to be either by a new road from the Turkey Shore Road, or by rail from the company's sidings via a movable bridge or caisson worked by hydraulic power, across the entrance to the new graving dock. The 1876 Act provided that on completion of the public quay the LNWR was to be permitted exclusive use of the inner harbour. By August 1875 a coffer dam for the new works had been completed and excavations for the quay walls and the graving dock started. Dredging was to total 452,000 cubic yards to obtain the required depth of water, the area of the harbour being increased from $10\frac{1}{4}$ acres to 24 acres with a uniform depth of 13ft at ebb tide.

In 1875 construction started on a new 750ft by 54ft warehouse on the east quay. The graving dock was opened on 16 January 1880, and the goods shed two months later. Total siding accommodation after completion of the works was 15 miles. The railway land at Holyhead now had an area of 43 acres, 23 of which had been reclaimed from water or waste land. The hydraulics, cranes, and capstans installed for the new harbour works were operated by three pairs of high pressure horizontal 80hp engines. To provide night-time illumination the harbour was electrically lit from three 60ft lattice columns by Siemens' lights, one on either side, and one at the south end. The trains were controlled from four signal boxes containing a total of 225 levers. *The Engineer* of 6 August 1880 noted that from figures at Holyhead for the year ending May 1880, the new works were designed to cope with daily passenger traffic of about a thousand, numerous goods and fish consignments from seven goods trains in and out daily, and a number of weekly specials, and yearly totals of 149,000 sheep, 127,000 pigs, 54,500 head of cattle, and 4,800 horses. These animals were provided with their own separate road and inclined way and bridges to get them from and to the import shed and the cattle lairage south of the Shrewsbury Road bridge.

### NEW HARBOUR, STATION AND HOTEL OPENED

To complete the job a fine new combined station and five storey red brick hotel were built, grandly fitting to the land termination of the LNWR's Irish passenger service. The plans were agreed in April 1876 but the contract was not let until 14 November 1877; it went to Messrs J. Parnell & Son, the price for the station and hotel being £64,807. The station, with the hotel above it, had an elevation length of 135ft, side walls at obtuse angles of 96ft 6ins in length, and projecting wings. Its situation at the angle of the east and west passenger quays, each 550ft long, 35ft wide, and with berth space each for two vessels, permitted passengers to transfer direct and with minimum difficulty between train and ship. The town front, with an approach road from the Shrewsbury Road overbridge, was provided with a covered porch and the rear circulating area with a veranda. The station platforms were 1,130ft and 1,260ft in length on the east and west sides respectively and communicated direct with the quays. Arrivals were at the east quay where conversely was the export goods shed, and departures went from the west side which also dealt with imported goods and cattle.

The harbour works and the new station and hotel were opened by the Prince of Wales on Thursday 17 June 1880. The Prince arrived at Holyhead at 8.30am, breakfasted in the hotel, and after various formalities boarded the new LNWR steamer *Lily* (see chapter 10 as to steamers at Holyhead at this time). With spectators at the harbour sides, steamers dressed overall, and sailors manning the yards, the *Lily* passed out of the harbour to the salutes of warships in the bay. On the Prince's return lunch was served in the goods shed, specially transformed into a pavilion fit for the occasion. The Prince's visit was commemorated by the placing of a large ornate clock in the station circulating area. Two fine photographs from the British Transport Archives are reproduced on p 287. Dated June 1880, it would seem that they were taken on the opening day. The upper photograph shows the *Earl Spencer* to the immediate left with, behind her and nearest, the *Isabella*. To the right of one of the lighting masts is the *Lily*, with maybe the Prince himself as the central figure on the port paddle box. The sun's shadows suggest the forenoon. In the lower photograph the *Lily*, dressed overall, as is the *Earl Spencer*, has presumably returned from the inaugural trip. In the background are the quays, station, and hotel.

With the opening of the harbour, station, and hotel, the railway development at Holyhead was virtually complete. Thus armed, and with the CDSPC excluded from the inner harbour, the struggle to transfer the mail contract to the LNWR's North Wall run was resumed with renewed vigour. Bitter and devious attempts were to be made by the railway company, aided by powerful friends in government office, which were staunchly and successfully to be repelled by the CDSPC and its supporters at Westminster and in Ireland. These happenings, and the further development at Holyhead up to the present time, are dealt with in volume 2.

CHAPTER TEN

## *Operating and Way and Works 1848-1880*

EARLY TRAINS AND TRAFFIC

The train service between Chester and Bangor commenced on 1 May 1848, but there were, apparently, no formalities on the opening day.[1] The *Chester Courant* of 3 May carried an official advertisement of the initial service, departures from Chester being at 4am (mail), 10am, 1.45 and 4.25pm; and returning from Bangor at 6.30 and 9.15am, and 3 and 7pm (no reference to the mail). The Sunday service consisted of the first and last of the above departures from Chester, and the 7am and 7pm from Bangor. *Bradshaw* for May 1848 shows the same times (appendix 3) but with the warning 'Holyhead Trains Incomplete—Accuracy uncertain'. Perhaps this explains a CHR advertisement in *Herepath's Journal* of 6 May which gives a different set of times. Chester to Bangor departure and arrival times respectively were: 8am arr 10.23; 10.15 arr 12.27pm; 1.45pm arr 4.08; and 4.25 arr 6.35pm. In the reverse direction: 7am arr 9.23; 9.15 arr 11.30; 3pm arr 5.15; and 7pm arr 9.23pm. The Sunday service consisted of the first and last weekday trains in each direction.

The first mail service on the opening of the Anglesey line in August 1848 has been noted in chapter 7. It brought Dublin within thirteen hours of London and the revised timetable from 1 August was as follows: from Holyhead, 9am local (returning from Llanfair dep 3pm), 2pm express and 6.20pm mail (these trains connecting by road between Llanfair and Bangor with trains on to Chester); from Bangor to Chester 6am

Parliamentary, 9.15 and 11am, 3.30pm express, 6pm, 7.50pm mail. Sundays from Bangor at 7am, 6.03pm and 7.50pm mail. Chester departures for Bangor were at 3.45am mail (connection Llanfair to Holyhead), 8am Parliamentary, 10.15am, 1.45pm, 2.45pm express (connection Llanfair to Holyhead), 4.30pm. On Sundays from Chester the 3.45am mail (connection Llanfair to Holyhead), 8am and 4.25pm. These timings remained virtually unaltered until January 1849 when a new timetable came into force with five trains each way on weekdays between Chester and Bangor: an early morning mail and an afternoon express, both connecting with corresponding Angelsey trains; and three stopping trains, morning, midday, and afternoon. There was also one afternoon stopping train from Llanfair to Holyhead. In the up direction on weekdays there were three stopping trains on the mainland and one in the morning on Anglesey, with an afternoon express and an evening mail from Holyhead to Llanfair, and from Bangor to Chester and Euston. On Sundays there were three trains in each direction on the mainland, one of which, the mail, operated as during the weekdays with connection to Holyhead. May of 1849 saw an additional morning Parliamentary train in each direction on the mainland.

Apparently, from the first, drivers reached speeds of 45mph, considered reckless by Lee who warned them in May 1848 that if they persisted they would be taken before a magistrate. Timekeeping must at first have been vague; the *Illustrated London News* of 23 December 1848 noted that the station clocks were regulated by the 'celebrated Craig-y-Don gun, which is 16min and 30secs after Greenwich time'. Commented the *News*, 'This cannot fail to prove of great inconvenience to travellers'. On the Irish Mail, however, things were arranged differently: from the very first a special pocket watch in a leather case, set to Greenwich time by the Admiralty, went with the train guard to Holyhead where it was handed to an officer of the Kingstown boat. Though timekeeping proper came with the introduction of the telegraph, this ritual was kept up until the start of he Second World War. Ordinary passengers, however, lured early to the local stations for their trains, were at least mollified from the first months of 1849 by the appearance of bookstalls of W. H. Smith & Co (the '& Son' came later). In May 1849 a special attraction on sale was a series of views of the Britannia Bridge.

During this period passengers were taken across the Menai Straits by Bicknell's coach, and a Mr Wright provided local connecting road services to the railway: three omnibuses at Bangor and two at Holyhead (taking ten inside and six outside passengers), were provided at a cost to the CHR of 25s (£1.25) each week; and there were two luggage vans (converted omnibuses but with outside seats for occasional passengers) at £1 per week. All bore the railway company's name. To ensure that passengers' portmanteaux should not go astray all Irish-bound luggage had the letter 'K' marked large upon it. The other connecting road services were arranged early in 1848. Mr Hughes was to meet all trains at Abergele; Mr S. Edwards of the Uxbridge Arms, Caernarvon, and John Roberts of the Mostyn Arms, Rhyl, were permitted to operate their coaches from Bangor and Rhyl station yards respectively. Edwards was also required to meet 'the Liverpool steam packets'. This relates to the services then operated between Menai Bridge and Liverpool, thrice-weekly by the City of Dublin Steam Packet Company's *Albert*, and a private vessel, *Cambria*, and twice-weekly by another private steamer, *Orion*. Coaches connected with these steamers from Caernarvon, and to Amlwch, Llangefni, and Holyhead on Anglesey. (In May 1849 the *Albert* was replaced by the *Prince of Wales*.) In July 1848 a coach for Ruthin was admitted to the yard at Rhyl, and a Mr Humphries undertook to run an omnibus between Beaumaris and Bangor station. Apparently this gave way to Bicknell's *Magnet* coach which started operating between Bangor station and Beaumaris in the summer of 1849.[2] *The Carnarvon & Denbigh Herald* carried advertisements from the coastal steamers in the autumn of 1848 showing fare reductions resulting from competition from the railway.

The CHR finance committee reported in February 1849 that

rail passengers carried from 1 May to 31 December 1848 were: first class 29,776; second 50,175; third 71,676; Parliamentary 35,266; and children 2,174; (total 189,067). Goods traffic consisted of 4,786 tons of miscellaneous freight; 7,239 tons of coal, lime, bricks, and stone; 9,710 pigs, calves, sheep, and produce; and 2,409 parcels. The CHR steamers took 4,798 first class passengers, 1,670 second, and 181 children (total 6,649). Gross rail receipts were: passenger £38,879, and goods and parcels £6,847. Deduction of working charges left £28,520 net. Total steamboat receipts, including parcels, were £3,446, but allowing for working expenses there was an overall loss of £5,695 which, set against the rail figure, left net receipts at £22,825. The number of passengers carried by rail during the first ten years is given in appendix 4.

Children's half-price tickets were introduced from 21 August 1848, and season and cheap tickets in April 1849. In May 1849 excursion tickets to Killarney followed, together with first and second class day return tickets between all stations at fare and a half, and to Manchester, Stockport, and Macclesfield on Saturdays available until Monday at single fare for the return journey. Through tickets to Cork were issued from 1 December 1849. Special excursion trains operated from the first: Thomas Cook arranged in May 1848 for an outing to Bangor.[3] Road excursions were also popular: in July 1849 Binger arranged with a Mr J. P. Hamer to run an excursion coach twice-weekly from Bangor station 'around Snowdon'.[4]

March of 1850 saw alterations to the timetables on the opening of the up line over the Straits (the first trains are noted in chapter 6). Dealing only with the through services, the first down train was the 8.45pm Irish Mail from Euston, dep Chester 3.09am, and arrive Holyhead 5.49am. The 9am Irish Boat Express from Euston left Chester at 2.55pm, arr Holyhead 5.15pm; and the 5pm Irish Mail out of Euston left Chester at 10.25pm and reached Holyhead at 1.05am. Packet departures were approximately half an hour later. The up service was similar: the Irish Mail left Holyhead at 1.35am, Chester arr 4.40 and Euston 1pm; the 2pm Irish Boat Express from Holyhead reached Chester at 5 and Euston at 11pm; and the second Irish Mail left Holyhead at 6.58pm, Chester arr 10.03, and reached Euston at 4.50am. Generally, the mail and express trains called at five or six of the principal intermediate CHR stations. Broadly speaking, the local services were continued much as before, though a Parliamentary train was put on which ran the whole length of the line in each direction, and there were additional stopping services between Chester and Bangor. To detail these would be tedious: the company tried several train alterations during this phase, one example of which will suffice. On 3 May 1850 the traffic committee ordered 'that a market train should be run on Fridays from Holyhead to Bangor as an experiment and also that a second and third class carriage should be attached to the afternoon goods train for the local accommodation of the line between Chester and Bangor'. Such niceties of timetable discussion could be extensive. On Sundays only the mail trains ran on Anglesey, but with a Parliamentary carriage attached since the mails catered only for first and second class.

From August 1851 through booking arrangements for passengers were introduced in co-operation with thirteen railway companies in England and Ireland. These were further extended on 1 September and again on 1 October when a faster train service was introduced, with the length of the stops at Chester and Crewe substantially reduced. From 1 February 1852 second class accommodation was provided in the express trains.[5] By 1853 there were nine trains each way on weekdays with the first up and last down having Parliamentary carriages attached on Angelsey, and four each way on Sundays. Through booking then extended to fifteen companies and eighty-three 'foreign' stations. In December 1853, during the squabble with the CDSPC, through booking was withdrawn from that company's steamers and the CHR even went so far as not to mention the mail steamer timings in the timetables. Though this resulted in an increase of passengers by the CHR boats they were, however, mostly of the poorer classes, Irish labourers and 'harvestmen'. Receipts in fact dropped and through booking was resumed for the CDPSC boats on 1 January 1855.[6]

Notices were printed and distributed in Ireland to attract labourers over to the English harvest. Wearing a black glazed hat with the words CHESTER & HOLYHEAD RAILWAY around it in bright yellow, an Irish-speaking porter attended the arrival of the harvestmen's trains at the Dublin station of the Midland Great Western Railway. The CHR traffic committee minute of 27 July 1854, which authorised the appointment, added as an after-thought that the gangers of each party of harvestmen should be instructed 'how to distinguish this man from the Touters of the City of Dublin Company'. The harvestmen were a rough lot: on an evening in September 1857, on the way home, with nothing to lose, and presumably truculent with liquor, large numbers of them arrived at Holyhead to find that their boat, the goods vessel, had sailed. They then took forcible possession of the express vessel after assaulting several of Captain Hirste's men and attacking his house. The ringleaders appeared before the magistrates who asked that in future harvestmen only be sent to Holyhead when a boat was ready. To this Binger replied that they had come from all quarters and that he had to send them on to prevent similar trouble at Chester.

Between 1855 and 1860 the timetables broadly showed a summer service of ten trains each way, including the mails and expresses, and eight in winter, with four each way on Sundays throughout the year. There were still no local Anglesey trains on Sundays, and the first up mail, leaving Holyhead at the unearthly hour of 2am, had Parliamentary carriages attached. On market days on Anglesey fourth class carriages were attached to the up morning and evening stopping trains from Holyhead and the down morning and evening stopping trains from Bangor. (It is not clear, however, in what way these carriages differed from the Parliamentary ones.) For Irish traffic, return tickets, available for 14 days, were issued at fare and a half. From June 1855 a new east-west mail service was commenced, connecting with the night Irish Mail trains at Crewe. Known as 'The Bangor Mail', this left Normanton in Yorkshire, where connection was made with mail trains to and from the north, at about 10.30pm (the timings varied through the years) and, running by way of Huddersfield and Stockport, met the down Irish Mail at Crewe at about 1am. In the reverse direction the evening mail from Holyhead connected at Crewe at about midnight with the 'Bangor Mail' which reached Normanton at about 2.45am. The last leg, between Huddersfield and Normanton, was over the metals of the Lancashire & Yorkshire Railway and was worked by that company's engines.

### ADDITIONAL STATIONS

Early stations, additional to those opened concurrent with the line on Anglesey were Ty Croes, first in *Bradshaw* in November 1848; Gaerwen, January 1849; and Valley and Bodorgan, both October 1849. There was an appeal for a station at Llangaffo on Angelsey but it came to nothing. More mainland stations came into use as follows: Bagilt (sic), first in *Bradshaw* in January 1849; Colwyn, October 1849; and Penmaenmaur (sic), November 1849. The current spelling of Bagillt and Penmaenmawr was adopted in the timetables in the early 1860s. Both stations must at first have been sparse affairs, for they were considerably rebuilt later: Penmaenmawr in 1865, 1868-9, and 1877; and Bagillt resited in 1871, with the old station being converted into two cottages. Gaerwen station was enlarged in 1871-2. The first Llandudno Junction station was planned as an interchange for passengers on the branch line as early as June 1858 but in September it was agreed that the branch trains should run into Conway station. Though this in fact happened, times for Llandudno Junction appear in the LNWR timetable for November 1858. Details of the branch and the junction station are given in volume 2. Llanfairfechan station was opened in May 1860, and Llandulas on 1 August 1862 (renamed Llysfaen in 1889 when a new station for Llandulas was opened about a mile nearer Chester).

In October 1852 it was decided to enlarge Bangor station which, as originally constructed, had a platform length of 260ft, occupying nearly all the space between the Bangor and

Bangor station 1848

Belmont tunnels.[7] Mr A. Lockwood's tender for £3,711 was accepted for the building works, and Mr Millar's of £746 for excavations. The station layout and working was described in a Board of Trade report on an accident which occurred on 17 September 1856. The practice at that time was for the two platform loop lines to be used for through running while the two centre lines were used for wagon storage. Perhaps because it was the original intention to run fast trains on the centre lines, the points were weighted so as to be open to the latter. As today, the points leading to the down platform were near the Bangor tunnel mouth. The arrangement was that all down trains whistled in the tunnel so that the points were held open for the platform line. The inevitable happened. On the day in question policeman Myddleton, on duty at the tunnel mouth, so far forget himself that having lowered the signal he omitted to turn the points and allowed the night mail from London to plough into the wagons. Having watched this spectacular arrival, during which a Post Office inspector, a mail guard, and four passengers were injured, he immediately absconded 'and has not been heard of since'. The inspecting officer was critical of the whole business and reiterated the widely-held fears concerning facing points in general. In 1857 Binger stated that after 31 May the running of the express through Bangor station would be attended with difficulty, as the main line had hitherto been used as a siding. He was instructed to warn the engine drivers to shut off steam on approaching and 'to take such precautions as experience may suggest'.[8] Three years later another accident occurred, this time in Bangor tunnel. On 15 October 1859 the royal train carrying the Queen arrived at Bangor up platform from Holyhead where the ss *Great Eastern* had been drawing large crowds (chapter 9). At Bangor the Queen's train delayed eight excursion and local trains and it was during the subsequent despatch of these, at intervals of ten minutes, that one of the excursions ground to a halt in the tunnel and was run into by the next. The collision was light and no vehicles were derailed. The tunnel, which was wet and full of smoke, was not protected by the electric telegraph, an omission which was rectified shortly after. Indeed, the general manager of the LNWR informed the Board of Trade that the telegraph was to be installed forthwith on the other tunnels on the CHR but as will be seen, these works were considerably delayed. Further improvements at Bangor in the period up to 1880 included a booking office on the down platform in 1869, extensions to the warehouse, booking offices, and waiting rooms, together with new track work, in 1876, and new refreshment rooms in 1878.

If operating at Bangor was questionable, that at Chester General was even more so. Some 480 yards to the west of the station, on the southerly arm of the triangle formed by the CHR with the Birkenhead line, there was a ticket platform for incoming trains. The joint goods station was immediately to the north of the station train shed, and between these there were two lines of rails used for the through goods trains. The track layout necessitated wrong line working for down goods trains as far as points immediately to the east end of the ticket platform. On 23 June 1855 a Great Western passenger train from Birmingham arrived at the ticket platform where, as was the practice, the engine was uncoupled and run round its train for the purpose of pushing it into the station. In the meantime a down goods train passed along the up passenger line and was just clearing the points in front of the ticket platform when the Great Western engine was backing onto its train. It did so 'with a certain impetus', and forced the rear two carriages into collision with the passing goods. One woman was injured. The pushing of trains from the ticket platform was, said Captain Tyler of the Board of Trade, an arrangement agreed upon by the joint station committee in August 1848. He roundly condemned the working at the station and appealed particularly for the operating procedure for goods trains to be altered.

Perhaps Captain Tyler was not informed of the other gyrations performed by Great Western engines at Chester. If not he was enlightened in October 1858 when the second accident involving locomotive movements in the vicinity of the station took place. After having pushed their trains into the station the Great Western engines then proceeded to about-face by the expedient of using the triangle, an operation rendered necessary by the turntable being just 2in too short. On the evening of 16 October a GWR engine was turning on the triangle when it was run into by a down passenger train for Bangor, the driver of which was 'in liquor', had started from the station without authority, and was running through all the signals. Once again Captain Tyler called for alteration to the working.

To return to the early stations: Colwyn was quite small, with only one room for the station 'agent'; and Lee was ordered to enlarge it in November 1857. In October 1856 Lord Chandos complained of the state of the furniture at Conway station, which had not been renewed, he said, since 1848 (did they, one wonders, renew things more rapidly at Euston?), and of smoking at the station by touters from the local inns. The original platforms at Conway were widened in 1857. On 20 November 1858 the station was severely damaged by fire, all the upstairs rooms being destroyed; repairs to and enlargement of the station, and additional works and sidings west of the tunnel, were carried out by 1861. The platforms were extended to the tunnel end in 1875.

In May 1864 Lee reported that the wooden station at Llanfair, which according to the company's minutes was never intended to be other than temporary, was decayed and in need of repair. He recommended that a permanent building be erected in brick or stone, but in the following month was instructed to keep the existing structure in order. On 13 November 1865, however, it caught fire. Neele relates that 'the first Llanfair was a rickety structure, the worst on the CHR, and when news came one night that it was on fire the engineer, Hedworth Lee, merely said "Let it burn!"'. On 18 January 1866 the tender of John Thomas of Bangor was accepted for a new station at a price of £2,200. Neele considered that most of the early CHR stations were too small. 'The platforms all too short for the work. The booking offices small, and the booking windows so insignificant in size, and so low that passengers had to bend down to ask for tickets from a clerk it was impossible for them to see.'

Generally, platforms were too low as well as too short. In the mid 1850s a Mrs McIntosh stepped off a train which had stopped at a CHR station in the confident assumption that she would find a platform beneath her feet. She was both disappointed and hurt and was eventually awarded damages of £450. No improvement to the platforms was seen, however, until the CHR came under Euston's control. In the 1860s the LNWR commenced raising the platforms at nearly all the stations, thus improving passenger safety. The standard LNWR platform height was fixed in 1860 at 20in from the surface of the rails, proposed to be altered to 3ft in 1867, but was finally agreed to be 21in in 1868, except for terminal stations where 3ft was adopted. These measurements were again confirmed in November 1879.[9]

In June 1864 plans were prepared for a new station, at Connah's Quay. No further action was taken until 1867, however, when land for the station had to be purchased from the Wrexham Mold & Connah's Quay Railway whose line passed under the CHR at that point. An agreement between the two companies as to the land was coupled with provisions respecting the WM & CQ's junction at the site with the CHR. Messrs Thomas & Sons of Bangor were given the contract for construction of the station, in February 1869, at a price of £1,540. The station was opened on 1 September 1870. In 1878 work started on the enlargement of the station at Rhyl, the contractor being J. R. Jones of Rhyl and the price £8,174, some £3,000 under the engineer's estimate. In the same year improvements were carried out at Holywell station. Stations opened after 1880, and further works, are dealt with in volume 2.

### BRITANNIA HOTEL, PARK, AND STATION

In chapter 7 mention was made of Morton Peto's interest in the Crystal Palace and Great Exhibition of 1851. With the exhibition finances in a bad way, and the guarantee fund to cover costs unable to get off the ground, it was Peto who saved the whole project from foundering when in July 1850 he personally started the fund by guaranteeing £50,000. At the same time he successfully recommended that Joseph (later Sir Joseph) Paxton's revolutionary design be adopted in preference to a hybrid effort proposed by the official building committee. Thus were the two men drawn together, and in the following month Paxton returned the favour by taking up a typical Peto scheme. The latter had, in his other undertakings, dabbled in hotels; when CHR chairman he did so again. There were 26 acres of spare land at Gorphwysfa, and 90 acres between the Britannia and Menai bridges. Paxton, together with Charles Reed, a Liverpool architect, was invited to suggest a design for an hotel and 25 acre park on the latter site. Another Peto scheme at this time was for the building of lodging houses on $7\frac{1}{2}$ acres of land near Abergele, where, according to Lee, 'the beach is very much better than that of Rhyl for bathing and is always preferred by visitors'.

By October 1850 agreement had been reached with the Commissioners of Woods and Forests for an approach road to the park and hotel over crown lands along the shore under the Menai Suspension Bridge. By January 1851 Reed had produced plans and elevations of a 300-bed hotel overlooking the Straits on the north side of the approach curve to the Britannia Bridge. Two wings, to be built later, were to provide a further 200 beds. Possibly because many German tourists came yearly to Bangor, only to find the hotels there fully booked, the 'Britannia Hotel' was to be based on continental models: the Three Kings at Basle, the Grant at Coblenz, and the Lamb at Vienna. The company's land not required for the park was to be sold off as building sites and it was hoped that a small township would spring up. To serve the development a new station, called the 'Junction Station' was to be erected; the new Caernarvon branch (volume 2) was to join the main line opposite the hotel. By April 1851 there was an offer to run a refreshment room on the station, by then known as 'Britannia Bridge'.

In May 1851 the contractors on the Caernarvon branch agreed rates for carriage of brick and stone to the hotel site. The local press noted that 'the works for the Monster Hotel . . . are in full operation. Several scores of labourers are employed in levelling the ground and others are occupied in forming the foundations. We are given to understand that no time will be lost in completing this stupendous adjunct to the Chester and Holyhead and the Bangor and Carnarvon Railways'.[10] In June work started on laying out Britannia Park, to Paxton's supervision, and July 1851 saw the first appearance in *Bradshaw* of Britannia Bridge station. By September 1851, however, financial difficulties had led to suspension of the hotel works. The CHR half-yearly meeting in March 1852 was informed that the directors were prepared to assist parties who might undertake to build the hotel. In the following month the board agreed that such inducements would include a 99-year lease of 25 acres for the hotel and park at a peppercorn rent; a commission for a similar period of 25 per cent on fares of passengers conveyed on the CHR to or from the hotel, to make with the hotel profits a return of 7 per cent on construction costs not exceeding £126,000; and an undertaking on the railway's part to make and maintain a station adjoining the hotel. There were no takers, and in August 1853 there was talk of Brassey joining with Peto (to whom by now the deeds of the park were pledged) to erect the hotel privately, with the same perquisites on passenger fares, but again nothing was achieved. Two years later it was decided that encouragement should be given by means of free tickets to private developers willing to erect 'villas' on the park site. In August 1856 orders were given for the sale of the Gorphwysfa lands; it was not until April 1861, however, that this took place at a price of £7,000.

Meanwhile, with proposed private development of Britannia Park, the need again arose for a separate entrance under the suspension bridge—the agreed road of 1850 had not been made—but the company was informed that it must now make a fresh application. At the same time—late 1857—plans were prepared for a new station at Menai Bridge to serve the development, and it was agreed that, when opened, the existing stations of Britannia Bridge, and Treborth on the Caernarvon branch, might be closed. (In fact Treborth remained open.) Adjoining the new Menai Bridge station there was to be an hotel, considerably smaller than the original proposal, leaving the remainder of the park area for development. The LNWR Chester & Holyhead committee approved plans of the station in March 1858, to be constructed at the sole expense of the CHR company, and on the following 1 October, Menai Bridge station was opened at the junction with the Caernarvon branch. At the same time Britannia Bridge station was closed. Little is known of the latter; it was situated $2\frac{1}{4}$ miles from Bangor station, which puts it near the Britannia Bridge on the Caernarvon shore. In an engraving published in the *Illustrated London News* on 23 March 1850, showing Stephenson driving the last rivet on the bridge, there is what appears to be a small station visible beyond the tube. This might have been in use by the contractors at the railhead and thereafter have become the passenger station, in lieu of a new structure, though there is no evidence to substantiate this.

In February 1858 the Menai Suspension Bridge entrance was approved by the Office of Works and instructions were given for its immediate construction. By the following November plans for a railway hotel at the station gave place to those of an intending private company for resurrection of the original 1850 proposal. Plans and a prospectus were submitted to the CHR board in December 1858 but, with the pending amalgamation with the LNWR, the subject was deferred. When negotiations with Euston broke down, and for a short time it seemed that the CHR might 'go it alone', Parliamentary powers were sought by the CHR to subscribe to the hotel development but eventual success of the negotiations resulted in final abandonment of railway interest in the scheme. In August 1865 another private company came forward, but failed to proceed. It was then briefly suggested that Britannia Park should become the home of the proposed North Wales University College, but it was eventually sold to a private individual for £10,500 in September 1868.

By 1857 Abergele was the scene of considerable housing development, and house tickets were issued by the CHR to intending developers. At this time Peto became involved in another hotel scheme. In November he and the chairman of the Birkenhead Railway sat on a committee to consider construction of an hotel at Rhyl. Despite LNWR remonstrances that the CHR was acting outside its powers, the company took fifty shares in the hotel scheme and Peto and the CHR secretary were elected to the new company's board. One of the promoters' advertised privileges for their patrons, as given in the prospectus, was that of a 'branch railway' from the CHR right up to the hotel. The railway press was frankly incredulous: when the CHR was on its beam ends, how could it afford such a thing? 'There's life in the old dog yet!', said a correspondent in the *Railway Times*. The CHR board minutes are silent as to later developments concerning the hotel and it is not clear whether this private venture went ahead.

### FREIGHT TRAFFIC AND FACILITIES

In January 1848 W. M. Comber, the CHR goods manager, reported that all the goods stations were incomplete and badly designed. Despite this flat assertion of incompetence on somebody's part, the first goods trains ran daily from 1 June 1848, leaving Bangor at 10am and Chester at 2pm, each with a journey time of about 4½ hours. In September 1848 Braithwaite Poole, the LNWR's goods manager, wrote asking Moorsom if North Wales merchandise could now be diverted to the CHR direct. Up to that time goods were sent to Liverpool and thence by sea to the North Wales coast. His suggestion was accepted. In the following month a goods wagon was attached twice-weekly to the Anglesey local train. An all-out effort was then made to build up the goods traffic. During 1849–50 sidings for coal and cattle at Aber and Bangor, and for coal at Conway, were put in, together with sidings to industrial works at Abergele, Penmaenmawr, and the Llysfaen limeworks. Much of the coal traffic came off the Mold branch (volume 2) and the collieries of the Malltraeth Vale on Anglesey also prospered from the opening of the freight service.[11]

Freight traffic increased sufficiently during the first year to necessitate engine turntables being installed at Mostyn and Rhyl in mid 1849, thus enabling the service to be increased to two goods trains daily in each direction. In April 1849 Comber and Poole reported that nearly all goods from Manchester to North Wales still came by canal to Liverpool and thence by sea to Flint, Mostyn, Conway, Bangor, and Caernarvon. Three carriers operated from Caernarvon to Portmadoc; from Conway a carrier went to Llanrwst; and at Rhyl, Eli Lewis was operating thrice-weekly to Denbigh. Liverpool traffic was considered to be almost untapped, the CHR being virtually unknown in that city. The two officers therefore suggested a joint venture with the S & C and Birkenhead companies:

> We would advise a comprehensive scheme adopted—to wit—The Baths on George's Pier (Liverpool), rented from the Corporation and converted into a general station; i.e. Booking Offices and Reception Rooms for Passengers and Goods. The scheme is perfectly feasible and practicable . . .[12]

This was not carried out, but the CHR did appoint a canvassing agent for the city, and open an inquiry office, first in James Street and from 1853 in High Street.[13] These presumably achieved some success, for by 1855 there were severe delays in working the goods traffic via Birkenhead and the LNWR reluctantly agreed that it should go via Warrington over the Birkenhead Lancashire & Cheshire Junction Railway, a route which incidentally permitted through transport without the necessity for transhipment at Birkenhead. Braithwaite Poole, the Northern Western officer in charge of developing the CHR freight traffic adopted a cautious approach. Sometimes this delayed potentially lucrative traffic agreements, to the annoyance of the CHR directors, who complained bitterly to Euston. In 1851, for instance, Muspratt's at Flint could not agree rates with Poole who wished to take all the firm's traffic but was unable to give a firm date for when he could arrange it. In the meantime all the traffic went by sea. Similarly, Poole had delayed an agreement for the carriage of stone setts from Conway because he was concerned over the recipient's inability to pay for a siding at the other end. Nevertheless, the freight traffic steadily increased. In April 1851 Peto inspected the goods facilities and ordered further works. Valley, Ty Croes, Bodorgan, Colwyn, and Bagillt were each to have sidings, and a goods shed, platform, and crane; Bodorgan and Llanfair were to have coal yards. Additional sidings were to be laid: to Admiral Dundas' siding at Queensferry; at Mold Junction; to Eyton's brick and tile works; and at many of the smaller stations. These works were mostly completed by March 1852 In November 1851 orders were given for a wharf and sidings at Conway Quay for slate and fish traffic and these were brought into use in December 1852.

Sidings went in at Talysarn, near Conway, in 1856; at Pendyffryn, $1\frac{1}{2}$ miles east of Penmaenmawr, in 1857–8, the same time as those at Llanarch-y-Mor, midway between Holywell and Mostyn; and to the Bychton Colliery near Mostyn, and to Eyton's colliery near Holywell, in 1859. In May 1860 Messrs Raynes Lupton & Co received permission to make an incline over the railway from their rocks on to land on the seaward side of the line at Penmaenrhos, so as to be able to supply stone to the company. In 1861 a siding was made to Sir Stephen Glynne's colliery at Sandycroft, and in 1862–3 sidings at Rhyl and to the Queensferry Alkali Co. In the latter year over £2,000 was expended on sidings at Llandudno Junction, presumably for interchange of traffic with the Conway Valley line and the Llandudno branch. Similarly, interchange sidings were put in at Gaerwen for the Anglesey Central line in 1871, and at Menai Bridge for the Caernarvon branch in 1872. In 1868 sidings were made to the Flint Marsh

Colliery. A goods shed was ordered for Flint in 1860, Llanfairfechan in 1865, Queensferry in 1870, and Menai Bridge in 1878. That year saw sidings put in at Mold Junction for the Bedford Colliery and the Pontypool Iron and Tin Plate Co. In August 1880 orders were given for additional facilities at Menai Bridge so as to remove cattle traffic from Bangor, where it had started on 1 August 1848, at the west end of the station.

January of 1852 saw a new fish service, leaving Dublin at 7pm and arriving at Manchester at 6.30 the following morning. There were other more specialised consignments: a Mr Pritchard of Llanrwst had recently started the Caernarvon oyster trade, and by 1852 beds were being established at Porthfarog near Llanfair for providing the English market by rail, bringing £1,000 a year in receipts to the CHR.[14] Slate traffic reached such proportions that in 1852 eight acres of land at Saltney were purchased from Mr W. E. Gladstone (shortly to become Chancellor of the Excheqeur) for a large open area to hold 80,000 tons of slates. By 1853 upwards of 1,000 tons a week went by rail and the quarries were hard put to keep pace with the demand. That year 185,000 head of cattle were carried, 47,400 of which came from Ireland, and in 1854 general freight receipts were £500-£600 a week higher than in the previous year. The Crimean War, however, adversely affected all traffic, particularly the slate trade. By September 1855, with a general cut-back in building throughout the country, the slate depot was stacked with unwanted slates to a height of seven feet over four acres.[15]

Total traffic receipts climbed from £57,481 for the half-year ending June 1850 to £114,750 seven years later. The period ending June 1858, however, saw a drop to £110,176, largely due to stagnation in trade and a consequent decline in mineral traffic. The steamer account was mostly in the red to varying degrees during the whole period. From 1856 it apparently moved into credit, but this was in fact due to a contribution from the LNWR.[16] The cattle traffic received a boost in May 1862 when the LNWR commenced a new service with the conveyance of some 250 head of cattle from Dublin to Manchester by special steamer and fast trains in just over twelve hours. This success, and the publicity it aroused, led to a like Liverpool service, with cattle shipped at Dublin reaching Edge Hill, Liverpool (where they were unloaded for the nearby market) in under twelve hours. Apparently the City of Dublin Steam Packet Company scorned such menial carryings; Neele remarks that its steamship officers, proudly taking the Royal Mail, always spoke of the railway vessels as 'pig boats'. But the swagger cloaked a jealous awareness that the North Western steamers were beginning to bring financial returns to their owners, that the cattle trade was a success, and that competition for the Irish passenger traffic was going to become more intense as time went by.

IRISH INTERLUDE 1860s TO 1880

After the introduction of the new Post Office timings of 1860 the LNWR did little to accelerate the Irish Mail service further, though in fairness Neele says that in 1863 the Irish Mail was the fastest train out of Euston. By 1875, for instance, there had been only minor improvements of some five or ten minutes over the whole journey between Euston and Holyhead, about $6\frac{1}{2}$ hours. The main traffic improvements were made in the express, a distinct from the mail, service, for between 1870 and 1880 the LNWR opened a new route to Greenore and improved the existing one to North Wall, Dublin.

It was, however, at Belfast that the company next aimed (map p 265). In 1863 the Dundalk & Greenore Railway had been incorporated to construct an 18 mile line from the Irish North Western Railway at Dundalk to Carlingford on Lough Carlingford, north-west of Greenore harbour on the east coast of Ireland. There it was to make a junction with the Newry & Greenore Railway, likewise incorporated in 1863, and there was to be a joint railway of the two companies to Greenore. By the LNWR (Traffic Arrangements) Act of 14 July

1864 (27–28 Vic cap cxciv) Euston made a determined bid for increased traffic from Ireland. The Act facilitated transmission and interchange of traffic between the LNWR and Irish North Western, Dundalk & Greenore, Newry & Greenore, Newry & Armagh, the Ulster, the Dublin & Belfast Junction, and the Dublin & Drogheda Railways, and also with the CDSPC and the Dundalk Steam Packet Company, and all the foregoing companies, as to sea traffic between Dublin, Kingstown, Dundalk, Greenore, Carlingford Bay, and the ports of Liverpool and Holyhead.

By the Dundalk & Greenore Railway Act of 1867 the LNWR contributed to that undertaking to the extent of £130,000, and undertook to work the line. Next there came a link with Holyhead. The LNWR (Steam Vessels) Act of 14 July 1870 (33-34 Vic cap cxix empowered the company to work steamships between Holyhead and Greenore, and on Lough Carlingford. The Act scheduled an agreement dated 1 July 1869 between the LNWR, the Irish North Western, and the Dundalk & Greenore, as to rail and steamship operations, including through booking, and an undertaking from Euston to work, as soon as the D & G was open, a service of daily sailings, except Sundays, between Greenore and Holyhead. The Act provided for the steamship powers to run until 31 December 1885, and also extended the existing steamship powers at Holyhead to the same date. At a meeting of the LNWR company in May 1870 at which the proprietors approved application for the steamship powers of that session, Moon stated 'it is necessary that traffic should be brought to the Chester and Holyhead otherwise it would not pay'. In the same session of 1870 the LNWR was empowered to join with the Lancashire & Yorkshire Railway in the latter's existing steamship service between Fleetwood and Belfast, so that Euston's approach to the northern Irish city was now two-pronged.

Meanwhile, with Moon as chairman and the LNWR's engineer in charge of construction, work on the Dundalk & Greenore Railway went ahead. On 21 March 1873 two

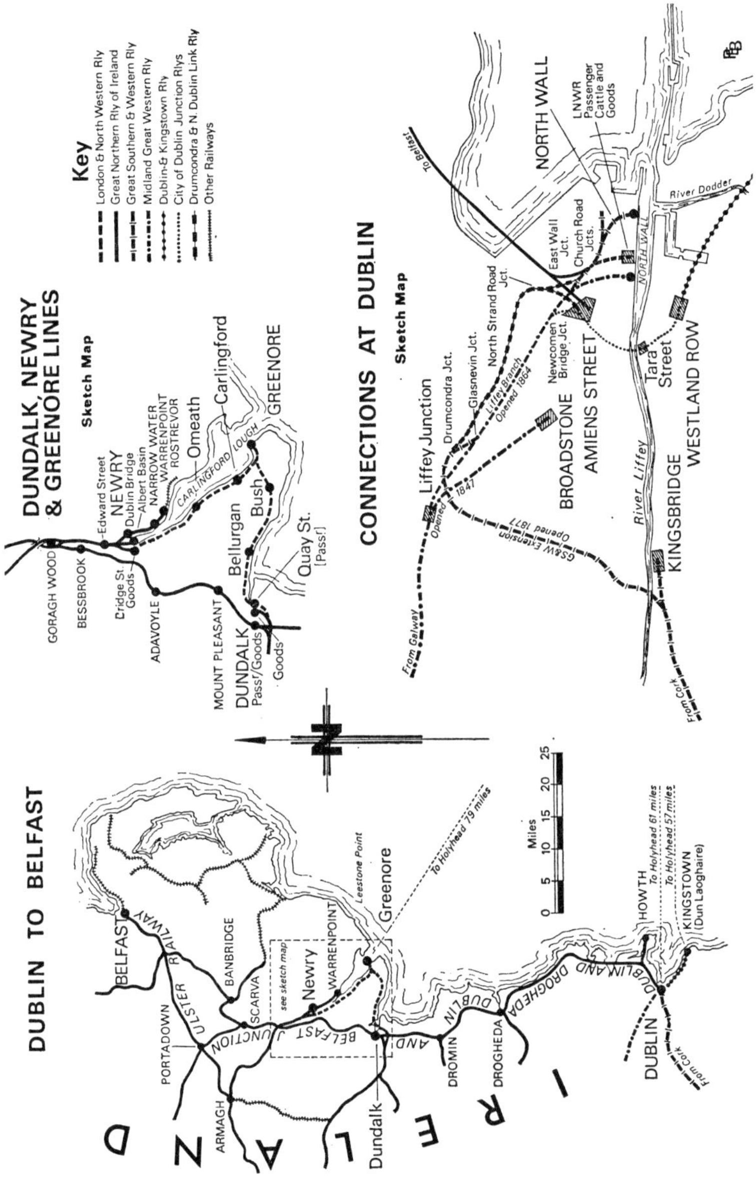

DUBLIN TO BELFAST
DUNDALK, NEWRY & GREENORE LINES
Sketch Map
CONNECTIONS AT DUBLIN
Sketch Map
Key
London & North Western Rly
Great Northern Rly of Ireland
Great Southern & Western Rly
Midland Great Western Rly
Dublin & Kingstown Rly
City of Dublin Junction Rlys
Drumcondra & N. Dublin Link Rly
Other Railways
IRELAND
BELFAST
ULSTER RAILWAY
BANBRIDGE
PORTADOWN
SCARVA
ARMAGH
see sketch map
Newry
WARRENPOINT
Leestone Point
Greenore
To Holyhead 79 miles
BELFAST JUNCTION
Dundalk
DUBLIN AND DROGHEDA
DROMIN
DROGHEDA
HOWTH
KINGSTOWN
(Dun Laoghaire)
To Holyhead 61 miles
To Holyhead 57 miles
DUBLIN
From Cork
Miles
0 5 10 15 20 25
GORAGH WOOD
BESSBROOK
Bridge St. Goods
ADAVOYLE
MOUNT PLEASANT
DUNDALK Pass/Goods
Goods
Edward Street
NEWRY
Dublin Bridge
Albert Basin
NARROW WATER
WARRENPOINT
ROSTREVOR
Omeath
Carlingford
CARLINGFORD LOUGH
GREENORE
Bellurgan
Bush
Quay St. [Pass]
From Galway
Liffey Junction
Opened 1847
Drumcondra Jct.
Glasnevin Jct.
Liffey Branch Opened 1864
North Strand Road Jct.
East Wall Jct.
Church Road Jcts.
NORTH WALL
LNWR Passenger Cattle and Goods
To Belfast
Newcomen Bridge Jct.
BROADSTONE
AMIENS STREET
GS&W Extension Opened 1877
River Liffey
Tara Street
WESTLAND ROW
KINGSBRIDGE
NORTH WALL
River Dodder
From Cork

Irish gauge tank engines were sent from Crewe to Greenore, the LNWR also supplying the rolling stock.[17] The line was inspected by Colonel Rich of the Board of Trade on 27 March and in April crews were selected for the two steamers which were to operate the Holyhead—Greenore service. The D & G was opened by the Lord Lieutenant of Ireland on 1 May 1873, from which date fixed-time sailings from Holyhead were introduced. The train and steamer times were: Euston dep 5.10pm, Holyhead arr 12.45am, dep 1.15, Greenore arr 6.50, dep 7.15, Dundalk arr 8am and Belfast arr 11am. The return journey left Belfast at 4.50pm, Dundalk 6.55, Greenore 7.30, Holyhead arr 1.55am, dep 2.15, and Euston arr 9.50am. By the LNWR (England & Ireland) Act of 30 July 1875 (37–38 Vic cap clix) further traffic and other arrangements were confirmed between the LNWR, the Irish North Western, and the Dundalk Newry & Greenore. This last company was the successor to the Dundalk & Greenore, which had absorbed the Newry & Greenore by Act of 1873. This Act authorised construction of a 13 mile line from Newry along the south side of Lough Carlingford to Greenore Point in lieu of that of the N & G Act of 1863. For this purpose the LNWR might subscribe £195,000 towards the works. Construction started early in 1874, there being a change of contractor due to poor workmanship in October of that year. The LNWR again supplied locomotives and rolling stock. The line was first inspected by Colonel Hutchinson of the Board of Trade on 21 July 1876, was opened for passenger traffic on 1 August, and was re-inspected on 5 September.

There is disagreement concerning the steamers first allocated to the Greenore service, in May 1873. Neele, who should have known, states that they were the LNWR's *Eleanor*, *Isabella*, and *Earl Spencer*, but in fact none of these vessels was completed by that date. On 9 May 1873 Captain Dent, the LNWR's marine superintendent, reported that 'the steamers *Edith* and *Countess of Erne* have made regular daily service between Holyhead and Greenore since 1st instant . . .'[18] From the same date the LNWR's steamer *Dodder* (an unfortunate name for a ship, but that of a tributary of the River Liffey at Dublin) commenced working a service between Greenore and Warrenpoint, on the north side of Lough Carlingford, where there was a railhead to Newry.

The *Eleanor* arrived at Holyhead from her builders on 26 August 1873. Presumably she went straight to the Greenore run, but in any event she ended her days on it, being wrecked on Leestone Point, County Down, in thick fog on 27 January 1881. That the *Countess of Erne* was still at Greenore in July 1873 is borne out by her running into and sinking the *Dodder* there that month. The *Dodder* was raised and returned to service in September 1874, and was replaced by the LNWR steamer *Mersey* on the Lough Carlingford service on 1 June 1880. On 15 September 1874 another new steamer, *Earl Spencer*, arrived at Holyhead from Liverpool, Captain Dent noting on 2 October that he hoped 'to put her on the Greenore service this week'.[19] On 8 September 1875 the *Edith*, working the Greenore run, collided with the company's *Duchess of Sutherland* off Holyhead and sank. During protracted attempts to raise her, the CDSPC's vessel *St Patrick*, outward bound with the mails to Kingstown, collided with the buoyancy tanks, on 29 October 1876. As there was no other CDSPC vessel available at Holyhead, a North Western steamer, *Shamrock* (see below), took the mails instead. The *Edith*, which incidentally cost £26,500 to build, was raised in December 1877 at the exorbitant cost of £33,000, and was returned to service on 3 December 1878. Neele's third supposed 1873 Greenore vessel, the *Isabella*, was launched at Laird's on 11 October 1877, arrived at Holyhead on 3 January 1878, and commenced running the regular night service to North Wall, not Greenore, on 23rd of that month.[20]

During the build-up of the Greenore route the LNWR had also been improving the North Wall service. There had for some time been a move afoot at Euston to encourage travel to America via Holyhead, Dublin, Cork, and Queenstown. Neele relates that in 1871 the timetables advertised the Chester—Holyhead line as being the 'Quick Route to America—One

Day saved', whereby the 8.25pm mail from Euston, and associated steamer service, connected across Dublin by road from North Wall with a special train from the Kingsbridge terminus of the Great Southern & Western Railway to Cork, and thence to Queenstown where called the North Atlantic liners.

Dredging of the Liffey at North Wall brought abandonment of the tidal service on 1 September 1873 when, as already at Greenore, fixed time sailings were introduced: Dublin North Wall dep 11am and 7pm, and Holyhead dep 1.30am and 5pm. The 7pm departure from North Wall was altered to 8pm in November and back to 7.30 in January 1874. The sea passage took about $5\frac{1}{2}$ hours. On 1 July 1876 a day express service was established between London and Dublin. The 9am express from Euston connected with the 5.15pm steamer from Holyhead, due at the North Western quay at North Wall at 10pm. Return timings were North Wall dep 9.30am, Holyhead dep 3pm and arr Euston at 10.40pm. The service was started with the new Laird steamer *Shamrock*, joined within a month by her sister ship, *Rose*. There was no cattle traffic by these vessels.[21] The new timings were superior to those provided by the mail boats to Kingstown, whose fares were regulated by the sub-contract with the LNWR and were pegged to the old price. This, together with the recent introduction of third class accommodation on the express trains, but not on the Irish Mail, took passengers away from the mail route and led to an increase in bitter feelings between the railway and the packet company. They were made worse by increased LNWR competition in 1880 with two new Laird vessels, *Lily* and *Violet*, sister ships to *Rose* and *Shamrock*, and built with hulls of Crewe steel. These two 1880 steamers were at Holyhead for the opening of the harbour (chapter 9) and on 24 June of that year, by arrangement with Watson of the CDSPC, *Violet* raced the mail packet *Ulster* out of Holyhead. After steaming one hour at 19 knots *Violet* gained three miles on her rival. On 1 July 1880 *Lily* and *Violet* were put on the North Wall run so that the LNWR now operated day and night express sailings

Page 269

*Aerial view of the railway harbour at Holyhead. Station at top left, Admiralty Pier in right foreground*

Page 270
CHR *paddle steamer* Cambria, *1848*

LNWR *paddle steamer* Eleanor, *1873*

OPERATING AND WAY & WORKS 1848-1880 271

in direct competition with similar services of the CDSPC.

The land connections at Dublin demand some explanation (map p 265). By Act of 1869 the Dublin & Drogheda Railway was authorised to make a branch, ¾ mile in length and to which the LNWR might subscribe, from its main line at Dublin to the LNWR at North Wall. In 1871 the Midland Great Western Railway secured powers for a 53 chain line from its Liffey branch to North Wall, and by Act of 1872 the Great Southern & Western was likewise authorised to construct a communication to North Wall. The 1872 Bill was promoted jointly with the LNWR, and was a repeat of an attempt deferred from 1871. It was violently opposed by parties interested in other Dublin schemes but received the Royal Assent on 25 July 1872. The LNWR subscribed £95,000 towards the GS & W works which consisted of four railways, connecting from near the Kingsbridge terminus, by a tunnel under Phoenix Park, with the Liffey branch of the MGW, the Dublin & Drogheda's North Wall extension line, and North Wall quay. The LNWR now had an interest in the GS & W and the D & D, and was entitled to vote at their meetings. Running powers as between the Irish companies were provided for in the 1872 Act as was the question of joint ownership of a portion of the line between their railways and that of the LNWR.

A new cattle landing was opened at North Wall in December 1875. The works on the connecting railways and the LNWR new station were pushed forward with vigour, and all were inspected for the first time by Colonel Rich of the Board of Trade on 1 March 1877. Meanwhile, the Dublin & Drogheda, the Dublin & Belfast Junction, the Irish North Western, and the Ulster Railways had successively amalgamated, ultimately to become the Great Northern Railway of Ireland, by Act of 1877. In August 1877 Colonel Rich again inspected the LNWR's North Wall station and the connecting Irish lines. The GNR (I) line from East Wall Junction to Church Road Junction and on to the LNWR North Wall line was opened on 1 September 1877, and the GS & W's extension line, also to

R

North Wall, on the following day.[22] According to Neele, however, the GS & W line came into use on 1 October, followed by the connection to the Liffey branch on 1 January 1878.[23] To complete the railways at Dublin as shown on the map, the line from Westland Row to Amiens Street and Newcomen Bridge Junction was authorised by Act of 1884, while that from Drumcondra Junction to the latter and to the GS & W's extension of 1872 was authorised ten years later.

### PERMANENT WAY AND WORKS 1850s TO 1880

The CHR track was first jointed with fish-plates experimentally between Saltney and Chester on licence from the Permanent Way Company in August 1855. The first general relaying took place in 1858–9, with 80lb to the yard rails, in preparation for the new mail service. On some parts of the line the new Bessemer steel-tipped rails were used, with the web and lower part of iron, notably on the approach curves to the Britannia Bridge (replaced by all-steel rails in 1869). Iron rails continued generally in use until 1876, however, when Webb was ordered henceforth to employ 84lb to the yard bull-headed steel rail on main lines and 75lb rail on the branches.[24] For many years the rail lengths were 30ft. By 1869 the condition of the CHR track was giving cause for concern, particularly on Anglesey where some seven miles, referred to as 'very much worn and thin', and 'rails much crushed', were still laid with old 75lb iron rails, 15ft in length. Despite remedial repairs the poor reports continued. In 1874 W. Smith the engineer at Bangor, who had succeeded Lee on the latter's death in 1873, was told to relay only where necessary. Even so, accidents directly attributable to permanent way were conspicuously few, perhaps because train speeds had not increased so much as might have been expected.

There were many improvements for safety during this period and several road overbridges and footbridges were substituted for level crossings. At Rhyl an overbridge was built concurrently with station improvements in 1863–4; at Mostyn an overbridge in 1865–6; at Prestatyn a footbridge in 1871; a road diversion and closure of George Earl level crossing on the Bangor Ferry Road in 1871; a road overbridge at Mold Junction in 1874; and a footbridge at Bagillt in 1875. In 1879–80 a bridge was erected for the slate traffic over the railway at Penmaenmawr, instead of the existing level crossing; and another such bridge at Penmaenbach was specifically authorised in the LNWR Act of 6 August 1880 (43–44 Vic cap cxlv).

Underbridges likewise received attention. During 1860–1 the timber viaducts at Flint and Bagillt were replaced by stone structures and in April 1862 Lee was instructed to cover with zinc such parts of the remaining wooden viaducts and bridges as was necessary to protect them from fire. The viaduct at Flint was replaced by an embankment during 1866-7; the wooden bridge over the River Llanfairfechan by an iron girder design in 1875–6; and perhaps most importantly, the Foryd Bridge was closed permanently to river traffic. For some years it had been a nuisance as regards maintenance, while the river traffic for which it was built had greatly declined. In March 1855 part of the machinery had failed and a new wrought iron bridge, of considerably less weight than the first one, had been constructed during the winter of 1855–6. By the LNWR (Additional Powers) Act of 7 August 1862 (25–26 Vic cap ccviii) the sections of the CHR Act of 1845 which required an opening bridge over the river were repealed, though the bridge itself, with the raising gear, was not to be altered without prior approval from the Admiralty. The LNWR Act of 1880 repealed this last proviso, and work on rebuilding as a fixed structure commenced in October 1880.

Storm damage by the sea was frequent. On 9 January 1849 some 20ft of walling was brought down at the west end of Penmaenbach tunnel and 250yd of wall were damaged at Colwyn; the sea also came over the wall at Talacre and Mostyn, and between the Foryd and Abergele the water came 18in above the rails. In late September 1851 the sea flooded to a depth of 2ft over the rails between Mostyn and the Talacre sea embankment. In 1852 there were more storms, followed by a particularly severe one in February 1853. By 1855 the CHR had carried out a general strengthening of the sea defences, particularly the walls at Colwyn and Penmaenmawr and at Connahs Quay where the railway embankment was raised by 4ft for half a mile. In February 1858 the sea wall at Bagillt was extensively damaged and both there and at Flint the walls were raised.

A storm in November 1859 was so severe that the engine fires were extinguished by the waves. At Penmaenmawr the side walls were broken down and the embankment washed out from under the timber covering at the tunnel, stopping all traffic. Joseph Locke inspected the damage and reported on 23 November. Immediate temporary repairs were made but new permanent and more substantial works were carried out by Lee to Locke's recommendation in August 1860. Nine years later a November gale swept the sea into the Rhuddlan Marsh at Foryd. The company argued with the Marsh Commissioners as to the latter's liability to keep their embankment, between the railway and the sea, in repair. The LNWR, meanwhile, strengthened the wall between Abergele station and the Foryd. On 20 November 1872 the sea wall between Penmaenmawr and Llanfairfechan failed again, and repair works were carried out with the aid of an engine adapted especially for the purpose with a 4 ton crane; the works were apparently still in progress in 1875, and a further expenditure on the wall of £55,000 was authorised in 1879.[25] The Rhuddlan Marsh embankment failed yet again on 30 January 1877, stopping all traffic. So as to protect their line the company took powers by the LNWR Act of 1880 to maintain the Rhuddlan Marsh embankment, and the existing trustees for the works, originally authorised some eighty years earlier, were relieved of their liability.

Undoubtedly the most catastrophic of the storms which lashed the railway was that which swept the North Wales coast on 17 August 1879 for, weakened by the floods of water, the Llandulas viaduct collapsed. Neele tells of what followed:

The principal breach was between Abergele and Llandulas; the stone viaduct over the usually trifling watercourse called the Dulas, having been undermined by the floods, and washed away by a raging torrent. For two days the flood remained so high that nothing could be done towards repairing the line at this place. I came down to the spot early on Monday, 18th, and went over the ground with Mr. Wood, who had made some temporary arrangements for carrying on the traffic by road; but it became necessary to largely improve the coach service between the two points of Colwyn and Abergele. The mails formed a difficulty, as they required more rapid transit than the heavy transfer of tourist passengers' luggage entailed, but the Post Office authorities had on the ground a Mr. Neville—an old guard and a skilled inspector—whose aid was invaluable ...

The breach took place on the 17th, and on the 25th, I was able to write to the papers announcing that the traffic ... was again resumed, and trains were running as usual.

Neele relates that he was on the spot all day on the 25th, and that the 3pm train from Holyhead was the first to pass over:

The line was carried across the Dulas on a temporary viaduct, sloped down from the main line, at a grade of 1 in 23; and the traffic was conducted over this single line, until the completion of the new viaduct. It was decided to replace the viaduct by one of steel, with seven spans, and its construction is one of Mr. Webb's most notable performances at Crewe Works. The viaduct is 224 feet long, the seven spans being 32 feet each; the crude pig iron for the work was converted into Steel, and the girders, 14 lattice and 28 plate, with the transverse portions, flooring plates, angle irons and all other parts, were ready at Crewe for erection within one week! Mr. Footner's men were employed night and day with the masonry of the eight piers, and the electric light was, for the first time, employed, to enable the night work to be carried out.

The new viaduct was brought into use on 14 September 1879[26], and on 3 October the LNWR locomotive committee noted that 'they cordially approve of Mr. Webb's action in this matter.' During the disruption to traffic trains had run via Shrewsbury, Bala, Dolgelly, and Barmouth, to the LNWR's Afonwen-Menai Bridge line (volume 2). Though passenger traffic used the temporary structure, as Neele says, goods trains continued to run via the Cambrian Railways' line between Dolgelly and Afonwen until the new viaduct had been completed. In consideration for the use of their railway, the Cambrian received from Crewe duplicate tender engine No 1881[27], a Sharp, Stewart 0–6–0, valued at £1,125. This became No 18 on the Cambrian list. It was estimated that the disaster cost the LNWR traffic worth £40,000, and the cost of reconstruction amounted to £25,000.

Accidents discussed so far in this chapter were caused by one or other of the following: general inefficient and slack operating, signalmen's errors, and the dangers inherent in the time interval system. Other contributory factors to accidents yet to be discussed include lack of adequate refuge sidings; inadequate, inefficient or no signals; lack of interlocking; late shunting in front of fast trains; and the casual leaving of loose vehicles, either on the main line or in such positions that they could foul traffic on the main line. Such general faults were common in different degrees to all railway companies at this time but it does seem that the CHR, and later the LNWR, were more than usually prone to general carelessness, and more dilatory or parsimonious with improvements to safety even when the benefits from their introduction were plain to see.

## MENAI BRIDGE JUNCTION 1865–70

In view of this attitude it is ironic that when a rare determined effort was made to avoid a generally common cause of accidents—in this case that of facing points in main lines—the CHR produced an unusual layout which necessitated peculiar operating movements. Menai Bridge Junction was the venue, where the Caernarvon branch joined the main line.

In 1865 the branch was still single tracked. It joined the up main line by points about 200yd on the Bangor side of Menai Bridge station, with the signal box on the high ground above. The branch crossed over the down main line 95yd to the west of the box. Down trains for Caernarvon ran past the station on the down main line and then set back, through points 420yd from the junction box, into the branch platform. There were thus no facing points at the junction and apparently no communication between the signalman and pointsman, 420yd distant. The junction was described in a Board of Trade report on an accident which occurred on the evening of 9 May 1865 when the 8.31pm passenger train from Caernarvon to Bangor, composed of tank engine, four carriages and a van, started from Menai Bridge station without proper authority and struck a down Holyhead train, running under clear signals. Both locomotives suffered damage and 25 passengers were injured. Captain Tyler of the Board of Trade recommended alterations to the layout but it was not until 1870, when the points were concentrated, that a direct junction was made from the main line to the branch. At the same time an additional platform was built for the down Caernarvon trains, and the existing tunnel subway extended to it.

Lack of adequate refuge sidings led to some serious accidents. On 8 November 1855 a heavy, double-headed, cattle train arrived at Conway from Chester. The sidings being full, the drivers were ordered to shunt on to the up main line to make way for a down passenger train. While pulling forward to clear the crossover they noticed that six wagons and a van had broken loose and remained behind in the Conway tube. Shortly afterwards these vehicles were run into by the following passenger train. Three passengers and a guard were injured. Blame attached to the brakesman on the cattle train, who had not gone back sufficiently promptly to warn the passenger train. Nineteen years of age, and from a pool of inexperienced shunters at Chester, he was nevertheless given charge of a heavy train, on a line for which he did not know the regulations, and had not been provided with watch, timetable, or rule book. It turned out that the refuge siding at Conway was occupied by the 7.25 goods from Chester which itself had arrived at Conway 38 minutes late after detention at the Foryd Bridge at Rhyl. This train had been forced to leave three vehicles on the up line and the cattle train drivers had had to deal with these before moving their own train. Other aspects mentioned in the Board of Trade accident report included premiums paid for keeping to or making up lost time, and 17 or 18 hours worked frequently at a stretch by the enginemen.

Though some additional signalling was carried out, the company policy on refuge sidings is made clear by Binger's report to the traffic committee in January 1856 that an extra siding at Conway, at a cost of £1,000, as recommended by Captain Tyler, was not considered to be necessary. This attitude by the CHR was coupled with one concerning signalling, on which LNWR policy was admirably, if cold-bloodedly, summed up by Richard Moon at that company's half-yearly meeting as late as February 1867. Commenting on the fact that £54,000 had been paid out in accident compensation during 1866, he told the meeting that 'some people say we should have more signals and flags, but there is a strong impression on the minds of the board that the company is rather over-signalled, and the difficulty is to hit the happy medium. The more signals we have, the more they confuse our drivers and staff . . . we must expect accidents'. The matter was, he said, to be left to the discretion of the directors. Thus refuge sidings and signalling improvements were looked on in the one case as 'unnecessary' and in the other as 'confusing'. This extraordinary and disastrous state of affairs continued until a really serious accident resulted.

### THE ABERGELE ACCIDENT

The terrible happenings at Abergele in the early afternoon of Thursday 20 August 1886 shook the board at Euston to its foundations. On that morning a pick-up goods left Crewe for

Holyhead. At Saltney Wharf two wagons, containing 7¾ tons of paraffin oil in 50 casks, were attached to the rear of the train immediately in front of the guard's van. The train arrived at Abergele at 12.15, performed some shunting, and then left for Llandulas (later Llysfaen). It arrived there at 12.24pm with 26 empty and 17 loaded wagons, the last two of which contained the oil. At a distance of 43yd east of the down platform at Llandulas, trailing points on the down line led to the Llysfaen lime sidings on the down side. One siding was 950ft long and afforded 768ft of clear road for wagons, while a loop on its south side gave a further 300ft of standing space. The sidings were level and the outlet was guarded by a dead-end siding. The main line falls towards Abergele at a ruling gradient of 1 in 100.

When the goods arrived, there were some wagons already in the sidings, and there was not room for the whole train in either siding. By shunting, however, all the train could have been safely distributed clear of the main line. The down Irish Mail was due to pass at 12.39pm. There were, therefore, fifteen minutes during which the goods train should have been shunted. The company's rules clearly directed that 'goods trains, when likely to be overtaken by a passenger train, must be shunted at stations where there are fixed signals at least ten minutes before such passenger train is due'. The correct action would, therefore, have been for the goods to set back into the sidings in two stages. Instead, the station master at Llandulas, the two brakesmen of the goods, and the guard, elected to do things their way, with disastrous results.

The six rear wagons and the brake van were first uncoupled and left on the main line, standing on the down grade. The van brake was screwed on, but the wagon brakes were unsecured. The driver then pulled the rest of the train forward, clear of the lime siding points. Eight or ten wagons were then fly-shunted into the sidings while the station master held the points. Next, incredibly, since all present should have known better, a loaded timber wagon, with a 'check' wagon on either side, was fly-shunted on the main line towards the seven standing vehicles. While shunting a fourth lot of wagons into the sidings the engine driver noticed the timber wagon and two checks strike the standing vehicles and a moment later all ten were on the move down towards Abergele. It was proved later that the shock of impact had broken the cog wheel on the brake in the van. The runaways were chased by the senior brakesman, but as they were gaining on him, the driver decided to go after them with his engine. Before he could do so, however, the brakesman signalled him to stop. For, around a bend, out of sight but within hearing, the Irish Mail had collided with the runaways.

The mail had left Chester at 11.47am, four minutes late, having taken on four extra carriages at the front of the train. It consisted of engine, tender, guard's van, two first class, a composite, and a second class carriage (these being the Chester portion), and a Post Office van and tender, a luggage van, a first class, three composites, and a guard's van. The mail passed through Abergele at 12.39 at about 40mph. Just $1\frac{3}{4}$ miles beyond Abergele, driver Arthur Thompson spotted the runaways a short distance ahead, until that moment obscured by a cutting. While he shut off steam, his fireman, Joseph Holmes, applied the brakes. With 'For God's sake, Joe, jump; we can do no more!' Thompson dived from the footplate. Holmes, however, did not follow him. Thompson heard one cry from his colleague; on the impact the tender went right over the engine and must have killed him instantly. The engine, tender, guard's van and three front carriages were instantly enveloped in a fierce searing fire as the paraffin oil, with an ignition point of 137 degrees Fahrenheit, caught the engine coals and exploded into flames. There was later a horrid rumour that a woman and children had been seen alive in the front carriage but Colonel Rich of the Board of Trade, who conducted the inquiry was certain that passengers in the front part of the train must have died instantly. According to driver Thompson, not a single human sound was heard from the roaring flames.

The fourth carriage and the front of the Post Office van were next alight. Despite minor injuries Thompson, with the aid of willing helpers, managed to uncouple the rear vehicles,

The Abergele accident 1868

which were drawn away by an engine which fortunately had come forward from Abergele. The Post Office tender was also saved as were some of the mail bags. In the first half hour distraught survivors, including the Duchess of Abercorn and her suite, were helped by men from a lineside factory and the Llysfaen lime quarries to clamber through dense smoke from the rear of the train. They were taken back to Abergele. According to the *Illustrated London News* of 29 August 1868, the Marquis of Hamilton, a passenger in the rear of the train, was quick-wittedly responsible for stopping the up Irish Mail, shortly due to pass.

The scene immediately after the accident was vividly described and depicted by eye witnesses, some of whom had been on the beach nearby, and contemporary press accounts are full of detail. Of the thirty-three victims, only the remains of Lord and Lady Farnham were definitely identifiable, from their crested watches. In those days the Irish Mail was more often than not patronised by the aristocracy. Three doctors had the sickening task of attempting identification; they could only say that there were ten males, thirteen females, and ten of sex unknown. Diamond necklaces, tiaras, rings, and many precious stones of considerable value were found in the evil-smelling wreckage. Gangs worked frantically to clear the debris to allow traffic through, and that evening the up and down Irish Mails were able to pass through over the up line.

Colonel Rich fixed the blame for the accident on the improper shunting, when the passenger train was due, for which he held the station master responsible. He censured the senior brakesman for not sufficiently securing the wagons and for the dangerous business of fly-shunting. He criticised the timetable, by which two goods trains were due to start the climb from Abergele to Llandulas, one at 12.5pm and the other at 12.15, when the down mail was due on the same line at Abergele at about 12.34. Llysfaen sidings had not been inspected or approved at any time by the Board of Trade. They were, according to the colonel, quite unfitted for the work, sometimes containing 29 or 30 wagons at times when goods trains of up to 50 wagons might be required to shunt there. He called for a siding sufficiently long, and for the block telegraph to be installed between Abergele and Llandulas. The carriage of gunpowder and paraffin was examined, and it appeared that there were no particular regulations as to these dangerous cargoes. Also, some of the carriage doors on the wrecked train had been found locked, and this practice was condemned. Colonel Rich concluded by saying that the railway companies generally allowed many of the rules for safe working to be broken daily, and that the railway staff frequently looked after their own interests at the expense of their duties, particularly on stations. Trains were thus made late. 'Although the Abergele catastrophe could not have been averted by the train being in proper time . . . it might have been much less fatal in its results. The mail train would have been quietly standing by the (Llandulas) distant signal when the trucks ran down the incline, instead of rushing to meet them at 40 miles per hour. The trucks, also, would have been moving at far less speed, and the paraffin casks might not have been broken by the collision.'

On 11 September 1868 Richard Bore reported that first class carriages Nos 204 and 352, composite No 218, second class No 49, Post Office No 19 and brake van No 6 had been entirely destroyed in the accident at a replacement cost of £1,700. There appears to be no note in the minutes as to the ultimate fate of the engine, 'Lady of the Lake' class No 291, *Prince of Wales*, though according to *The Journal of the Stephenson Locomotive Society* for January 1955, it was in stock until 1906. On 15 October 1868 instructions were given to lengthen the Llysfaen sidings by 100yd, and to purchase a strip of land in Abergele churchyard for a private railed-off mass grave for the victims. Neele, whose account conflicts in detail with that of the Board of Trade, noted that 'At the close of the inquest, at which I was present, the brakesmen were brought in guilty of manslaughter, and fled to avoid apprehension; in somewhat doubtful taste the Company did not object to their flight'. Perhaps remembering his previous utterances on signalling and accidents, Richard Moon was severely shocked by the news of the Abergele disaster. At the half-yearly meeting, on the day after the accident, that seemingly unbending man was so overcome by emotion that he was forced to give place to his deputy on the platform.

For many years a small, white, wooden post, on which was marked a cross surmounting the date 'August 20—1868', served as a memorial to the victims at the site of the accident. It was situated at the foot of the embankment on the up side at approximately $36\frac{1}{2}$ miles from Chester (near the modern $215\frac{1}{2}$ mile post). A century after the accident the wooden post was replaced by a similarly inscribed 2ft high slate in the same position, and this is today maintained by the District Engineer.[28] The last words on Abergele can be taken straight from the modern sectional appendix to the working timetable. Under 'Local Instructions' may be found the following: 'LLYSFAEN—Trains for the sidings at the East end of the station must be shunted inside immediately on arrival, and all shunting operations must be performed inside the sidings'.

A very similar, though less severe, accident to Abergele occurred at Holywell on 16 September 1868. Again shortage of siding space had caused an up goods train to shunt clear of the following 1.15pm passenger train from Bangor, and into the path of the 2.40pm down express from Chester. Happily only one passenger was slightly shaken by the collision. The driver of the express, who had found the signals against him, had then perceived them lowered. The signalman, thinking that he would wish to draw forward to take water, as he had done on three previous days, had lowered the signals assuming that the goods train had cleared back on to the up line. Lieutenant Colonel Hutchinson conducted the inquiry and noted that a complete remodelling of the siding arrangements at Holywell, and at Chester, Mold, Flint, Prestatyn, Rhyl, Abergele, Llandulas, Bangor, and Holyhead, was about to be effected, with the establishment of adequate refuges on both sides of the line, so that in future goods trains might safely shunt clear of passenger trains. He concluded with a plea for the introduction of the block telegraph system, instead of time interval. 'Had it been in operation it might very possibly have prevented the present accident.'

While siding works were in progress there was another accident when in the early morning of 30 September 1870 a goods train arrived at Mostyn nine minutes before the 6.15am stopping passenger train from Chester was due. The goods had several vehicles to pick up from Mostyn, and some to leave in the coal sidings on the north side of the line and in the goods yard on the south side. Despite the 10-minute embargo on shunting before passenger trains were due, a complicated set of movements was commenced, made more irresponsible in that there was dense fog. At some point during these proceedings the passenger train was heard approaching, its exhaust magnified between high walls on the approach curve. It hit the tender of the goods train, whose engine was thrown off the the rails. Speed, however, had been reduced, damage was negligible, and none of the vehicles on the passenger train left the rails. In this case the signals, which were on the absolute block system between Mostyn and Eaton Sidings, one mile to the east, were at first correctly against the passenger train. The signalman had gone off duty early, however, and during the exchange with the relief man he unfortunately inferred that the goods train was clear of the main line. The relief signalman thereupon telegraphed to Eaton Sidings where the signals were lowered. They remained at danger at Mostyn only because at the last moment the relief man saw the goods engine, through the fog, on the main line. The lights had already been put out, however, and the semaphores were barely visible. Nearly all the staff were to blame in some way, but Colonel Rich specifically stated that the station signal at Mostyn should be raised and the points and signals interlocked.

Despite previous accidents—only some of which have been mentioned—and official criticisms, yet another such collision occurred as late as 26 July 1879. On a wet, clear morning a Crewe carriage works excursion train ran into three wagons left on the down main line at Connah's Quay station. Twelve persons were injured. In this case it was pure forgetfulness on the part of the signalman. The wagons were left during shunting operations and, oblivious of their presence, the signals were lowered. At the last minute the signalman saw the wagons and raised the signals but it was too late. The excursion was travelling fast and the rails were greasy. Though the signalman was obviously at fault, Colonel Yolland of the Board of Trade pointed out that if the excursion had been fitted with continuous brakes throughout, instead of the four front and four rear vehicles in a train of fifteen carriages (the much-vaunted Clark-Webb system), the driver might have been able to pull up sooner.

Apart from proven human error, accidents sometimes happened from truly freak causes. On 6 December 1856 a wagon was blown by the wind up a gradient of 1 in 170 at Conway on to the main line and was struck by the 2am up mail. On 14 March 1857 a coke wagon was blown off a siding at Holyhead in front of a mail train, and on the very next day exactly the same thing happened at Bangor. That month two nine-year-old children were whipped in school at Holyhead for placing stones on the line. On the early morning of 19 December 1862 the up Irish Mail hit an empty coal truck standing on the main line near Mold Junction. The engine and almost the whole train were hurled from the line but providentially the few passengers escaped with nothing worse than cuts and bruises. The night was dark and stormy with a strong north-westerly wind and the latter had plucked the wagon out of a siding nearly five miles away and, with the help from the gradients, had deposited it at Mold Junction. Colonel Yolland noted that the company intended constructing catch sidings so as to stop such occurrences in the future. The wind also caused other mishaps: on 18 January 1875 a platelayer's hut was blown on to the line at Penmaenrhos to be reduced to matchwood by the down Irish Mail.

Lastly, the slaughter of animals along the Chester and Holyhead line was at one time of gargantuan proportions. For example, taking the first quarter of 1875 alone: 4 January, sheep at Bangor; 12 January, sheep at Colwyn; 26 January, sheep at

Page 287
*Two views of Holyhead new harbour, June 1880 (see p 243)*

*Holyhead new station and hotel, c 1880*

Penmaenmawr; 8 February, sheep at Rhyl; 2 March, sheep at Colwyn; and 28 March, two donkeys at Valley. One can only conclude that it was certainly an eventful life for both enginemen and passengers in those days.

### SIGNALLING AND TELEGRAPH WORKS TO 1880

Some of the signalling shortcomings have already been noted. Signals which were installed in the early days were often either badly sited, inefficient, or improperly worked. A combination of all these faults, together with that of shunting too late in front of a passenger train, led to an accident near Penmaenmawr on 10 April 1854. The accident was primarily caused by a preceding argument between the various officials concerned about verbal orders only having been given to the brakesman which were at variance with others given to a goods foreman at Conway. This had delayed the 1.15pm goods train from Chester and it arrived at Wright's Siding, used for loading stone sets quarried at Penmaenmawr, no less than 1 hour and 9 minutes late. While shunting into the siding, which was ¾ mile west of Penmaenmawr station, six wagons were left on the up line and were run into by the 6pm up passenger train from Bangor. One passenger was injured. The siding had distant signals in each direction under the control not of railwaymen but of the agent for the quarry proprietors. Before shunting commenced the lever for the up line distant was set to danger but the wire had gone slack and the signal did not respond. In any case, the passenger train, which was on time and thus due within three minutes of the start of shunting, could not have stopped as the driver's view was obscured until the last moment by Penmaenmawr tunnel. The CHR traffic committee immediately put a man in charge of the signal, his wages to be paid by the quarry owners.

The use of the time interval system of operating also led to accidents. On 10 May 1856 a goods train was despatched at 11.33pm from Conway to Bangor and the down mail train, which was five minutes late, was allowed to follow at 11.50

The goods went along at 20mph, but when within three miles of Bangor a fault developed and it was reduced to a crawl. At Penlan Mills, 1½ miles from Bangor, the mail caught it up. Speed was reduced at the time of impact so that there was no damage and no injury to passengers. The Conway signalman had warned both the goods and the mail drivers of each others' presence but all had gone blithely ahead. Captain Tyler of the Board of Trade condemned the existing regulation of five minutes' time interval, with caution shown thereafter. He also called for the telegraph to be installed.

> The true cause of the collision is sufficiently evident. Two trains were started from Conway for Bangor, a distance of fourteen and a quarter miles, the one to travel at the rate of twenty miles an hour, and the other, following it seventeen minutes afterwards, to travel at a speed of forty miles an hour.
>
> Under these conditions, simple calculation will show that the latter ought to have overtaken the former, in its ordinary course, in eleven and one third miles, at three miles from Bangor, or about the place where the leading engine first began to fail, and although it did go a little farther, in spite of the partial failure of one of its engines, before it was run into, yet this was simply because the drivers did not keep precisely to what they call their usual speed.

The telegraph, as noted when discussing the Bangor accident of 1856 (p 252), was introduced in some tunnels at an early date. In October 1859 Lee was authorised to erect huts for working the telegraph through Belmont, Bangor, and Llandegai tunnels. Five years later the wooden huts at each end of Penmaenbach tunnel were replaced by brick ones, presumably as a precaution against rock falls.

The placing, and in some cases absence, of early signals occasionally caused confusion and accidents. On 2 August 1856 the position of the Rhyl semaphore contributed to a slight collision. The 1.40pm pick-up goods from Bangor reached Rhyl at 3.45, five minutes late. Two wagons were to be left and two taken on. The greater part of the rain was left on the main line, with the brake van 285 yards outside the station signal, supposedly protecting it, while the engine shunted and then went to the coke stage. As it was returning, the goods wagons were struck by an up express passenger train, running to time and due to stop at Rhyl. It appeared that frequently the passenger train entered at one end of the station as the goods was leaving at the other, a practice frowned upon by the Board of Trade inspecting officer, particularly as the recognised place for the goods to shunt clear of the following express was at Prestatyn, $3\frac{3}{4}$ miles beyond Rhyl. The station master had apparently asked for the provision of a distant signal west of the station but to no avail. The one semaphore, at the station building, though at danger, was obscured or made indistinct by red brickwork and could not, said Colonel Wynne, be held to apply to a train 285 yards on the wrong side of it. The outcome of the accident was that the time interval between the goods and the passenger train was increased from 15 to 20 minutes; the brakesmen were fined and cautioned for not putting the goods into a siding, or going back to protect their train. An auxiliary, or distant, signal was erected as requested by the Board of Trade.[29]

In an accident at Abergele in June 1858 the station signals were described as consisting of two arms on one post, worked by wires by the policeman at a public level crossing 150yd away. Again, the use of distant signals was recommended. The late 1860s saw the first of a string of signalling improvements which, by 1880, had brought operating to a degree of safety which was bettered only with the developments of the twentieth century. In February 1867 improved spectacle signals were ordered to be substituted in all cases for those then in use on the LNWR. In September of that year an agreement was made with the signal engineers, Messrs Saxby & Farmer, for the supply of brick signal cabins, junction and station semaphores on 25ft posts either in wood or wrought iron, and patent point and signal lever apparatus, together with all necessary equipment such as gongs, ground discs, etc. Up to that time the various LNWR divisions had each constructed and erected their own signals. Lee's CHR division signal works were at Conway where he turned out, at the special request of the traffic department, 30ft high semaphores, unlike the other divisions which made 25ft signals. He was ordered henceforth to conform to 25ft except where in special cases the additional height was required.

On 25 March 1868 there was an accident at Chester when a passenger train from Holyhead was turned into the goods yard and there rammed a GWR goods train. Although in fact caused by a tired and muddled signalman pulling a wrong lever, Lieutenant Colonel Hutchinson, the inspecting officer, pointed out that the accident would have been prevented by proper interlocking of the points and signals, and he suggested that in future the levers should be painted in different distinguishing colours. 'It is to be regretted', he said, 'that the system of interlocking signals and points has not yet been introduced at an important station like Chester'. There was a similar accident on 18 September 1868 of which the exasperated Colonel Hutchinson reported, 'This collision occurred owing to a mistake made by the *same* signalman, in the *same* cabin, with the *same* lever handles in that cabin, as was the case in the accident on the 25th March . . .' But, he continued, 'I am happy to be able to report that before the occurrence of this accident, viz, on the 31st July, orders had been given for the remodelling of the whole of the Chester Yard on the locking principle, and also that arrangements are in progress whereby the objectionable system alluded to in my former report, of keeping signalmen on duty for 18 hours at a spell on Sundays, will be obviated'.

In December 1867 the way and works committee ordered that the block telegraph be installed between Chester and Saltney, used jointly with the GWR, and in February 1869 the train telegraph was ordered for the remainder of the CHR to Holyhead, to include fifteen new 'huts', at a total cost of £3,450. In the following September, orders were given for the train telegraph to be completed throughout the LNWR main lines, but a minute of the commitee of 21 October 1869 infers that the system was already in full operation on the CHR. The block telegraph, however, was still in embryo form; in November 1869 it was decided that it should 'be tried' on the Liverpool—Manchester and Manchester—Leeds lines.

Lack of the protective block system was held responsible for an accident in Penmaenrhos tunnel on 16 July 1869. The 6.55am pick-up goods from Bangor left Colwyn station at about 11am, with 37 heavily-laden wagons and eight empties. Toiling up the 1 in 100 grade, the engine stalled with the whole train in the tunnel. The brakesman put down a fog signal but then picked it up again for fear the explosion might frighten a nearby horse which was harnessed to a carriage in which were a man and a woman! Though he put down another fog signal, this was in fact too near the tunnel to be of any use. The usual procedure with a following passenger train at Colwyn was to detain it at the station until a preceeding goods train had been seen to enter the tunnel, $1\frac{7}{8}$ miles from the station and visible on a clear day. Thus, into the goods train ran the 9.15am passenger train from Holyhead, consisting of engine, tender, and fourteen vehicles. The signals at Colwyn were clear, and the passenger train passed the station without stopping at 11.25am. The collision took place five minutes later. The driver saw the goods brakesman in the act of placing a signal, with a red flag under his arm, but the speed was then 40mph and he was only able to reduce it to 10mph before the impact.

Though Colonel Yolland noted that the goods engine was underpowered, and that the staff had been lax, his real criticism was of the lack of the block system and the continued use of the time interval in despatching trains. 'The London and North-Western Railway Company are engaged at present in making arrangements for the introduction of their own particular system of working traffic, with the assistance of the electric telegraph, over this section of their line, and these arrangements are nearly completed; but I am not prepared to say that if it had been in operation the collision would have been avoided.' In other words, only a proper block system would do. Up to this time it had been the practice for signals to show a 'line clear' indication as normal, but the gradual extension of lock and block brought in the regulation as a hard and fast rule that they should normally stand at danger. In February 1870 the LNWR directors reported to the half-yearly meeting that though they had doubts as to the advantage of the absolute block system, they were, 'in deference to the Board of Trade', experimenting with it on portions of the line. More likely, it was to public opinion that they were bowing. From now on progress became more rapid. On 20 October 1870 the way and works committee ordered that the absolute block system should be adopted on the CHR and work went ahead immediately. May of 1871 saw plans for rearrangement of station signals, an additional block post between Gaerwen and Bodorgan, and provision of additional refuge sidings at Rhyl and Mold Junction. In the following November the committee ruled that all points and signals on the main line were to be interlocked.

By early 1872 there was much activity on the signalling. In January the 'speaking telegraph' was ordered for the whole of the CHR, and in February work was sanctioned for moving the distant signals further back where necessary so as to give sufficient early warning for fast trains. While works progressed there was an accident on 2 July 1872 when the down Irish Mail ran into a train of wagons which had failed at Valley due to lack of steam. They had been despatched from Bangor after learning that the mail was running an hour late, and at that time the protective absolute block was not yet operational on that section. Mold Junction received a new signal box, up and down main distant, starting, and siding signals in 1873 as did the Caernarvon branch junction at Menai Bridge. In that year the LNWR decided to manufacture all the locking and signal apparatus itself.[30] In July 1874 the way and works committee authorised erection of a shed at Llandudno Junction for the 'signal-making department', though in all probability this also had something to do with the works on the Conway Valley line (volume 2).

The signalmen at both ends of Rhyl station were joined telegraphically in 1875, and interlocking and new signalling went in at Foryd Junction for the Vale of Clwyd line (volume 2). In late 1875 the mechanical gongs between the east and west boxes at Rhyl, Bangor, and Gaerwen were replaced by electric communication. In May 1877 all distant signals were ordered to be notched to the now familiar fishtail-pattern.[31] Ty Croes and Valley stations were connected to the telegraph on the Bangor—Holyhead circuit in 1877, and at the same time, as the Chester—Rhyl circuit was overcrowded, a new circuit was set up between Chester and Holywell, with intermediate posts at Mold Junction West, Connah's Quay, Flint, and Dee Bank. In 1878 certain of the level crossings between Mostyn and Rhyl were fitted with electric train indicators.

Though much had thus been done to avoid accidents there were still loopholes. On 8 July 1875 fourteen passengers, of whom two died, were injured when a Great Western Paddington—Birkenhead train was divided on a pair of facing points between Chester station and the junction with the CHR. Though the main junctions were all interlocked, the points on a slip road at Chester had no locking bars. It was an accident similar to that at Wigan on the North Western some two years before, and matters were made worse by the fact that the slip road points had never been passed by the Board of Trade as fit for use. Human error also over-rode the block system. On 27 December 1879 an up goods train failed for lack of steam between the Britannia Bridge and Menai Bridge station. The signalman forgot it was there and the following 2.10 am mail from Holyhead ran into it.

Nevertheless, the period of twenty years since the CHR became part of the greater North Western organisation had seen many improvements to the track, stations, and signalling. The next twenty years witnessed yet more, culminating in widening to four tracks of most of the main line as the traffic grew, both from main line and branch sources. These latter years, together with the build-up of the branch system, and the improvements generally and development of traffic in North Wales to the present time, are covered in volume 2.

## Appendices

### APPENDIX 1a  DATES OF OPENINGS OF MAIN LINE

| Description | Length m c | Date | Notes |
|---|---|---|---|
| Chester—Saltney Jct | 1 67 | 4.11.1846 | For Shrewsbury & Chester Railway traffic |
| Saltney Jct—Rhyl | 28 09 | 14.10.1847 | 'Experimental train' |
| Rhyl—Conway Tubular Bridge | 14 33* | 16.11.1847 | Special train from Chester |
| Llanfair—Holyhead | 20 41* | 31. 3.1848 | Contractor's special train |
| Conway Tubular Bridge | — | 18. 4.1848 | First special train over up line tube |
| Chester—Conway Tubular Bridge | 44 30* | 24. 4.1848 | Public excursion train |
| Chester—Bangor | 59 57 | 1. 5.1848 | Passenger traffic |
| do | do | 1. 6.1848 | Goods traffic |
| Llanfair—Holyhead | 20 41* | 1. 8.1848 | Passenger traffic (Goods traffic shortly thereafter by mixed train) |
| Conway Tubular Bridge | — | –. 1.1849 | Down line tube |
| Bangor—Llanfair and Britannia Tubular Bridge up line tube | 3 35 | 5. 3.1850 | Special train over up line tube |
| do | do | 18. 3.1850 | First passenger train over up line tube |
| Britannia Tubular Bridge | do | 19.10.1850 | Down line tube |
| Holyhead station to Admiralty Pier | 0 72 | 20. 5.1851 | |

\* Approximate distance

APPENDIX 1b

## DATES OF STATION OPENINGS &c AND OTHER WORKS UP TO 1880

| Location | Distance from Chester m c | Date | Notes |
|---|---|---|---|
| Chester General station | 0 0 | 1. 8.1848 | |
| Chester tunnel | 0 50* | 4.11.1846 | Originally about 475yds. Later part opened out |
| Dee Bridge | 1 37* | 4.11.1846 | Failure of bridge |
| | | 24. 5.1847 | Reopened |
| | | 26. 7.1847 | Rebuilt 1870–71 |
| Queensferry station | 7 04 | 1. 5.1848 | |
| Connah's Quay station | 8 70 | 1. 9.1870 | |
| Rockcliffe tunnel | 10 40* | 14.10.1847 | 98yd. See Appendix 1a |
| Flint station | 12 33 | 1. 5.1848 | |
| Bagillt station | 14 36 | –. 1.1849 | Resited 1871 |
| Holywell station | 16 56 | 1. 5.1848 | |
| Mostyn station | 20 08 | 1. 5.1848 | |
| Prestatyn station | 26 27 | 1. 5.1848 | |
| Rhyl station | 29 76 | 1. 5.1848 | Enlarged 1878 |
| Foryd Bridge | 30 75* | 16.11.1847 | See Appendix 1a. Closed to river traffic 1862. Rebuilt as fixed structure 1880–81 |

# APPENDICES

| Location | Distance from Chester m c | Date | Notes |
|---|---|---|---|
| Abergele station | 34 18 | 1.5.1848 | See Appendix 1a |
| Llandulas viaduct | 36 62* | 16.11.1847 | Collapse of viaduct |
|  |  | 17.8.1879 | Temporary viaduct open |
|  |  | 25.8.1879 | New viaduct opened† |
| Llandulas station | 37 71 | 14.9.1879 | Renamed Llysfaen 1889 |
| Penmaenrhos tunnel | 38 40* | 1.8.1862 | See Appendix 1a |
|  |  | 16.11.1847 | 487yd |
| Colwyn station | 40 31 | –.10.1849 | Enlarged 1857 |
| Llandudno Jct station | 44 43 | –.11.1858 | First station |
| Conway Tubular Bridge | 44 60* |  | See Appendix 1a |
| Conway station | 45 27 | 1.5.1848 | Damaged by fire 20.11.1858 |
|  |  |  | Enlarged 1860–61, 1875 |
| Conway tunnel | 45 40* | 1.5.1848 | 74yd |
| Penmaenbach tunnel | 47 20* | 1.5.1848 | 700yd |
| Penmaenmawr station | 49 56 | –.11.1849 | Rebuilt 1865, 1868–69, and 1877, the latter dates being enlargements |
| Penmaenmawr tunnel | 50 60* | 1.5.1848 | 254yd later extended to 453yd |
| Llanfairfechan station | 52 34 | –.5.1860 |  |
| Aber station | 54 37 | 1.5.1848 |  |
| Llandegai tunnel | 58 40* | 1.5.1848 | 506yd |

| | | | |
|---|---|---|---|
| Bangor tunnel | 59 25* | 1. 5.1848 | 913yd |
| Bangor station | 59 57 | 1. 5.1848 | Enlarged 1852, 1869, 1876, 1878 |
| Belmont tunnel | 60 15* | 5. 3.1850 | See Appendix 1a |
| | | | 726yd later shortened to 615yd |
| Menai Bridge station | 61 09 | 1.10.1858 | Enlarged 1870 |
| Britannia Bridge station | 61 77* | –. 7.1851 | Closed 1.10.1858 |
| Llanfair PG station | 63 16 | 1. 8.1848 | Damaged by fire 13.11.1865 |
| | | | Rebuilt 1866 |
| Gaerwen station | 66 00 | –. 1.1849 | Enlarged 1871–72 |
| Bodorgan tunnels | 71 40* | 31. 3.1848 | See Appendix 1a |
| | | | 413 and 115yd |
| Bodorgan station | 72 40 | –.10.1849 | |
| Ty Croes station | 75 18 | –.11.1848 | |
| Valley station | 80 76 | –.10.1849 | |
| Holyhead first station | 84 08* | 1. 8.1848 | Closed –.9.1851 |
| Holyhead second station | 84 30* | –. 9.1851 | Closed 17.6.1880 |
| Holyhead third and present station | 84 35 | 17. 6.1880 | |
| Admiralty Pier | 85 30 | 20. 5.1851 | Pier built 1824 |

\* Approximate distance

† BR permanent way records say 22.9.1879

APPENDIX 2

OFFICERS OF THE CHR AND LNWR HOLYHEAD DISTRICT
1844–1880

*Secretary*
| | |
|---|---|
| George King | 1844–1848 |
| Alexander Gifford | 1848–1850 |
| Edward Brooks | 1850–1852 |
| Robert S. Mansel | 1852–1859 |

*General Superintendent*
| | |
|---|---|
| James Owen Binger | 1848–1875 |
| E. M. G. Eddy | 1875–1878 |
| Ephraim Wood | 1878– |

*Resident/District Engineer*
| | |
|---|---|
| Hedworth Lee | 1847–1873 |
| W. Smith | 1873– |

*Goods Manager*
| | |
|---|---|
| W. M. Comber | 1847–1862 |
| E. Farr | 1862–1869 |
| J. Fred. Mason | 1869–1877 |
| Joseph Guest | 1877–1879 |
| T. Henshaw | 1879– |

*Marine Superintendent*
| | |
|---|---|
| Captain Thomas Hirste | 1850–1862 |
| Captain P. H. Risk | 1862–1865 |
| Captain C. B. C. Dent | 1866– |

APPENDIX 3

OPENING PASSENGER TRAIN SERVICE    CHESTER—BANGOR
MAY 1848

Extracted from *Bradshaw*

| Up | Weekdays | | | | Sundays | |
|---|---|---|---|---|---|---|
| | 123 | 1&2 | 1&2 | 123 | 123 | 123 |
| | am | am | pm | pm | am | pm |
| BANGOR | 6.30 | 9.15 | 3.00 | 7.00 | 7.00 | 7.00 |
| Aber | 6.43 | — | — | 7.13 | 7.13 | 7.13 |
| Conway | 7.05 | 9.48 | 3.33 | 7.35 | 7.35 | 7.35 |
| Abergele | 7.31 | — | — | 8.01 | 8.01 | 8.01 |
| Rhyl | 7.41 | 10.19 | 4.04 | 8.11 | 8.11 | 8.11 |
| Prestatyn | 7.50 | — | — | 8.20 | 8.20 | 8.20 |
| Mostyn | 8.05 | — | — | 8.35 | 8.35 | 8.35 |
| Holywell | 8.13 | 10.43 | 4.28 | 8.43 | 8.43 | 8.43 |
| Flint | 8.23 | — | — | 8.53 | 8.53 | 8.53 |
| Queens Ferry | 8.36 | — | — | 9.06 | 9.06 | 9.06 |
| CHESTER | 8.53 | 11.25 | 5.10 | 9.23 | 9.23 | 9.23 |

| Down | Weekdays | | | | Sundays | |
|---|---|---|---|---|---|---|
| | 1&2 | 123 | 123 | 1&2 | 1&2 | 123 |
| | am | am | pm | pm | am | pm |
| CHESTER | 4.00 | 10.00 | 1.45 | 4.25 | 4.00 | 4.25 |
| Queens Ferry | — | 10.17 | 2.02 | — | — | 4.42 |
| Flint | — | 10.30 | 2.15 | — | — | 4.55 |
| Holywell | 4.36 | 10.40 | 2.25 | 5.01 | 4.36 | 5.05 |
| Mostyn | — | 10.48 | 2.33 | — | — | 5.13 |
| Prestatyn | — | 11.03 | 2.48 | — | — | 5.28 |
| Rhyl | 5.05 | 11.12 | 2.57 | 5.30 | 5.05 | 5.37 |
| Abergele | — | 11.22 | 3.07 | — | — | 5.47 |
| Conway | 5.39 | 11.48 | 3.33 | 6.04 | 5.39 | 6.13 |
| Aber | — | 12.10 | 3.55 | — | — | 6.35 |
| BANGOR | 6.10 | 12.23 | 4.08 | 6.35 | 6.10 | 6.48 |

Note: *Holyhead Trains Incomplete—Accuracy uncertain*

APPENDIX 4

CHR RAIL PASSENGERS 1848–1858

Half-year ended:

| | |
|---|---|
| 30 June 1848 | 46,138 |
| 31 December 1848 | 142,929 |
| 30 June 1849 | 119,911 |
| 31 December 1849 | 185,912 |
| 30 June 1850 | 157,108 |
| 31 December 1850 | 238,623 |
| 30 June 1851 | 190,388 |
| 31 December 1851 | 273,689 |
| 30 June 1852 | 226,242 |
| 31 December 1852 | 345,226 |
| 30 June 1853 | 277,941 |
| 31 December 1853 | 354,417 |
| 30 June 1854 | 316,025 |
| 31 December 1854 | 381,411 |
| 30 June 1855 | 314,010 |
| 31 December 1855 | 453,170 |
| 30 June 1856 | 340,684 |
| 31 December 1856 | 385,708 |
| 30 June 1857 | 293,352 |
| 31 December 1857 | 399,997 |
| 30 June 1858 | 267,925 |

Extracted from Parliamentary Accounts and Papers

# References

## Notes to Chapter 1

1. Much of the information on the early mail service and connections is drawn from Parliamentary Papers, State Paper Room, British Museum, and Watson, Edward, *The Royal Mail to Ireland* (1917).
2. Robinson, Howard, *Carrying British Mails Overseas* (1964) p 53
3. Ibid, p 72, though on p 77 Robinson says Skinner transferred in 1799.
4. Hughes, D. Lloyd, and Williams, Dorothy M., *Holyhead: The Story of a Port* (Denbigh 1967) p 34 et seq.
5. Smiles, Samuel, *Lives of the Engineers* Vol 2 (1861) p 436.
6. Rolt, L. T. C., *Thomas Telford* (1958) p 111.
7. Hughes, Mervyn, 'Telford, Parnell, and the Great Irish Road', *Journal of Transport History* Nov 1964 Vol 2, No 4.
8. Smiles, p 438.
9. *Boswell's Life of Johnson* Vol 5, ed. Hill, George Birkbeck, (Clarendon Press, Oxford 1950) pp 446–7.
10. Smiles, p 445.
11. Ibid, p 459.
12. Rolt, p 127; Smiles, p 459.
13. Owen, Sir David J., *The Ports of the United Kingdom* (1948) p 250.
14. Watson, p 112.
15. Robinson, p 120.
16. Body, Geoffrey, *British Paddle Steamers* (Newton Abbot 1971) pp 55–6.
17. Watson, p 124.
18. Ibid, p 140.

| | |
|---|---|
| 19 | Whishaw, Francis, *The Railways of Great Britain and Ireland* (1842) p 62 et seq. |
| 20 | Robinson, p 122. |
| 21 | Ibid, p 123. |
| 22 | Vale, Edmund, *The Mail Coach Men of the Late Eighteenth Century* (Newton Abbot 1967) pp 237–8. |
| 23 | Watson, p 111. |

## Notes to Chapter 2

| | |
|---|---|
| 1 | Herepath's *Railway Magazine* Feb 1836. |
| 2 | Ibid, July 1836. |
| 3/4 | Report of the Railway Commissioners for Ireland 1838. |
| 5 | *The London Gazette* Nov 1836. |
| 6 | Herepath's *Railway Magazine* Oct 1838. |
| 7 | Ibid, 13.3.1841. |
| 8 | Smiles, Samuel, *The Life of George Stephenson* (1857) pp 370–71. |
| 9 | *The Dictionary of National Biography.* |
| 10 | Herepath's *Railway Magazine* Feb 1839. |
| 11 | Ibid, May 1839. |

## Notes to Chapter 3

| | |
|---|---|
| 1 | Report from the Committee on London—Dublin Communication 1840. |
| 2 | Herepath's *Railway Magazine* 23.5.1840. |
| 3 | *The Dictionary of National Biography.* |
| 4 | Herepath's *Railway Magazine* 18.12.1841. |
| 5 | DNB. |
| 6 | *Railway Times* 18.3.1843. |
| 7 | Ibid 15.4.1843. |
| 8 | Ibid 10/24.6.1843, 28.10.1843. |
| 9 | Chester & Holyhead Railway board 12.12.1843. Min No 15 reproduces Walker's report. |
| 10 | *Railway Times* 24.2.1844. |
| 11 | CHR board 3.6.1844. |
| 12 | Ibid 12/13.12.1843. Mins Nos 16–29 record negotiations up to 13.12.1843. |
| 13 | CHR first general meeting 30.8.1844. |
| 14 | CHR board 8.2.1844. |

## Notes to Chapter 4

1. *The Dictionary of National Biography.*
2. Attributes remarked upon in the railway press.
3. DNB.
4. Details from files of the *Chester Chronicle*, 1845.
5. *Herepath's Journal*, 23.8.1845 (prospectus)
6. Ibid, 11.10.1845.
7. Chester & Holyhead Railway board, 6.5.1846.
8. *Herepath's Journal*, 8.8.1846.
9. Ibid, 21.11.1846.
10. CHR board, 3.3.1847.
11. Ibid, 11.11.1846.
12. *Herepath's Journal*, 14.10.1848.
13. Details of Thompson's architecture kindly supplied by Mr Oliver F. Carter, FRIBA.
14. CHR traffic committee, 11.1.1848; CHR board, 12.1.1848.
15. *Herepath's Journal*, 8.4.1848.
16. CHR board, 12.4.1848.
17. Clark, Edwin, *The Britannia and Conway Tubular Bridges* Vol 1 (1850) p 3; and Parry, Edward, *Parry's Railway Companion from Chester to Holyhead* (1848) p 113.
18. CHR board, 8.10.1845.
19. Ibid, 11.11.1846; 9.12.1846.
20. Carter, Oliver F. See note 13.
21. *Illustrated London News*, 9.8.1848.
22. DNB.
23. Neele, George P., *Railway Reminiscences* (1904) p 372.

## Notes to Chapter 5

1. CHR board, 18.3.1844.
2. Clark, Edwin, *The Britannia and Conway Tubular Bridges*, 2 Vols (1850).
3. CHR board, 19.2.1845.
4. Clark, p 22.
5. Ibid, p 26.
6. Ibid, p 27.
7. Ibid, p 29.
8. *The Dictionary of National Biography.*
9. Clark, pp 32, 50.

| | |
|---|---|
| 10 | Ibid, pp 473–4. |
| 11 | Ibid, p 482. |
| 12 | Ibid, p 483. |
| 13 | Ibid, p 534. |
| 14/15 | CHR board, 13.5.1846. |
| 16 | Ibid, 8.7.1846. |
| 17 | Ibid, 29.7.1846. |
| 18 | Clark, pp 496–7. |
| 19 | CHR board, 14.10.1846. |
| 20/21 | *Herepath's Journal*, 14.2.1847. |
| 22 | Clark, pp 625, 667. |
| 23 | Ibid, pp 593, 611. |
| 24 | Ibid, p 724. |
| 25 | *Herepath's Journal*, 31.7.1847 (Advt). |
| 26 | Berridge, P. S. A., *The Girder Bridge* (1969) p 11. |
| 27/28 | Clark, p 534. |
| 29 | *Herepath's Journal*, 6.11.1847. |
| 30 | Clark, pp 640–42. |
| 31 | Ibid, pp 645–6. |
| 32 | Ibid, p 585. |
| 33 | Ibid, p 647. |
| 34 | Ibid, pp 654–5; *Herepath's Journal*, 14.10.1848. |
| 35/36 | Clark, p 658. |

## Notes to Chapter 6

| | |
|---|---|
| 1 | Clark, Edwin, *The Britannia and Conway Tubular Bridges*, p 546. |
| 2 | CHR board, 19.1.1849. |
| 3 | I am indebted for this thought to Mr Oliver F. Carter, FRIBA. |
| 4 | Clark, p 557. |
| 5 | Ibid, pp 540–44. |
| 6 | Ibid, p 670. |
| 7 | Ibid, p 680. |
| 8 | *Railway Times*, 23.6.1849. |
| 9 | Clark, p 684. |
| 10 | Ibid, p 483. |
| 11 | Ibid, p 617. |
| 12 | Ibid, p 696, but on p 724 Clark gives the date as 9 November. |
| 13 | Ibid, p 696; *Railway Times*, 1.12.1849. |

| | |
|---|---|
| 14 | Ibid, pp 705–6. |
| 15 | *Carnarvon & Denbigh Herald & North & South Wales Independent*, 9.3.1850. |
| 16 | Ibid, 23.3.1850; *Illustrated London News*, 23.3.1850. |
| 17 | Clark, pp 710, 724; *Herepath's Journal*, 24.8.1850. |
| 18 | *Herepath's Journal*, 26.10.1850. |
| 19 | *Illustrated London News*, 23.10.1852; Neele, George P., *Railway Reminiscences* (1904) p 455. |
| 20 | LNWR permanent way, works, and estate committee, 19.8.1874. |

Notes to Chapter 7

| | |
|---|---|
| 1 | CHR board, 3.3.1847. |
| 2 | *Herepath's Journal*, 27.5.1848. |
| 3 | CHR board, 6.9.1848. |
| 4/5 | Ibid, 10.1.1849. |
| 6 | *The Dictionary of National Biography*. |
| 7 | CHR board, 16.9.1852. |
| 8 | Ibid, 8.12.1852, 10.2.1853. |
| 9 | LNWR Chester & Holyhead committee, 4.8.1857. |
| 10 | *Railway Times*, 9.5.1857. |
| 11 | LNWR C & H committee, 2.10.1857. |
| 12 | CHR board, 18.12.1857. |
| 13 | Ibid, 12.5.1858. |
| 14 | Watson, Edward, *The Royal Mail to Ireland* (1917) pp 174–81. |
| 15 | *Seventh Report of the Postmaster General*, 1861. |
| 16 | *Railway Times*, 6.10.1860. |

Notes to Chapter 8

| | |
|---|---|
| 1/2 | BRB archives. A box of correspondence concerning early locomotives at Wolverton. |
| 3 | *The Engineer*, 14.5.1920. |
| 4 | For the Stephenson information I am indebted to Mr Brian Reed. |
| 5 | LNWR general locomotive committee, 13.4.1849. |
| 6 | *The Locomotive*, 15.4.1909. |
| 7 | LNWR Crewe locomotive committee, 19.9.1848, 3.10.1848. 17.10.1848. |

T*

| | |
|---|---|
| 8 | LNWR general stores and locomotive expenditure committee, 25.9.1860. |
| 9 | CHR traffic committee, 15.11.1850. |
| 10 | CHR finance committee, 6.3.1848. |
| 11 | LNWR Crewe locomotive committee, 1.1.1850. |
| 12 | Stuart, D. H., and Reed, Brian, *Loco Profile 15—The Crewe Type* (Windsor 1971). |
| 13 | This and later locomotive information in part from articles 'Locomotives built at Crew Works', *The Journal of the Stephenson Locomotive Society*, 1953–5. |
| 14 | LNWR locomotive committee, 18.7.1861. |
| 15 | LNWR permanent way, works, and estate committee, 18.9.1862. |
| 16 | LNWR locomotive committee, 10.12.1869. |
| 17 | BR records, Chief Civil Engineer, Euston. |
| 18 | Dunn, J. M., correspondence in the *Railway Magazine*, June 1958. |
| 19 | Ahrons, E. L. *Locomotive and Train Working in the Latter Part of the Nineteenth Century* (Cambridge, 1952) Vol 2, p 14. |
| 20 | Neele, George P. *Railway Reminiscences* (1904) p 127. |
| 21 | LNWR locomotive and mechanical engineering committee, 14.7.1865. |
| 22 | Ahrons, pp 22–3. |
| 23 | CHR traffic committee, 23.12.1850. |
| 24 | Parliamentary Papers, Reports, Committees, 1852–3, Vol 38, State Paper Room. |
| 25 | CHR half-yearly meeting, 7.9.1853. |
| 26 | LNWR Chester & Holyhead committee, 20.6.1856. |
| 27 | LNWR locomotive committee, 2.7.1862, 3.10.1862, 16.10.1862, 15.4.1864. |
| 28 | Ibid, 11.3.1870. |
| 29 | Ibid, 3.10.1862, 5.12.1862, 3.7.1863, 15.12.1864. |
| 30 | Ibid, 12.3.1875, |
| 31 | *Railway Times*, 11.4.1863. |
| 32 | LNWR locomotive committee, 12.9.1873; *The Journal of the Stephenson Locomotive Society*, Sept 1955, pp 306–7. |
| 33 | Neele, pp 191, 204. |
| 34 | CHR traffic committee, 6.12.1850. |
| 35 | LNWR locomotive, carriage and Crewe committee, 7.10.1854, 2.12.1854. |
| 36 | LNWR locomotive and mechanical engineering committee, 6.5.1864. |

## REFERENCES

### Notes to Chapter 9

1. *The Dictionary of National Biography.*
2. CHR board, 10.2.1846.
3. Ibid, 9.9.1846.
4. CHR half-yearly meeting, 10.2.1847.
5. CHR board, 7.7.1847; minutes of evidence before Select Committee on CHR (Extension at Holyhead) Bill, 15.6.1847.
6/7. Deposited plans, House of Lords Record Office.
8/9. Contracts with Rigby are in the keeping of the Archivist to the BRB. There is much detail on the quarry railway and breakwater works in *Holyhead: Story of a Port*—see note 4, chapter 1.
10. Letter from Hawkshaw, 30.9.1857, appended to Civil Service Estimates for 1859. Parliamentary Reports, Accounts, Papers, etc. State Paper Room.
11. Ibid, and Rendel's evidence before Committee on London—Dublin Communication, June 1853.
12. Civil Service Estimates for 1859.
13. BRB Historical Records.
14. Details from contract, BRB Historical Records.
15. CHR traffic committee, 31.5.1851.
16. Same as note 10.
17. LNWR Chester & Holyhead committee, 1.1.1858; LNWR traffic committee, 28.1.1859.
18. Report upon the Harbours of Holyhead made to the Board of Trade, 1869.
19. Bennett, Alfred Rosling, *The Chronicles of Boulton's Siding* (1927).
20. *Locomotive Magazine,* August 1905; *Railway Magazine,* July and September 1961.
21. LNWR C & H committee, 7.11.1856.
22. *Illustrated London News,* 22.10.1859.
23. CHR traffic committee, 7.7.1848, 21.7.1848.
24. *Carnarvon & Denbigh Herald & North & South Wales Independent,* 24.5.1851.
25. CHR traffic committee, 31.5.1851.
26. CHR board, 11.6.1851.
27. CHR half-yearly meeting, 11.9.1851.
28. Jackson, Thomas, *The Visitor's Handbook for Holyhead* (1853).
29. CHR traffic committee, 22.6.1855.

30 Ibid, 18.12.1852; CHR board, 13.6.1855, 11.7.1855; *Holyhead: Story of a Port*, p 106.
31 LNWR locomotive committee minutes as given; 'Locomotives built at Crew Works', *The Journal of the Stephenson Locomotive Society*. 1955 p 17–18.
32 LNWR permanent way, works, and estate committee, 20.7.1865.
33 LNWR locomotive and mechanical engineering committee, 18.1.1866; Neele, George P. *Railway Reminiscences* (1904) p 138.
34 LNWR permanent way, works, and estate committee, 21.2.1866, 22.8.1866.
35 LNWR locomotive and mechanical engineering committee, 14.8.1868.
36 Neele, p 242.
37 LNWR permanent way, works, and estate committee, 18.8.1870, 20.10.1870; Neele, p 139.
38 Details of works 1873–80 from minutes of LNWR permanent way, works, and estate committee; *Railway Engineer*, July 1880; *The Engineer*, 6.8.1880.

## Notes to Chapter 10

1 *Chester Chronicle*, 15.5.1848.
2 CHR traffic committee, 18.4.1848, 21.7.1848, 7.7.1849.
3 Ibid, 23.5.1848.
4 CHR board, 9.5.1849, 7.11.1849; CHR traffic committee, 18.8.1848, 21.4.1849, 20.7.1849.
5 *Herepath's Journal*, 24.1.1852.
6 CHR half-yearly meeting, 7.3.1855.
7 Parry, Edward, *Parry's Railway Companion from Chester to Holyhead* (1848) p 109.
8 LNWR Chester & Holyhead committee, 1.5.1857.
9 LNWR permanent way, works, and estate committee, 17.10.1867, 14.11.1867, 23.4.1868, 19.11.1869.
10 *Carnarvon & Denbigh Herald & North & South Wales Independent*, 24.5.1851.
11 *The North Wales Chronicle and Advertiser for the Principality*, 17.5.1851.
12 CHR traffic committee, 21.4.1849.
13 Ibid, 16.7.1853.
14 Ibid, 3.12.1851, 24.4.1852.

## REFERENCES

15  CHR half-yearly meeting, September 1855.
16  *Bradshaw's Shareholders' Guide*, 1859 p 33.
17  LNWR locomotive and mechanical engineering committee, 16.12.1871, 10.4.1873.
18  Ibid, 9.5.1873.
19  Ibid, 2.10.1874.
20  Ibid, 6.2.1878.
21  Ibid, 14.7.1876, 11.8.1876; Neele, George P. *Railway Reminiscences* (1904) p 214.
22  *Bradshaw's Shareholders' Guide*, 1878.
23  Neele, p 219.
24  LNWR permanent way, works, and estate committee, 13.10.1875.
25  Ibid, 20.2.1873, 18.11.1874, 16.7.1879; locomotive committee, 10.1.1873.
26  Neele, p 237.
27  LNWR locomotive committee, 9.1.1880.
28  Information from the Area Manager, British Rail, Llandudno Junction, Oct 1971.
29  LNWR C & H committee, 5.9.1856.
30  LNWR permanent way, works, and estate committee, 18.6.1873.
31  LNWR locomotive committee, 11.5.1877.

## *Acknowledgements*

There is no separate bibliography; published works and periodicals consulted are referred to in the chapter notes.

The foundations of this book rest on official records of the Chester & Holyhead Railway and the London & North Western Railway in the BRB archives; and information obtainable from the House of Lords Record Office; the State Paper Room and Reading Room at the British Museum, and the Museum's Newspaper Library at Colindale; the Public Record Office; and the Museum of British Transport at Clapham. To all these I tender my thanks for facilities to inspect original source material. Particularly, for their friendly, courteous, and most knowledgeable help, I am indebted to the staff at the House of Lords Record Office, and to Mr E. H. Fowkes, Archivist, British Transport Historical Records, and his staff led by Harry Whatson. Without easy access to the records in Mr Fowkes' care much of the company history in this book could not have been told. That such a complete coverage of original and interrelating records concerning transport history as listed above is still freely available within the capital city for ease of cross-reference, is a situation which it is hoped will long survive.

My cousins, Mr John R. Bulmer, and his brother, the late Mr Kenneth J. Bulmer, both gave generously of their time to answer questions and volunteer information. Their father and my great-uncle, the late Captain Julian Ralph Bulmer, joined the London & North Western steamer service at Holyhead in 1900 and rose to become commodore-captain, as master of the *Hibernia*, before his retirement in July 1939. Mr John Bulmer also introduced me to Mr C. S. A. Dobson, the House of Lords Librarian, who provided some most interesting material concerning his great-grandfather, George Clarisse Dobson, resident engineer during construction of the Holyhead harbour of refuge.

I wish to thank Mr Terence Barry of Burgess Hill for reading the text throughout and for his most constructive and detailed criticism. My thanks also go to Mr David Joy of Hebden, Skipton-in-Craven, Yorkshire, for the final editing.

Mr Oliver F. Carter of Wigton, Cumberland, very generously made available his study of Francis Thompson, the architect, together with much useful professional information on the buildings and structures on the CHR; Mr Francis F. Clough of Upper Colwyn Bay gave much time to correspondence, with useful information and references; and Mr Roger B. Wilson of Cheltenham kindly provided material from the Hutton House Transport Collection. Other friends who have contributed in various ways, either with sources of reference, or written or photographic material, and to whom I am most grateful, are: Mr Frank Bell of Holyhead; Mr Harold D. Bowtell of Gatley, Cheshire; Mr Stirling B. Dickson of Bangor; Mr John Edgington in the PR & PO office, British Rail, Euston; Mr M. F. Higson of Harrow; Mr John Marshall of Bolton; Mr Brian Reed of Windermere; Mr R. F. Roberts of Hinchley Wood, Surrey; Mr David Tee of Brampton, Cumberland; Mr L. Ward of Chiswick; and Mr R. A. Williams of Egham, Surrey.

I am likewise most grateful to the following for their kind help: Mr W. R. Parry, Curator, the National Trust, Penrhyn Castle, Bangor; the Area Manager, British Rail, Llandudno Junction; and the librarians at the Institution of Civil Engineers, the Institute of Transport, and the University College of North Wales. Much help and advice came from local sources: Anglesey County Library, Caernarvon County Record Office, Chester Public Library, Colwyn Bay Public Library, Denbighshire County Library, Flint County Record Office, and Westminster City Library. I am obliged to the Trustees of the British Museum for the portrait of James Meadows Rendel; the National Maritime Museum, London, for the portrait of

Captain Moorsom RN; the Science Museum for photographs of illustrations as credited; and Aerofilms Limited for the photographs of Conway and Holyhead. Messrs W. Heffer & Sons Ltd kindly gave me permission to quote from E. L. Ahrons' *Locomotive and Train Working in the Latter Part of the Nineteenth Century*.

My father, the late Mr Victor Edward Baughan, took an early interest in the photographic work of this book.

Finally, my thanks again to my wife Anne for her continued help and encouragement during the preparation of the manuscript.

# Index

Abergele, 46, 256, 259
Accidents:
Abergele (1858), 291; (1863), 204; (1868), 278-84, **281**; memorial, 284; Bangor (1856 & 1859), 252; Britannia Bridge (1879), 295; Chester (1855 & 1858), 253; (1868), 292; (1875), 295; Connah's Quay (1879), 285; Conway (1848), 118; (1855), 277; Dee Bridge (1847), 104-11, **105**; Holywell (1868), 284; Llandulas viaduct (1879), 274-6; Llanfaelog boiler explosion (1848), 120; Menai Bridge Junction (1865), 277; Mostyn (1870), 285; Penlan Mills (1856), 289; Penmaenmawr (1854), 289; Penmaenrhos (1869), 293; Rhyl (1856), 290; Ty Croes (1861), 203-4; Valley (1872), 294
Acts of Parliament:
Act of Union (1800), 15; Chester & Birkenhead Rly (1837), 29; Chester & Crewe Rly (1837), 29; Chester & Holyhead Rly (1844), 46; Completion (1845), 96; Chester Extension and Amendment (1847), 56-7, 87; Holyhead Extension and Amendment (1847), 212, 214; (1848), 146; (Increase of Capital) (1849), 122; (1858), 176-7; Railway at Holyhead (1859), 235; Dublin & Drogheda Rly (1869), 271; Dublin & Kingstown Rly (1831), 20; Dundalk & Greenore Rly (1867), 264; Dundalk Newry & Greenore Rly (1873), 266; Grand Junction Rly (1840), 29; Great Northern Rly (Ireland) (1877), 271; Great Southern & Western Rly (1872), 271; Harbours Transfer Act (1862), 215; Holyhead Docks & Warehouses Co (1869), 239-40; Holyhead Harbour (1847), 212; Improved Postal & Passenger Communication with Ireland Act (1855), 170, 176, 218; London & North Western Rly (1846), 63; (Additional Works) (1858), 177; (Chester & Holyhead) (1861), 237; (Additional Powers) (1862), 238, 273; (Traffic Arrangements) (1864), 263-4; (New Works & Additional Powers) (1869), 238; (Steam Vessels) (1870), 264; (Holyhead Old Harbour) (1873), 240; (England & Ireland) (1875), 266; (New Lines & Additional Powers) (1875), 240-1; (New Lines & Additional Powers) (1876), 241; (Additional Powers) (1879), 178; (1880), 273-4; Midland Great Western Rly of Ireland (1871), 271; Shrewsbury & Chester Rly (1847), 86
Adams, William, 240
Admiralty, 17, 21, 22, 37, 41, 45, 50, 91, 96, 144, 148-9, 153, 155-7, 208, 212, 215-6, 221, 226
Admiralty Pier, Holyhead, 18-20, 145, 149-50, 194, 208-9, 211, 213; map, 217; 218, **220**, 221, 226, 228, 230-2, **234**, 235, 237-9
Ahrons, E. L., 186, 194-5
American War of Independence, 13
Amlwch, 246
Amos, Mr, 129
Anglesey (*see* separate headings)
Animals killed on line, 286, 289
Appold, J. G., 132
Archer, Henry, 23-36
Architecture, 73-4, 85, 87, 122
Auckland Lord, 153
Avalanche tunnels, 85

Back, Capt, 41
Bala, 24, 26, 31, 36, 40
Balaclava Railway, 171
Bangor, 14, 16, 22, 26, 256
Bangor & Porthdynllaen Railway, 36, 40-3, 62

315

316   INDEX

Bangor & Carnarvon Railway, 178
Barlow, Peter, 25, 35
Barmouth, 24, 37
Beaufort, Capt F., 27
Beaumaris, 12, 14, 74, 146, 246
Beechey, Capt, 37
Belfast, 263, 266
Bessemer rails, 272
Bethell, Bishop Christopher, 55
Bethesda, 16
Betts, E. L., (*see* Contractors)
Bettws-y-coed, 16
Bidder, George, 40, 93, 126, **133**, 142
Binger, James Owen, 79, 169, 173, 188, 191, 222, 236, 247, 252, 300
Birkenhead, 30, 71-2, 155
Birkenhead Railway, 72, 259
Birkenhead Lancashire & Cheshire Junction Railway, 72, 175, 177
Birmingham & Gloucester Railway, 183
Board of Trade, 38, 70, 73, 78, 146, 203, 215, 235, 237-9, 253, 291, 294; Inspections, 80, 82, 117, 120, 132, 138-9, 227-8, 235-6, 271; Accident Reports, 204, 252-3, 277-8, 280, 282, 284-6, 290-2
Bookstalls, 246
Boothby, J. B., 46, 230
Bore, Richard, 200, 283
Boulton, William, 225
Braithwaite, John, 43
Brakes, (*see* Rolling Stock)
Brassey, Thomas, (*see* Contractors)
Breakdown train, 205
Breakey, William, 59
Bridge rails, 131
Bridges (general), 82, 110, 272-3
Britannia Hotel and Park, 256-9
Britannia Tubular Bridge, 50-1, 58, 64, **84**, 90, **133**, **136**; First design, 91; description, 123; conference of engineers, **133**; experiments and mode of construction, 97, 100; contracts, 98, 101; first and last stones, 98, 128; masonry work, 123-5; bricked recesses, 129-30; permanent way, 131, 272; tube construction and floating, 102-3, 124, **125**, 126-8, 131, 138; raising the tubes, 128-32; accidents, 130; roofing, 131, 140; opening the bridge, 132-3; cost, 135; first trains, 132, 135, **136**, 139, 189; Board of Trade experiments, 139; preserved cylinder head, 141; rust, 141; other tubular designs, 142
British Association, 138
British Transport Commission, 237

Broad gauge, 61, 63, 72-3, 213, 238
Brunel, Isambard Kingdom, 25, 37, 62, 71, 113-14, 126-7, 132, **133**, 138, 142, 169-70, 218, 225
Brymbo, 187
Buddicom, William B., 189
Burgoyne, Col J. F., 25
Bury, Edward, 42, 183
Bury Curtis & Kennedy, 146, 181, 183-4
Butterley Iron Co, 100, 103
Bwlch-y-Fedwen, 24

Caernarvon, 23, 246
Calls on shares, 64, 67
Cambrian Railways, 276
Capel Curig, 16
Carlingford, 263
Carlisle Pier, 180
Carriage sheds, 205-7
Carriers and carters, 260
Carno, 24, 37
Cast iron, 82, 91, 95, 98, 104, 108-10
Cawkwell, William, 178
Chains for tubular bridges, 92, 94-6, 99-100, 103, 111-12, 137
Chancellor of the Exchequer, 32, 38, 50, 159, 214
Chandos, Lord, 161, 171-2, 174-6, 178, 235-6, 254
Chat Moss, 36
Chester, 21, 29-30, 32, 43, 86-8
Chester & Birkenhead Railway, 24, 28-9, 43, 46, 49, 86
Chester & Crewe Railway, 24, 28-30, 32-3, 37, 43, 46, 177, 189
Chester & Ellesmere Canal, 61, 71, 109
Chester & Holyhead Railway: First meeting, 38; provisional committee, 39; Bill in Parliament, 43; Ogwen—Llanfair line, 45-6, 55-6, 91, 95, 97; first directors, 46, routes at Bangor, 55; contracts let, 57-8; cutting first sod, 60; finances, 46, 49, 67, 89, 121-2, 135, 150, 154-5, 157-9, 161-3, 176, 214, 264; opening dates (*see* Appendix 1a); relations with LNWR, 154-5, 158, 162-80; and Peto, 156; final meeting, 178
Chester & West Cheshire Junction Railway, 71
City of Dublin Steam Packet Company (CDSPC), 22, 144, 153, 155-7, 162-6, 168-70, 174-5, 178-9, 218, 221, 226-8, 246, 263-4, 268
Clark, Edwin, 71, 88, 90, 100, 114, 116, 124-7, 130-2, **133**, 140, 142
Clark, John, 200

# INDEX

Clark, Latimer, 130, 132, **133**, 140, 142, 200
Claxton, Capt Christopher, 113-15, 126-7, **133**, 138, 142, 169
Clerk, Sir George, 45, 50
Coalbrookdale Iron Company, 100, 103, 132
Collett, William Rickford, 46, 50-1, 53, 61, 63, 70, 78, 91, 120, 122, 146, 150, 154, 211-12
Comber, W. M., 77, 173, 259-60, 300
Commissioners of Woods and Forests, 17, 45, 90, 215, 231, 256
Commissioners of Works and Public Buildings, 215
Committee on London—Dublin Communication, 35-7, 82, 215
Committee on Post Office Communication with Ireland, 27, 39
Committee on the Conveyance of Mails by Railway, 170
Contractors:
  Betts, E. L., 57-8, 60, 64, 76, 98, 155-7, 161, 171, 228; Brassey, T., 57-8, 86, 155-6, 161, 171; Chester, C. H., 207; Cropper, J., 57-8; Cropper & Bell, 79; Ditchburn, 101, 103, 146; Evans, J., 57, 98, 101-3,; Garforth, 101, 103; Giles, G., 231; Gregson, 57; Grissell & Peto, 155-7 (*see* Peto); Harding J., 57-8; Hemingway, J., 98; Horton, J., 103; Hughes, T., 76; Jackson, T., 57-61, 64, 77, 79-80, 98, 188; Jones, J. R., 255; Lockwood, A., 252; Mackenzie, W., 57, 98; Mare, 101, 103, 126, 132, 146, 159; Millar, 252; Morris, J., 76; Nowell, B., 98, 101; Parnell & Son, 242; Pauline, G., 99, 101; Pearson, C.,98; Rigby, Messrs, 213, 216, 221-7, 238; Scott & Edwards, 240; Stephenson, J., Thomas, J., 254-5; Warburton Bros, 206; Warton & Warden, 57, 64, 69
Conway, 12, 17, 21, 43, 67, **134**, 192
Conway ferry crossing, 15, 17, 21, 30
Conway reservoir, 192
Conway Suspension Bridge, 17-18, 114, **134**,
Conway Tubular Bridge, 46, 77, 80. **134**, First design, 91; description, 112; contracts, 98, 101; first stone, 98; tube construction and floating, 102-3, 112, 118, 188; raising the tubes, 117-19; first train, 117; Board of Trade inspections, 117, 119; roofing, 131; permanent way, 119
Cook, Thomas, 247
Cork, 41, 231, 247, 267-8
Corwen, 22
Creed, Richard, 42, 47, 188
Crewe, 30, 183, 189-91, 197, 200
Crimean War, 171
Cropper, Edward, 46
Crystal Palace, 255-6
Cubitt, W., 27-8, 40, 137

Dalkey, 55
Darbyshire, S. D., 175
Dee Bridge, 70, 104-11
Denbigh, 12, 260
Dent, Capt C. B. C., 239, 266-7, 300
Distances, 27 (*see* Appendix 1b)
Ditchburn & Mare, 146-7
Dobson, George Clarrise, 223-4
Dolgelly, 37, 62, 276
Drummond, Thomas, 25
Dublin, 20, 23, 146, 165, 264, 271-2
Dublin & Belfast Junction Railway, 264, 271
Dublin & Drogheda Railway, 175, 264, 271
Dublin & Kingstown Railway, 20, 31
Dublin (North Wall), 179, 267-72
Dublin time, 42
Duff, Adam, 46
Dundalk, 263-4
Dundalk & Greenore Railway, 263-4, 266
Dundalk Newry & Greenore Railway, 266
Dundalk Steam Packet Company, 264
Dundas, Admiral, 47
Dun Loaghaire, 19

Eagle and Child, 12 (*see* Royal Hotel)
Eastern Counties Railway, 146, 156
Easton & Amos, 103
Eccles, 193
Edge Hill, 30, 263
Edmundson ticket machines, 79
Edwards, S., 246
Electric & International Telegraph Company, 140
Electric lighting, 241, 275
Electric Telegraph Company, 40
Engine sheds, (*see* Locomotive sheds)
Euston, 122, 200
Eyton's Works, 47, 261

Facing points, 252, 276-7, 295
Fair, Capt, 41

Fairbairn, Thomas, 94, 99, 137
Fairbairn, William, 94-6, 98-101, 103, 110, 135-8, 142
Ferrers, W. E., 46
Festiniog Railway, 23
Ffestiniog, 24
Fishguard, 49
Footbridges, 238, 272-3
Forster, Frank, 63, 69, 77, 98, 100, **133**, 142
Foryd Bridge, 77, 80, 273, 278
Foster, John 16
Franklin, Benjamin, 13
Fuller, Francis, 56
Furniture, 147, 254

Gas lighting, (*see* Rolling Stock)
Gauge Commission, 63
General Steam Navigation Company, 144
Gifford, Alexander, 53, 129, 131, 300
Giles, Francis, 30-1, 35-6, 38-9, 42
Gladstone, William Ewart, 45, 145, 262
Glyn, George Carr, 42, 45-6, 55, 63, 89, 145, 158, 211
Glyn, Hallifax, Mills & Company, 121, 154, 159
Gordon, Rear-Admiral Sir James, 37
Gorphwysfa, 121, 256-7
Goulbourn, Henry, 50
Government House, Holyhead, 224
Graham, Sir James, 50
Grand Junction Railway, 22, 29-30, 42-4, 46-51, 63, 71, 86, 196
Grand Trunk Railway of Canada, 161, 171
Great Eastern Steamship Company, 225
Great Exhibition (1851), 140, 161, 167, 231-2, 255
Great Holyhead Railway, 32-3, 37-8
Great North & South Wales & Worcester Railway, 62
Great North Road, 16
Great Northern Railway, 177-8
Great Northern Railway of Ireland, 271
Great Southern & Western Railway of Ireland, 153, 230, 268, 271-2
Great Welsh Junction Railway, 61
Great Western Railway, 25, 37, 42. 61, 72, 155, 158, 174-5, 177-8, 189, 253-4
Greenore, 263-4
Greenwich time, 42, 245
Grenfell, Pascoe St Leger, 46
Grey, Sir George, 138

Griffith, Richard, 25
Grosvenor, Lord, 39
Grove, Sir George, 88
Guest, Sir John, 46
Gunpowder, 77, 221, 283
Guyot, Monsieur Jules, 138

Haigh Foundry, 182
Harecastle, 29
Harrison, Capt, 225
Hawkshaw, Sir John, 218, 221-2, 224, 226-7, 235
Hawthorn & Company, 182, 185
Head, Sir Francis, 126, 137, 140
Hemingway, John, **133**, 142
Herepath, John, 38-9
Hibbert, Mrs Leonora, 232-3
Hirste, Capt Thomas, 168, 173, 300
Hodgkinson, Eaton, 94, 97
Holyhead, (early 1800s), 11, 13-14, 17-18, 21
Holyhead, (early packet services), 12-14, 18-21
Holyhead Docks & Warehouses Company, 239-40
Holyhead Gas Company, 232
Holyhead Harbour, 17-18, 27, 37, 39, 41, 45, 50, 135, 150, 154, 159, **269**; 1846 plans, 209-12; pier extension line, 212, 229-37; quarry railway, 213, 221, 224-5; stone tipping, 215, 221-5; proposed extension railways, 212, 215; Great (north) Breakwater, 214, 216, 221-4; proposed packet piers, 209, 212-6, 218, 221, 226-7, 235; storm damage, 223; harbour area, 224, 241; expenditure, 224; lighthouse, 224; gasworks, 233; Great Eastern Jetty, 226-8; harbour works (1860s), 237-9; (1870s), 240-3; fish jetty, 239; graving docks, 19, 240-1; station and hotel (1880), **288**, new station and harbour works open, 242-3
Holyhead Mountain, 11, 213, 221-2
Holyhead Railway or Tramway Company, 212
Holyhead Road, 15-17, 21, 42, 82
Horses, 90, 236
Houses of Parliament, 124, 155
Howard & Company, 99, 103
Howth, 15, 17, 19-20
Huddart, Joseph, 15
Hudson, George, 43, 145
Huish, Capt Mark, 47-9, 80, 161, 165, 167-8, 178
Hutchinson, Col, 266, 284, 292
Hydraulic presses, 100, 103, 117-18, 129-30, 140

# INDEX

Institution of Civil Engineers, 94, 110, 137
Irish Mail Coach, 12, 15, 17-18, 21-2, 26
Irish Mail Train, (*see* Train services)
Irish North Western Railway, 264, 266, 271
Irish Railway Commission, 25-7
Iron, tenders for, 100; Government inquiry on, 109-10

Jackson, William, 46, 153, 155-6, 158-9
Jenkins, John, 32, 35-6
Johnson, Samuel, 17
Jones, Christopher Hird, 46
Jones & Potts, 181-2, 186

King George IV, 19
King, George, 53, 57, 85, 136, 182, 184-5, 188, 196, 212
Kingstown, 19, 20, 27, 180, 264
Kingstown & Dalkey Railway, 55
Kitson & Company, 182, 186

Labouchere, Henry, 39, 45, 145-6
Laird, John, 46, 94, 99, 122
Laird's (shipbuilders), 146, 267-8
Lancashire & Yorkshire Railway, 178, 250, 264
Lancaster & Carlisle Railway, 60, 187, 189, 191
Land purchases, 56
Lang, William Oliver, 169-70
Lavan Sands, 14
Ledsam, Joseph Frederick, 46
Lee, Hedworth, 70, 78-9, 132, 139, 141, 173, 192, 207, 213, 233, 235, 245, 254, 272, 274, 290-1, 300
Leestone Point, 267
Level crossings, 46, 56, 79, 82, 85, 235, 238, 272-3, 291
Lions at Britannia Bridge, 124
Liverpool, 20, 27-8, 30, 39, 153, 260
Liverpool & Birmingham Canal, 61
Liverpool & Manchester Railway, 22, 31, 36, 48, 77, 193
Llangefni, 246
Llanrwst, 260
Llysfaen limework sidings, 260, 279, 283
Locke, Joseph, 35, 48, 126-7, **133**, 142, 218, 274
Locomotives:
 Early CHR, 30, 147-8, 181-7; on Anglesey, 188-9; correspondence with Tayleur, 184-5; Crewe type, **151**, 189, 191-2; early Grand Junction and L&M, 189, 205, 236; fuel and grease, 187, 190, 192; 'Raven' class, 190; 'Lady of the Lake' or 'Problem' class, 191, 194-5, 283; tank engines, 191, 235-7, **288**; North London engines, 191-2; 'Precedent' class, 195; 'Newton' class, 196; liveries, 196; Holyhead broad gauge, 224-5; locomotives for Irish lines, 266; Cambrian, 276; crane engine, 274; named: *Anglesea*, 189; *Cambria*, 225; *Cambrian*, 189; *Cerberus*, 190, 192, 194, 237; *Columbine*, 205; *Conway*, 189; *Courier*, 190; *Dwarf*, 205; *Ellesmere*, 189, 191; *Engineer Bangor*, 205; *Glendower*, 189; *Holyhead*, 225; *Huskisson*, 191; *Lady of the Lake*, frontispiece, **219**; *Llewellyn*, 189; *Mammoth*, 190; *Menai*, 189, 191; *Pegasus*, 189-90; *Penmaenmawr*, 189; *Pheasant*, 192; *Powis*, 189; *Prince of Wales*, 189, 283; *Queen*, 225; *Rocket*, 190; *St David*, 189; *St Patrick*, 189; *Snowdon*, 189; *Stanley*, 189; *Sybil*, 192; *Velocipede*, 190, **219**; *Watt*, 194
Locomotive sheds, 147, 205-6
Locomotive troughs, 192-4
London & Birmingham Railway, 22, 26, 42-4, 46-51, 63, 71, 79, 183, 196, 211
London—Dublin communication, 16, 122
London & North Western Railway: Incorporation, 63; battle with Shrewsbury companies, 71-2; working agreements with CHR, 147, 162-3, 171-3, 182, 190; CHR lease, 158, 171; Chester & Holyhead committee, 173-4; amalgamation with CHR, 178; shortage of motive power, 183-5; takes CHR engines, 183-7; lease with Board of Trade at Holyhead, 238; Irish services to Greenore, Dublin and Belfast, 263-272, **265** (map)
London & South Western Railway, 156
London Tilbury & Southend Railway, 161
Longridge & Company, 182
Lonsdale, Earl of, 51
Lucas, John, 142
Ludlow, 23-4, 62

Mail contracts, 143-4, 146, 149-57, 170, 174, 178, 226
Mail service (early), 11-15, 19-22, 26-7, 30
Mail service (railway), 50-1, 64, 78, 148-9, 178-80, 192, 227

## INDEX

Mail service (steamer), 145, 148-9, 153, 155, 157-8, 167-71, 227
Mail service payments, 50-2, 143-4, 148-9, 150, 154, 168, 174-5, 178-9
Malltraeth, 36, 120, 191, 260
Manchester & Birmingham Railway, 29, 63
Manchester Sheffield & Lincolnshire Railway, 176-8
Mangles, Ross Donnelly, 46
Mansel, Robert S., 300
McConnell, J. E., 183-5
Menai Bridge Junction, 276-7, 294
Menai Straits:
 Ferry crossing, 14-15, 17, 21; proposed bridges, 17-18, 26, 32, 45, 90-1; tides, 126, 128; Nelson statue, 142
Menai Suspension Bridge, 17-18, 30-2, 38, 40-2, 45, 89, 90, 148, 188, 256
Midland Railway, 177
Midland Great Western Railway of Ireland, 249, 271
Milford, 12, 153, 174
Military, 29, 64
Miller & Ravenhill, 94
Mills, Charles, 53
Missionary readers, 58-9
Mochdre, 192-4
Mold Railway, 159, 178, 188, 197, 260
Moon, Sir Richard, 178, 192, 195, 236, 264, 278, 283-4
Moorsom, Capt Constantine Richard, 46, **66**, **133**
 Resident director, 53-4, 57, 70, 73, 77-8, 85, 100, 112, 116, 121; CHR chairman, 122, 125, 135, 141-3, 144, 149, 154-5, 157; leaves chair, 160; LNWR chairman, 178; death, 178; and locomotives, 182, 184-5, 187, 196; and traffic, 259; and Holyhead, 209, 229-30; evidence on navvies, 59-60, and steamers, 167
Moorsom, Admiral Sir Robert, 54
Mostyn, Lord, 193

Nant Ffrancon Pass, 16
Nasmyth & Company, 181, 183, 186
Navvies, 29, 58-60, 64, 76-7, 101, 124
Neele, George P., 195, 200, 203, 254, 263, 266-7, 272, 274-6, 283
Newry & Greenore Railway, 263-4, 266
New Steam Packet Company, 19
North European Steam Navigation Company, 161

North Lancashire Steam Navigation Company, 143
North Midland Railway, 51, 58, 73, 79
North Staffordshire Railway, 177
North Wales & Dublin Railway & Harbour Company, 43
North Wales cost road, 14-16
North Wales Mineral Railway, 69-70
North Wales University College, 259

Offices of CHR, 53, 87, 122, 260
Omnibuses, 109, 230, 233, 246-7
Openings of lines and stations, (see Appendix 1a and 1b)
Ormes Bay, 26-8, 32, 35-9, 43
Oxford, 23-4
Oxford & Birmingham Railway, 63
Oxford Canal, 31
Oxford Worcester & Wolverhampton Railway, 63

Page, Edward, 180
Page, Thomas, 43
Paraffin, 280, 283
Parkgate, 14
Parnell, Sir Henry, 15-16
Parry, Edward, 60-1, 70
Parry's Island, 18, 241
Pasley, General, 70, 91, 93, 105, 111-2
Passengers carried, 169, 247, 302
Paxton, Sir Joseph, 256-7
Peel, Sir Robert, 39-41, 44-5, 50-1, 54, 91, 146, 209
Pembroke, 62, 169
Penmaenbach, 14, 26, 273
Penmaenmawr, 14, 17, 26, 273
Penmon stone, 74, 112, 123
Pennant, Col, 85
Penrhyn, Lord, 193
Permanent way, 79, 82, 119, 131, 135, 173, 238-9, 252, 272, 276-7
Peto, Sir Samuel Morton, **160-1**
 Early career, 155-6, 161-2; proposed CHR lease, 156-8; financial involvement, 159; CHR chairman, 160-78, 231-2, 256, 259, 261; criticism of, 171, 173
Pigeon House Dock, 19
Pilbeo Rock, 18
Pilotmen, 135
Platforms, 254-5
Police, 60, 64
Pontoons, 114-6, 124, 126-7
Poole, Braithwaite, 77, 165, 259-61
Porth Dafarch, 19
Porth Dynllaen, 23-4, 26-8, 30-2, 35-7, 39, 41-2, 45, 61-2

INDEX 321

Portmadoc, 23
Portpatrick, 153
Postmaster General, 12-13, 22, 51, 146, 179
Post Office, 12, 19-22, 64, 78, 80, 150, 153-4, 170-1, 174-6, 178, 191, 195, 204, 227
Post Office steam packets, 13, 19-21, 80
Post stages, 11-12
Potter, William, 46
Press gang, 13
Prince Albert, 141
Prince of Wales, 132, 141, 224, 242-3
Prince Napoleon, 226
Provis, W. A., 18

Queenstown, 267
Queen Victoria, 132, 141, 252

Railway Clearing House, 166
Railway Department, (see Board of Trade)
Ramsbottom, John, 191-3, 195-6, 205-6, 236-7
Rastrick, John Urpeth, 23
Reed, Charles, 232, 256
Refuge sidings, (see Sidings)
Rendel, James Meadows, 44, **66**, 86, 92, 96
  Early career, 208-9, 223; and Holyhead Harbour, 209, 211-13, 215-16, 218, 222-3, 231; breakwater construction, 222; death, 218
Rennie, John (the elder), 15, 17, 19, 41, 208
Rennie, Sir John, 61, 92
Rhuddlan Marsh embankment, 274
Rhyl hotel, 259
Rich, Col, 266, 271, 280, 282-3, 285
Ringsend, 19
Rivers:
  Aber, 193; Cefni, 120; Dee, 14-15, 29; Dodder, 267; Dulas, 275; Foryd (estuary of the Clwyd), 77, 80, 192; Liffey, 19, 267-8; Llanfairfechan, 273; Ogwen, 45; Severn, 92
Riveting, 94, 102, 124
Robert Stephenson & Company, 181-2, 186
Rolfe, Charles, 128
Rolling stock:
  Proposed CHR (1846), 197; of Shrewsbury & Chester Rly, 197-8; shortage of, 197-8; freight wagons, 197-8; CHR wagon livery, 198-9;

transferred to LNWR, 198; 'Rainhill train', 199; sleeping carriages, 205; in Abergele accident, 283; carriages and wagons (1880), **288**; brakes, 199-200, 203, 286; driverguard communication, 203-4; footwarmers, 197; lighting, 197, 199; wheel tyres, 203-4
Roney, Cusack Patrick, 167
Ross, Alexander, 78, 90, 98, **133**, 142
Ross, Capt, 235-6
Rowton Moor, 43, 46
Royal College of Music, 88
Royal Danish Railways, 161
Royal Family, 132, 141, 222, 224, 226
Royal Hotel, Holyhead, 12, 135, 226, 232-3
Ruabon, 69-70
Runcorn, proposed bridge, 18
Runcorn stone, 112, 123
Running powers, 72, 260, 271, 276
Ruthin, 246

St Asaph, 21
St George's Harbour & Chester Railway, 28, 32
St George's Harbour & Railway, 28
St George's (Irish) Steam Packet Company, 79, 168
Sailing packets, 12-15, 18
Salt Island, 18-19, 208, 213, 218, 227, 230-1, 235
Saltney, 69, 72
Saltney Junction, 71
Saltney slate depot, 262
Samuda, Messrs, 54
Sandars, Francis, 56
Sea defences, 46, 67-8, 273-4
Select Committee on Atmospheric Railways, 54
Select Committee on Communications between London and Dublin, 166-71
Select Committee on Railway Labourers, 58
Sheffield Ashton-under-Lyne & Manchester Railway, 31
Sheringham, Lieut, 27
Shrewsbury, 15-16, 22, 24, 30-1, 35-6, 42, 62
Shrewsbury & Birmingham Railway, 71
Shrewsbury & Chester Railway, 69-72, 80, 104, 109
Shrewsbury Oswestry & Chester Junction Railway, 69-70
Shropshire Union Railway & Canal Company, 86

Shunting, 277, 279, 282, 284-6, 289, 291
Sidings, 260-1, 277-9, 282-4, 289, 291, 294
Signal boxes, 79, 241, 277, 290-2, 294-5
Signalling and telegraph, 70, 79, 118-19, 235, 239, 241, 252, 277-9, 283-5, 289-91; early signals, 290-1 spectacles, 291; signal heights, 291; interlocking, 292, 294-5; block telegraph, 283-5, 292-5; signals normally at danger, 294; notched distants, 295
Simmons, Capt J. L. A., 82, 106-9, 117, 119-20, 132, 138-9, 228
Skinner, Capt J. M., 11, 13-14, 20
Smiles, Samuel, 16, 31, 69
Smith, Lieut Col Sir Frederick, 35, 38
Smith, Thomas, 46
Smith, W., 272, 300
Smith, W. H. & Son, bookstalls, 246
Soldiers Point, 213-5, 223
Soup kitchens, 223
South Eastern Railway, 155-6
South Stack, 11
South Wales Railway, 49, 62, 91-2, 174
Staff, 79, 147, 173, 196, 228, 277-8, 292, 300
Stafford, 21, 61, 180, 199-200
Standing orders, 38
Stanley, W. O., 44, 191
Stanley Sands embankment, 16, 46, 73
Stations, dates of opening and distances, 297-9; fires at, 254
Aber, 73-4, 76, 193, **202**, 260; Abergele, 73-6, **75**, 284; Bagillt, 73, 76, 250, 261, 273; Bangor, 73-4, 76, 192, 246, 250-3, **251**, 260, 284; Bodorgan, 73-4, 76, 250, 261; Britannia Bridge, 256-8; Chester, 86-8, **87**, **152**, 199-200, 253, 284; Colwyn, 73-4, 76, 192, 250, 254, 261; Connah's Quay, 73, 255; Conway 73-4, 76, 254; Conway Bridge, 73; Conway Quay, 261; Derby, 87; Flint, 46, 73-4, 76, **201**, 262, 284; Gaerwen, **220**, 250, 261; Greenfield, 76; Holyhead, 180, 192, 199-200, 213, 228-33, 238, 242-3, 284; in (1880), 287-8; Holywell, 73-4, 76, 192, 255, 284; Liverpool (proposed), 260; Llandudno Junction, 250, 261; Llandulas, 250, 279, 284; Llanfaelog, 73; Llanfairfechan, **202**, 250, 262; Llanfair PG, 73-4, 76, 254, 261; Llangaffo (proposed), 250; Llysfaen, 250; Menai Bridge, 73-4, 258 262, 276-7; Mochdre & Pabo, 194; Mold, 284; Mostyn, 73-4, 76, 272; Penmaenmawr, **202**, 250; Penmynydd, 73; Prestatyn, 73-4, 76, 192, **201**, 273, 284; Queensferry (also Queens Ferry and Queen's Ferry, 73, 76, 262; Rhyl, 73-4, 76, 192, 246, 255, 272, 284; Treborth, 258; Trefdraeth, 73; Ty Croes, 73-4, 76, 250, 261; Westland Row, 20; Valley, 73-4, **220**, 250, 261
Steamers:
Admiralty: 19-22, 26, 38, 143-5, 148-50, 153
CHR and LNWR: CHR boats ordered 146; in first service, 148; threat to lay up, 150, 154; mortgaged, 154; service (1853), 166-70; and (1860), 179-80; receipts, 247-8; 'Pig boats', 263; Holyhead—Greenore, 264-7; steamship powers (1870-85), 264; Fleetwood—Belfast, 264; North Wall service, 267-72
Named: *Albert*, 246; *Anglia*, 147; *Banshee*, 145, 148, 158; *Cambria*, 147-8, 246, **270**; *Caradoc*, 145, 148; *Connaught*, 179; *Countess of Erne*, 266-7; *Dodder*, 266-7; *Doterel*, 22; *Duchess of Sutherland*, 267; *Earl Spencer*, 243, 266-7, **287**; *Eblana*, 158, 168; *Edith*, 266-7; *Eleanor*, 266-7, **270**; *Great Britain*, 113, 169; *Great Eastern*, 113, 169, 225, 252; *Great Western*, 113; *Hibernia*, 147, 163-4; *Isabella*, 243, 266-7, **287**; *Ivanhoe*, 19; *Leinster*, 179-80; *Lightning*, 20; *Lily*, 242-3, 268, **287**; *Llewellyn*, 145, 148, 157-8, 168, 226; *Mersey*, 267; *Meteor*, 20; *Munster*, 179; *Orion*, 246; *Otter*, 22; *Prince Arthur*, 158, 168; *Prince of Wales*, 94, 246; *Rose*, 268; *Royal Sovereign*, 20; *St Columba*, 145, 157-8, 168; *St Patrick*, 267; *Scotia*, 147; *Shamrock*, 267-8; *Sprightly*, 22; *Talbot*, 19; *Ulster*, 179, 268; *Violet*, 268; *Zephyr*, 22
Steamship Owners' Association, 144
Stephenson, George, 30-2, 35-40, 42, 44, 48, 53-4, 94, 118, 143, 208
Stephenson, Robert, **65**, **133**
Early years, 40; and Locke, 48; appointed CHR engineer, 53; and atmospheric railways, 55; and construction of CHR, 56-8, 64, 67-9,

73, 76-7, 85-6, 89; and tubular bridges, 89-142; Ware Bridge, 92; evidence in Parliament, 95-6; and Dee Bridge disaster, 104-111; MP for Whitby, 111; and General Pasley, 93, 111; and Brunel, 113; in accident at Conway, 118; argument with Fairbairn, 135-8; offered knighthood, 138; payments to, 140; physical toll on, 140; dinner to, 141; and Royal Family, 141; other tubular bridges, 142, 161; and CHR locomotives, 181-2; and Holyhead Harbour, 209, 211; death, 142
Stevens & Sons, 79
Storms, (see Weather)
Stourbridge Iron Works, 100
Swansea, 12, 62
Swan with Two Necks, The, 12
Swift, Dean, 14
Sychnant Pass, 14

Tal-y-bont, 90
Tamworth, 167, 193
Tanat Valley, 16
Tan-y-Bwlch, 24
Tayleur, Edward, 184-5
Tayleur & Company, 181-2, 184, 187, 189
Tech Hill, 25
Telford, Thomas, 16-18, 33, 42, 90, 142, 208
Thomas, John, 124
Thomas, William Henri, 46, 53, 78, 122, 146
Thompson, Francis, 73-4, 85, 87, 98, 112, 122, 142
Thompson, William, 46, 122
Thorneycroft & Company, 100
Through booking, 164, 170, 247-8, 264
Tickets, 247, 249
Time interval system, 289-91, 293
Timetables: (1848), 244, 301; (1850s), 247-9; Euston—Greenore, 266; North Wall, 268
Traffic:
Early coastal, 260; passengers and freight, 247, 262, 302; harvestmen, 248-9; Irish goods and cattle, 165, 242-3, 263, 268
Train formations, 180, 203, 277, 279-80
Train speeds, 42, 50, 170, 180, 183, 189, 191-2, 194-5, 204, 236, 245, 263, 272, 280
Train services:
First contractors' trains, 78, 80; excursions, 80, 135, 247, 285; Irish Mail train, 148, 167, 170, 180, 190-1, 195, 199-200, 203, 205, 244-5, 247-8, 263, 280; threatened withdrawal of Anglesey trains, 150; day express, 174; first (1848) service, 188; in (1850s), 247-9; goods service, 259-60; Holyhead Pier working, 233, 236; Bangor—Llanfair (1848-50), 80, 148, 246; market train, 248; Bangor Mail, 249-50; Llandulas viaduct diversions, 276
Travelling Post Office, 22, 167, 170, 180, 199, 280, 282
Trawsfynydd, 24
Treasury, 21, 27, 35, 37, 45, 50-2, 56, 64, 143-5, 149, 157, 209, 211-12, 214, 221, 226
Trent Valley Railway, 187
Trevithick, Francis, 132, 183, 189-91, 206
Treweryd Pass, 24
'Trent' run, 194
Tubes: 91-100, **125**; method of raising, 100; weight, 115; rust, 119; (see Britannia and Conway Tubular Bridges)
Tunnels: Bangor, 55, 61, 85, 252, 290; Belmont, 61, 86, 290; Bodorgan, 120; Conway, 85; Llandegai, 61, 85, 290; Northgate Street, 70-1; Ormes Bay (proposed), 36; Penmaenbach, 36, 44, 46, 67, 85, 273, 290; Penmaenmawr, 36, 44, 67-9, **68**, 77, **83**, 274; Penmaenrhos, 76, 82, 293; Rockcliffe, 82; Trefdraeth (proposed), 37; Windmill Lane, 71
Turnpike roads, 12, 15-16
Turntables, 207, 254, 260
Ty Croes, 203-4
Tyley, Capt, 204, 253-4, 277-8, 290
Tyrrell, Timothy, 47-8

Ulster Railway, 264, 271
Uniacke, John, 29-30, 37
Uniforms, 60, 79
United States of America, 13, 33, 41, 194, 267

Vale of Neath Railway, 174
Velin-heli, 128
Vernon & Company, 99
Viaducts: Cegyn, 85; Flint, 273; Llandulas, 274-6; Malltraeth, 120; Ogwen, **81**, 85; Penmaenmawr, 68-9, **68**, **83**; timber, 273
Vignoles, Charles, 23-8, 31-2, 35-7, 40, 42, 126

Vulcan Foundry, 184-5

Walker, James, 41, 48, 50, 55, 90, 106, 208
Waterloo Bridge, 16
Water pumping engines, 192
Watson, William, 155-7, 166, 168
Waverton, 43
Weather and storms, 32, 64, 67-9, 126, 131-2, 141, 204, 232, 273-5, 285-6
Webb, Francis W., 196, 206, 237, 275-6
Wellington, Duke of, 45, 141
Welsh language, 55, 59, 77-8
Wicklow, Earl of, 41-2
Wigan Branch Railway, 31
Wigram, Messrs, 146
Wild, Charles H., 88, **133**, 142
Wood, Ephraim, 275, 300
Wolverhampton, 24, 35, 61
Wolverton, 183, 185-8, 232
Worcester, 23-4, 37, 42, 61-3
Worcester & Porth Dynllaen Railway, 61-3, 86
Wrexham Mold & Connah's Quay Railway, 255
Wrought iron, 92, 98, 104, 110
Wynne, Capt (Col), 80, 291

Ynys Rug, 18
Ynys-y-Moch, 17-18
Yolland, Col, 286, 293